P9-DMZ-014

"PERHAPS PETER'S STORY WILL
HELP . . ."
Barbara Peabody

THE SCREAMING ROOM
A MOTHER'S JOURNAL OF HER
SON'S STRUGGLE WITH AIDS—
A TRUE STORY OF LOVE,
DEDICATION, AND COURAGE

"The most compelling and poignant story
of AIDS comes not from a doctor or professional writer but from Barbara Peabody."
San Francisco Chronicle

"What Peabody has done to humanize the
crisis is unequaled to date . . . it needs to
be mandatory reading for everyone."
Donald I. Abrams, M.D.
Assistant Director, AIDS Activities
San Francisco General Hospital

"THE SCREAMING ROOM is one of the
most outstanding books yet written about
AIDS."
San Francisco *Bay Area Reporter*

"THE SCREAMING ROOM should be required reading for all of us."
Los Angeles Times

THE SCREAMING ROOM

A MOTHER'S JOURNAL OF HER SON'S STRUGGLE WITH AIDS— A TRUE STORY OF LOVE, DEDICATION, AND COURAGE

BARBARA PEABODY

AVON
PUBLISHERS OF BARD, CAMELOT, DISCUS AND FLARE BOOKS

AVON BOOKS
A division of
The Hearst Corporation
105 Madison Avenue
New York, New York 10016

The Oak Tree Publications edition contains the following Library of Congress
Cataloging in Publication Data:

Peabody, Barbara.
   The screaming room.

   1. Vom Lehn, Peter, 1955–1984—Health.   2. AIDS (Disease)—Biography.
3. Peabody, Barbara.   4. Mothers—   5. Patients—United States—Biography.
I. Title.
RC607.A26P43   1986   362.1'9697'9200924   [B]   86-768

First Avon Printing: September 1987

Dedication

The Screaming Room is dedicated to:

My mother, Frances Wilson Peabody,
whose example and teachings
gave me the strength to be there for Peter

My children, Maria, David, and Jonathan,
whose love and loyalty
helped me to help their brother

All AIDS patients everywhere, and their families

And to Peter
I wish he were here

Acknowledgments

I wish to thank Chris Matthews, M.D., J. Allen McCutchan, M.D., and Phyllis Spechko, R.N., C.A.N.P., for their unique personal caring, professional dedication, and untiring battle against AIDS. Without their encouragement, this book might not have been written.

I also wish to thank the nurses on 10 East, whose genuine concern and lack of fear made Peter's six hospital visits at UCSD Medical Center bearable. Their excellent care helped us and continues to help so many others. And to all medical specialists, IV nurses, laboratory and X-ray technicians, pharmacists, and social workers who have joined the battle—thank you.

Special appreciation to Irene Milton, Beth Ingram, Larry Platt, and Paul Lapolla at Oak Tree for their faith in my story. And my heartfelt thanks to Susan Wiseman, whose literary skill and empathetic editing helped turn my journal into a book.

Gratitude also to Fernando Segui and Joe Hebert for their valuable assistance in word processing.

Barbara Peabody
May 1986

Prologue
Gray Morning

Sunday, December 4, 1983

"Oh, my God, no-o-o!" My cry pierces the quiet, San Diego morning. I am cold, shaking uncontrollably. I clutch the blankets around me.

"He has a very rare kind of pneumonia called pneumocystis pneumonia, or PCP. That's one of the two diseases that confirms the diagnosis of AIDS." The calm, doctor-voice of my ex-husband Walter, 2,500 miles away in Virginia, starts to break.

I can't speak.

"He's in St. Vincent's Hospital," Walter continues. "I'm going to New York this afternoon. He's been there since Wednesday but has been too sick to call us. Maria tried to call him this morning and his roommate told her Peter was in the hospital, so she called him there and then called me. I've already spoken to him and to one of his doctors."

Suddenly, a torrent of words. "How is he? How did he sound? What do you know about AIDS? What's going to happen? Should I go today, too?" Stupid questions. Why do I ask them? *Damn, Peter, why are you so far away?*

"I'm afraid I don't know very much about AIDS," Walter answers apologetically. "There hasn't been much in the medical journals. But I'll get there about five and call you back as soon as I can. I don't know if you should come east now or wait and see how he progresses."

"All right. Call me as soon as you can. 'Bye."

I hang up and stare into space, my body still shaking. I am cold, frightened.

I try to remember what I've read about AIDS. Damnit— what did that article say, where did I see it? Why didn't I pay more attention? After all, Peter is homosexual, and I know it affects homosexuals, as well as Haitians, hemophiliacs, and intravenous drug users. I remember reading that doctors are baffled by its random attacks on these unrelated groups. No clear-cut chain of infection. A gradually debilitating disease as immune defenses fail and diseases invade freely.

What else? I curse my ignorance. It can't be true. Peter is only 28, still trying to put his life together. It's not fair.

The Sunday morning grayness feels suffocating. I must get up, do something, keep busy. I have to notify people. First, my youngest sister Louise, in New York—see if I can stay with her and her husband David indefinitely. My mother in Maine—she can call my brother Sandy on Long Island. My sister Charlotte in San Francisco.

And my other kids, how will they take this?

There's analytical, logical David, immersed in computers at the University of Texas in Austin, but also sensitive and loving. Though he and Peter fought when small, they've grown closer since David was in college in New Hampshire, the three years between them shrinking. They've visited each other, going skiing in New Hampshire, Peter showing his kid brother around New York. Peter's homosexuality makes no difference to David. David'll be all right.

What about Maria? She already knows Peter's sick, of course, but I better speak to her myself. I know she's terrified. She and Peter are very close. She's always accepted him for what he is. My two musicians—Peter aspiring to an operatic career, Maria to being a symphony percussionist or even a conductor, just starting to prepare at Peabody Conservatory in Baltimore.

And Jonathan, "Number Three Boy" we used to call him. He worries me most. Only 23 and already the youngest assistant manager in a chain drugstore where he's worked since he was sixteen. He has let complete absorption in his job distract him from the hurt of Walter's and my divorce nine years ago. I've often thought of him as the most wounded of my four children, the least able to express the anger and pain caused by his ruptured world.

He was upset to learn, at 18, of Peter's homosexuality. He never suspected. Until then, he thought of Peter as quite a ladies' man, maybe even envied his easy wit and charm with the opposite sex. The girls where he worked always begged for an introduction to his good looking brother whenever he dropped in. That image was shattered, surprisingly enough, by me. I assumed he knew Peter was gay.

"Maybe you shouldn't laugh too hard. We have them in our own family, you know," I chided him one day as he was joking about a gay customer in his store.

"Who?" he asked, puzzled.

"Well, you do realize your Uncle Sandy is homosexual, don't you?"

"I hadn't really thought about it . . . but yes, I know he's never been married . . . guess it occurred to me."

"He's not the only one," I continued.

Doesn't he know?

"Who else? I can't think of anyone."

"Surely you know Peter is, don't you?" I asked gently. His expression changed from puzzlement to disbelief.

"Well, just now as you say it, there isn't anyone else it could be . . . no, I never thought about it," he answered slowly. I thought I saw apprehension in his eyes and quickly reassured him.

"Jonathan, don't be afraid of this. I believe that homosexuals are born homosexual. It's not something you acquire or learn. Frankly, it doesn't matter. What matters is that he's your brother and you love him. What either of you do with your sex life has nothing to do with that relationship. I didn't realize you didn't know."

His smooth young face still looked troubled. At 18, slim and handsome after losing adolescent chubbiness, I was afraid that this knowledge might shake his hard-won self-confidence. He seemed upset about it for several days. I could only hope he'd work it out for himself, gradually.

But I don't know if he really has. Peter had been in New York for four years when Jonathan learned of his homosexuality. Except for occasional visits, he's never had a chance to become close to Peter and accept him. I hope he can cope with this. I know he'll be afraid to declare openly that his brother is homosexual and has AIDS, and I fear that he'll keep everything bottled up inside. And now, more than ever in his life, I think he'll need support to avoid being torn between guilt about and love for his brother.

The calls are completed and I stare into space.

Louise and her husband David were shocked. They'll call Peter, said I can stay with them, and apologized that their loft apartment is in an almost unlivable state. She'll try to get me more information on AIDS. Her neighbors are gay and may help.

My mother, ever stalwart, wanted to know what she could do to help and if I plan to go to New York. I said I'd let her know when I decide. Charlotte, too, offered help. There's nothing she can do right now.

My kids? It's hard to tell. Jonathan and David were quietly stoic. They asked if they should go to New York. I said I didn't know. We know so little about AIDS that it's hard to make plans. Maria's voice was tense and anxious, close to tears. She can arrange to go to New York on Wednesday.

Now I must speak to Peter.

The line crackles, hums. 3,000 miles disappear.

"Hello?" Peter's voice, weak, shadowy.

"Hi, Peter. It's Mom."

"Well, hi!"—as if it's an ordinary Sunday call. "How'd you know I was here?" I can barely hear his voice.

"Dad told me. He called this morning. How are you feeling?"

"Pretty good, I guess."

What else can he answer; "Terrible, I might die"? Small talk, but words are unimportant. We don't mention AIDS. He's alive, he's talking to me.

"I love you," I say in closing.

"I love you, too," he answers, his voice soft. We haven't said that to each other since he was a little boy.

I hang up the phone and cry.

1

Tuesday, December 6

I don't know how I got through the last two days, anxiously waiting by the telephone for more news. Walter called Sunday afternoon, after talking more with Peter's doctor. Peter was in serious but stable condition then, but nothing could be predicted. More indecision.

Sunday night, I made a plane reservation for Monday morning, then canceled it after Walter's call. If Peter improves and wants to come to San Diego, shouldn't I wait till I can go bring him back? Then again, what if he doesn't improve? I should be there. It's so far and expensive. I can't afford to jet back and forth between coasts. I slept fitfully Sunday night.

Somehow, I found the presence of mind on Monday to investigate facilities for AIDS patients in San Diego, just in case. I called the Medical Center at UCSD, the University of California in San Diego, and asked if they had an AIDS clinic. As a teaching hospital, I thought surely they must be the main resource for coping with such a disease locally. Might as well think positively and hope Peter will want to come here.

The operator connected me with the Owen Clinic. After many rings, a young man answered. I explained that my son was sick with pneumocystis in New York, might be out here soon, and that I desperately needed information on

AIDS. He informed me kindly that Owen Clinic, staffed by volunteer doctors and nurses, was open two nights a week and, though created as a health clinic for homosexuals, was now seeing almost all the local AIDS patients, of which there were 38 diagnosed.

A support organization was also forming, called the AIDS Project. I called the number he gave me but had to leave my name and number on an answering machine. A Dr. Hal Frank finally called back after 6 P.M. Sensing the hysteria in my voice, he spoke calmly and compassionately about the support group and told me to get in touch if Peter returned with me.

I left the telephone long enough to have dinner with neighbors. Though gone but an hour, Walter called again, leaving a message on my answering machine.

"Barbara, Peter is still stable. He's on oxygen and his fever is still high."

Calm so far, then . . . "I think you'd better come." His voice quavered.

That did it! Enough vacillation. The fear in his voice convinced me I should go to my son. I remade my reservation for 7 A.M. this morning, and threw clothes into a suitcase. I canceled a catering job I was to do this week, called the kids, my mother, my sister, to tell them I was leaving. I arranged for a friend to take me to the airport.

I am flying eastward now, to New York and Peter. I hate flying. I like my feet on the ground and the illusory feeling that I'm at least partially in control of my life. This airborne interim between one place and another always makes me uneasy. Today, though, I almost love this unnatural machine that shrinks the time and distance between my sick child and myself.

My mind wanders erratically between past and present. I see Peter as a child—his greenish eyes circled by long, black eyelashes, his wiry body. Thick, light brown hair falling into his eyes. Then I remember him as I last saw him, just over a week ago, when most of the family gathered at my sister Charlotte's in San Francisco for Thanksgiving and her son's wedding.

Peter was thin, so thin. His clothes hung loosely on his

5'10" frame. His face was flushed, and I wondered if he'd been under a sunlamp. How stupid! And most disturbing: the gaunt, aged look. I kept glancing at him, puzzled. Well, I convinced myself, he *is* 28. Some men, especially if slender, start showing lines in their faces around 30 don't they?

I remember, too, his insatiable curiosity that led him to read voraciously, and the thirst for experimentation that took him from dissecting record players as a child to trying drugs as a teenager: "I wanted to know what it felt like." His headlong rush into life started at birth with his precipitous delivery, finding his obstetrician totally unprepared, not to mention his mother. Peter wasn't going to wait for anything. *Why did you always rush into everything, Peter?*

Rushing in, trying out, getting hurt, giving up too soon, crashing in disappointment—whether it was a project, a dream, other people; *even yourself, Peter. Always starting with such high expectations but never learning to use an unsuccessful experience and reconstruct from your mistakes. Your father and I must have failed in this, not teaching you the tough persistence, discipline, and patience needed to survive in your "instant culture," where instant gratification is an end in itself. Your life turned into a series of unrealistic highs and drastic lows. You've always been more fragile than my other three, Peter, bent on following a seemingly self-destructive path.*

I sit with fingers childishly crossed, willing the miles to speed by, willing Peter to live, wishing I knew how to say a rosary, although I'm not Catholic. It might be comforting—and diverting—to work my fingers through the beads, mechanically reciting ancient litanies. Oh, my God—what if something happens while I'm up here? Panic jerks me upright. No, that can't happen, no!

I sit back, my mind wandering again, trying to piece things together and find a pattern to Peter's life. Remembering.

Bright and inquisitive as a baby, pushing away when held, trying to see, to touch, to move. Never one to cuddle like the other three. And yet clinging strongly to family traditions and holidays, even as an adult.

Remember when you organized the surprise Christmas visit to me in Scottsdale, even paying Jonathan's way from Santa Fe?

Curious fingers always into everything, reaching and grasping. I swear his arms grew ten feet the minute we entered a supermarket. I always had music playing in the house, and he loved music, could sing nursery songs in perfect pitch at age two.

An introspective child, prone to intellectual activities. He used to draw and write so well, had unusual twists of imagination. His family-scene drawings were done with bizarrely clever humor. And later drawings of machines and space rockets had complicated, intricate details. Like most children growing up in the 1960s, he was fascinated with space exploration, astronomy, and electronic gadgetry.

He also wrote imaginative and well-constructed stories in school. And later, when he toured Europe at 16 with the school choir, his long letters home were filled with witty commentaries on Europe, his traveling companions, and their escapades in outwitting their chaperones. I smile now, remembering his return from that two-month trip. Despite his air of independence and world-weary sophistication, he was so glad to be home again that he cried—just for a second—when we met him at the Albuquerque airport.

There was always something different about him, though. My other three children were fat, placid, cuddly babies. Peter was wiry and hyperactive, always struggling for independence. Yet he hated violence and rough-and-tumble playground fights. He always held back and apart, much as my younger brother Sandy always had. I wonder if there's some meaning in that—Sandy is homosexual, too. Peter always reminded me so much of Sandy, not just in school, but even as a baby.

I look out the window and see that the plane is just crossing the desert. I glance at my watch. God, I must be patient. Relax. There's several hours yet till I can be with Peter. I let my mind continue to wander.

I can't explain why, but I often wondered if Peter were

homosexual. Not the worst thing that could happen, I thought. After all, my brother is gay, I have many gay friends, it just wouldn't matter. He's my son and I love him.

In high school, however, Peter dated girls, two or three quite steadily. He was very popular. That led me off track—maybe I was wrong. But he confirmed it when he visited me in Tucson after a year in New York and told me he was gay. He thought I should know, and he wanted to know how I felt about it.

"Well, it's no surprise, Peter. I don't feel angry or embarrassed. I admit, though that it *does* make me sad for you, because I don't think homosexuality is a very happy way to live. There's discrimination and derision, either a constant fight or living a lie. And I want more than anything that you be happy. This'll just make it harder for you."

He listened carefully, looked relieved when I finished. I'm sure he had only realized and accepted it himself in the last year.

"I'd like most to have a monogamous relationship, you know, live with someone eventually. I'm not interested in this flitting around stuff," he told me.

The plane bumps slightly. I notice that the "Fasten Seat Belt" sign flashes on. Damn my paranoia and sweaty palms. "Just a little turbulence," the pilot assures us. I try to ignore it and return to my reflections.

I was most concerned when I learned Peter was using drugs. We were living in Santa Fe when Peter came home after his freshman year at the University of Colorado and told his father and me that he'd quit school and wanted to go to New York to study music. He seemed depressed, and finally, after much prodding, he revealed to us that he had been using drugs. He'd taken LSD at least six times during the ninth grade—yet we'd never noticed. That was the year we returned from Santo Domingo, one of many moves. I felt such a deep sense of failure as he talked. He told us he smoked pot in high school, and how hashish, marijuana, and LSD were easily available.

He was so depressed that June that we felt we had to

intervene, try to find out what was wrong. We ended up finding him a psychologist. He saw him willingly until he left for New York in March. I don't really know if it helped him. He seemed less depressed but didn't talk about it. I wonder now if his depression was drug related, adolescent blues, or perhaps related to his homosexuality— evidence of his own fight at this time either to accept or reject his true nature.

Walter and I had been seeing a marriage counselor ourselves for four months. We were still seeing him when Walter decided to separate and move out that September, saying he needed to "live his own life."

What a mess! What chaos that year was! My marriage desperately needed readjustments. After close to 20 years of child raising, I was finally making progress as an artist. I had cofounded a cooperative gallery in Santa Fe, was selling my own work, and meeting people in my own field, other artists.

Walter, in contrast, seemed to get grayer and grayer, talking only about disease and death until I thought I'd go crazy.

Our lives diverged more and more, and we had less and less to talk about. He took his frustrations out on the children. I poured mine into painting, ignoring the whole situation, until it came to the point of no return—either a repair job and back on track or separation. We opted for repair and the marriage counselor, and I thought things were much better. Then Walter announced at noon on Friday of Labor Day weekend that he was leaving.

I never want to go through all that again! Trying to cope with the children's hurt and anger as well as my own, trying to pay all our expenses on the $500 a month that Walter gave me. Jobs for untrained English majors were rather scarce in Santa Fe.

I remember Maria, nine years old at the time, taking out her anger by beating up everyone at school, David and Jonathan uninterested in seeing their father at all, and Peter trying to be grown up and hoping Walter and I could remain friends.

For your sake Peter, I tried.

But I had too much hurt, too much resentment that Walter had left after 20 years of marriage and family, leaving me to finish raising the children while he pursued "living his own life." I felt as if my whole adult life had been thrown into the garbage can, along with the chicken bones and onion skins.

Peter moved into a small apartment in November that year, shortly after our separation. Sort of a preparation for going to New York in March and living on his own. He did such a touching thing that Thanksgiving. He invited the other children, myself, and Walter for dinner in his new home. He hoped so pathetically that holidays would always be the same, that the family traditions would remain.

But things change, Peter, everything changes. And we have to adapt all the time, no matter how much it hurts. I'm sorry, Peter. I couldn't do it your way.

Now Peter's desperate illness will throw Walter and me back together. I hope, for Peter, that I can keep the old resentments from surfacing. I know Walter needs me there—I could tell by his quavering voice on the answering machine—but he can't lean on me for support. We're strangers now.

"Would you like something to drink?" The flight attendant interrupts my thoughts. "No, no thank you." She serves the gentleman next to me and moves on.

I should try to sleep. I've hardly slept for two nights, and I know I'll sleep little once I get to New York.

But I'm too keyed up. I'm thinking of a long telephone call last February and Peter's casual mention of an annoying diarrhea he couldn't throw off and his doctor couldn't diagnose. This doctor said he'd picked up an intestinal parasite in the Chinese restaurant where he worked. The doctor prescribed Flagyl®, but Peter had a terrifying reaction—couldn't remember things, felt disoriented, and had to discontinue it even though it halted the diarrhea somewhat. Then he took Lomotil®, also ineffective, and he lost ten pounds. He started calling more often after that, which was unusual. His excuse was that he was planning a surprise eightieth birthday party for my mother in April, in Portland, Maine.

And what a fabulous birthday party it was. We all arrived gradually for 24 hours. Charlotte and I first from California; Louise and her family from New York; David and his girlfriend Karen from Texas; Maria from Michigan; Sandy from Long Island; and finally Peter, dashing for a plane after work in New York to arrive in the middle of our big dinner at an Italian restaurant the night before the big party. All four of us and six of the nine grandchildren. He and Karen stayed up until three A.M. that night, talking and talking. They got along instantly.

The next day, Peter slept until five in the afternoon, and we were worried. But after all, he was exhausted. And he ate boiled sweet potatoes daily. His doctor had prescribed them to replace minerals lost through the constant diarrhea.

How dumb I was not to suspect anything! I should have insisted on knowing more. I guess I attributed it to his depression, knowing that he hated his waiter job in the Chinese restaurant, and his general lack of success in what he loved most—music and theater.

Twice Peter left New York to audition as a baritone for the Baltimore Opera Company, rehearsing intensively and with high hopes—and twice he was rejected. And he'd been gone now for nine years, supporting himself as a waiter, meeting nothing but discouragement in his musical career.

I remember another long conversation we had last summer. I was so worried about Peter at the time, anxious without knowing just why. Even across 3,000 miles, I knew something was wrong.

I never thought of AIDS.

On a July night, Peter called and said he was thinking of leaving New York. He was saving money to come to San Diego with his lover, Frank, to look for a job in the theater. I was surprised—he loved New York City so much—but delighted that he might be nearer. I thought a smaller city might give him a better opportunity for developing his musical career—the "big fish in a little pond" idea.

You weren't really tough enough for New York, Peter, not competitive enough.

Aren't we there yet? Two more hours. I don't know what I can do, but I feel like things will be better if I can just get to Peter. Oh, why did I wait so long to decide to go to New York? Why didn't I *do* something sooner?

On September 3rd this year, I tried and tried to call and wish Peter a happy birthday. I found out later he'd gone to my brother Sandy's in Southampton for Labor Day weekend. He told me he was so tired that he slept the whole weekend. He still had the nagging diarrhea, changed doctors in September. The new one asked if Peter had ever heard of "AIDS panic," implying hypochondria, and did more tests for intestinal parasites. Again, negative results. I, in ignorance, didn't know there could be a connection between the diarrhea and AIDS. If only I'd known the early symptoms, maybe I could have persuaded him to seek better treatment, to look for doctors actively involved in AIDS care. Damn! So much precious time lost!

A few weeks after his birthday, Peter and Frank, whom he'd been with for two years, broke off their relationship but decided to remain friends. I asked Peter if he was upset. No, he told me, the whole thing had become burdensome. I didn't believe him for one minute, knowing how fond he was of Frank. Glibly, he said he always had his family—and his ridiculous cat, "Kitty." We laughed. He'd just found a new waiter job in a Japanese restaurant and was excited. The owners were kind to their employees, the tips excellent, and now he could pay off debts and plan a future away from New York. Good. At last he was trying to pull his life together.

I tighten my seat belt as the pilot informs us that we are about to land in Chicago. Thank God I don't have to change planes—just hold my breath until we move on to New York. Not much longer.

I kick myself mentally. Why hasn't it ever occurred to me that Peter could have AIDS? I try not to blame myself. I've never read more than one article on AIDS—something in *Time* or *Newsweek*—and "pre-AIDS symptoms" weren't mentioned. I had the impression that AIDS hit suddenly and death was immediate. Even so, my instincts have been telling me that something was terribly wrong. I should have done more.

Maybe I've been too wrapped up in my own life, too trusting that his medical care was adequate. I've enjoyed the last two years in San Diego. It's been like eternal vacation living alone, responsible for no one else since Maria went off to school. I've painted like a fiend, walked the beaches, made a few friends—not many. I've been enjoying my own company. I feel like I'm finally finding direction in my art. Always before, I'd no sooner get rolling than Walter would have us moving elsewhere again. I figured out once that every move cost me four to six months out of my own work. A lot of time.

I've done enough of my own moving around, I think ruefully. I didn't like it, though. Two years after the divorce, I rented out the Santa Fe house and moved with Maria to Tucson, looking for a new start. Peter was already in New York, David off to Dartmouth College, Jonathan choosing to stay in Santa Fe with Walter and his new wife to finish high school.

Just Maria and I alone, and I didn't know a soul in Tucson! Not a good idea. Maria made friends quickly in school, but I was lonely and even more depressed. Four months of therapy helped me learn to depend on myself and gain self-confidence.

After two years in Tucson, we moved to Scottsdale, where there was more activity in the arts. I sold the Santa Fe house—sad, but I needed the money, and my life began to straighten out.

Scottsdale was a new city, no history, perfect for a new life. We liked it. I got my work into some good galleries (though still not enough sales), painted, and with steady payments from the sale of the Santa Fe house—plus Walter's child support and my small alimony—I had less financial worry.

I started a small catering business to earn extra income. It was barely underway when Maria heard of Interlochen Arts Academy in Michigan, won a scholarship, and left for her junior and senior years of high school. I was glad for her, but sad to see her leave. We were so close after living together alone for five years.

Okay, I remember thinking. This is a good time to decide: move or stay? I was tiring of the endless, hot summers, and free to move on without disrupting Maria's life. How about San Diego? I'd visited there several times and liked it. Do it! I did, and haven't regretted it.

Well, if all goes well and Peter comes back with me, my life will change again. That's okay. I've had a good vacation, and first and foremost I'm a mother. I believe that my kids should be as independent as possible, yet I want them to feel they are always welcome home. There's always a refuge if they need it. Peter needs me now.

Looking back, fitting the pieces together, I can see that you suspected what was wrong with your body. You're too bright not to have known. That's why you started calling everyone more often. That's why you came to San Francisco last week. You were pulling away from New York and drawing back into the family, needing our warmth and support—the refuge—though not daring to explain why.

Oh, Peter, why didn't you tell us? Did you think we might not care?

My hands are cold. I'm not sure if it's because of my nervousness about flying or because I'm afraid. Afraid of what I'm flying toward, of what I may find out. Could I have done something, anything, to prevent this?

When we were all at my sister Charlotte's home for Thanksgiving and her son's wedding—just nine days ago—I was surprised that Peter came from New York since he was trying to save money. The gauntness, the aging in his face, the deep lines—I was shocked. His hair seemed to be thinning, too. His face was strangely rosy. He coughed a deep, dry cough at night.

David finally took you to the emergency room in Berkeley. The doctor there gave you a prescription for cough medicine but never even took your temperature, nor asked you any questions. Why didn't he take your temperature?

Why didn't he listen to your lungs? Why didn't he take an X-ray? Why didn't I ask these questions then?

Before the wedding that Saturday, Peter told me he tried to buy a suit or jacket in New York. Nothing had fit without needing extensive alterations. Instead, he bought a new shirt, tie, cranberry sweater, and tan trousers. He also bought new loafers but had to use two pairs of shoe liners to fill them in.

"Does this look all right?" he asked me anxiously. "It's not very formal, and I'm not sure if it all matches."

"You look great!" I told him. But he looked so thin. "This is California. You don't have to be formal, you know." I smiled brightly, but my heart lurched at how loosely his trousers hung.

"Thanks. I wasn't sure," he said, turning. "And I'll kill anyone who says how thin I am. I'm getting *tired* of that," he said, reading my mind.

The day after the wedding, Peter wanted to see San Francisco. And I wanted time alone with him. We left the family and drove into the city, losing our way several times but enjoying the picturesque, painted houses and the hilly streets. We parked at Fisherman's Wharf and walked slowly, gawking at tourist merchandise, then stopped for tea. He talked more about his relationship with Frank, insisting that all was for the best. But I could see the hurt in his eyes. Losing, letting go, is so hard, I know. I felt his pain.

You wanted to go to the top of a hill to see the sun go down. Sunset was always your favorite hour, ever since we lived in Santa Fe and I used to call you to see a spectacular sunset through the kitchen window while preparing dinner.

Now, in San Francisco, the sky glowed red and orange the moment we crested the hill, flaming the entire sky and throwing the city's silhouette into dark blues and purples. It was magnificent. We watched it in silence.

"Well, now I've seen San Francisco, my next trip will be San Diego," he told me as we drove slowly back down the hill.

If I'd only known then, had followed my instincts, Peter

could have come back to San Diego with me right away, been admitted to UCSD Medical Center before getting so dangerously ill. But no. He took the red-eye flight back that Sunday night, worked a full shift Monday and Tuesday nights, and collapsed on Wednesday. Thank God, Frank took him to St. Vincent's Hospital. Peter had promised me he'd see a doctor right away on Monday. For some reason he didn't.

"Oh, Peter, I hope you'll be able to make the trip back with me.

"Ladies and gentlemen, we are now making our final approach into La Guardia Airport in New York City. Please fasten your seat belts and observe the no smoking sign that the captain has turned on. Thank you."

At last, I'm here. And I survived the flight, as always, despite my unrealistic fears. Now I must go help my son survive.

This is real fear.

2

Tuesday, December 6 (continued)

Finally, after late planes, lost luggage, finding a taxi to the hospital, it's already eight o'clock. I get off the elevator. What a dilapidated, old place! A quick query at the nurses' desk, run down the hall, it's on the end. Into Peter's room.

"Hey! You can't go in like that. You gotta put on a mask, these gloves, a gown—here." A nurse stops me at the door. I stare at her in surprise, shocked.

"He's in respiratory isolation. You have to put these on every time you go in, take them off when you come out. This is to protect you from what he has and also to protect him, so you don't bring him anything now that his immunity is down." She hands me a yellow cotton gown and ties a mask over my face.

I seethe. I've come so far and can't touch my son, he can't see my face. Damn. I slide on the rubber gloves and enter.

Peter is sitting up, his face red with fever, but he appears alert. A large, green oxygen tank stands next to the bed and he holds a transparent green mask in his hand. His breathing is shallow. Walter sits in an old, vinyl armchair beside the bed.

"Hi, Peter." I smile, but he can't see my face under the mask. "Hi, Walter."

21

"Well, hi," Peter answers, as if I fly to New York daily. "How was your trip?"

"You know very well that the best trip would be terrifying for me," I answer, laughing.

Peter knows how much I hate to fly. I relate funny details of the trip, hoping to amuse him. Walter laughs, remembering my fear of flying. From time to time, Peter covers his face with the green mask but doesn't want to leave it on.

"The doctors say I can get out of here in a week," Peter tells me. I try not to appear startled. How could this be true? "I've been thinking. I'd like to go out to California—to San Diego—with you for a while . . . if that's okay."

"Of course, I'd love to have you."

"I've got lots of plans for when I get out of here and settled out there. I really want to make a new start."

"That's great, Peter." He talks on, his voice soft and his breathing labored. I listen as though from a distance, hearing, "When I get out . . . When I can . . . When . . . ." He's saying *when*, there's no *if* about it. He's fighting. He hasn't given up, as I feared he might have, as he's done before.

Soon, it's obvious Peter is tiring, and we should leave him. My gloved hand touches his leg under the blanket. I don't dare kiss or hug him for fear of infecting him. Oh, how I want to!

"See you tomorrow, have a good sleep tonight," I tell him.

Outside the door, Walter and I take off masks and gloves and stuff them into the bag labeled "Infectious Waste." The yellow gowns go into "Infectious Linens." I feel as if Peter were a leper and resent the precautions that keep us from touching.

"Just a minute . . . I want to leave Louise's number with the nurse, in case they need to call during the night," I tell Walter as we walk down the hall. His hotel, he tells me, has telephone service only at the desk, which isn't manned at night. There's no way to notify him if there's an emergency.

Walter suggests getting something to eat, and I readily

agree. I've barely eaten since leaving San Diego. We leave the hospital and duck into a restaurant two blocks away.

Walter looks morose, orders only a small salad.

"Is that all you're going to eat?"

"I'm not hungry," he answers, distressed.

"Walter, you have to eat more than that." I feel an impatient twinge of resentment. Am I going to have to mother him again, tend to his suffocating needs for attention? Anger and bitterness worm their way through the past nine years of loosely flung topsoil.

No, I won't do it, I won't give support. He has a wife for that, and I must build my strength for Peter, for myself, for my other children. Bury it. I must deny his need for my strength and refuse to slip into the old patterns.

"You know we have to stay strong for Peter. We've got to eat right, keep up our own resistance, too, so we don't give anything to him," I say.

Walter looks at me gratefully. "I'm so glad you're here," he says, eyes filling.

"I am, too," I say briskly. Don't weaken, don't fall back. "I should have come right away, but I didn't know what to do. Tell me what's happening. What are his chances? What . . . what can we expect? And if he survives this pneumonia, what then?"

"His chances of surviving aren't good, they told me." His father-eyes glisten, but his voice is calmly professional. "He waited so long to get help that he's extremely weakened. He was so sick when admitted. At least, every day he lives is a good sign."

"I think we should get more opinions, find out what's being done in research on AIDS, see if there's anything else that can be done for pneumocystis. If he pulls through this . . ." I hesitate as the tears of uncertainty and anguish surface. "If he pulls through, we're going to need to know all we can. Where else are they doing research—New York Hospital, Mt. Sinai, Columbia, where? Maybe tomorrow you could start calling around."

He glances up, his face frightened. "Don't ask me to do that, I can't do it."

"Why not?" I ask, after a shocked pause.

"I just can't," he repeats, shaking his head sadly.

"Well, I could do it," I say finally, "but you're a doctor, you speak the language. They wouldn't even talk to me, and we must learn all we can."

He doesn't answer. I feel anger and shock, impatience at his refusal to make inquiries. Does he want to lose Peter without a fight? Would it be easier to him to give up, not have to bear watching Peter die from subsequent infections? That would be so selfish. Peter wants to live and we *have* to bear the pain.

Perhaps he's afraid he'll seem "pushy" to his colleagues. But what's pushy about a father seeking his colleagues' help for his dying son?

I'm tired from the trip, the stress. I fight the urge to shriek at him in frustration. All right, all right. I'll do it myself. We finish eating and leave, he to his small hotel and I, by taxi, to my sister and her family in their SoHo loft.

The taxi leaves me at the door of the dark, sooty warehouse on Wooster Street, not far from the hospital, where my sister and her husband, David Stoltz, live with their two teenage children. Louise and David are both artists, and they struggle in this creative area of New York City to live and work among their fellow artists. Their loft is on the sixth floor, and Louise comes down in the clanking elevator to take me up. The elevator opens directly into the loft.

The loft is vast, dark, cold. A bare light bulb hangs over a long oaken table, creating an oasis of light. We rush to its welcome as if it could warm us, sit on the oak chairs and sip wine.

"I told you it would be freezing cold here," Louise says. "If we could just get the city to give us a building permit, we could make improvements—heat, plumbing, new wiring, and put in walls. It's all so political in New York, you know. Anyhow, how are you?"

"Tired," is all I manage to say. I can't begin to verbalize the fear, the frustration, the determination.

"Here's an AIDS booklet the two gay guys next door

lent me. Also, I've been asking around, and have a list of people and places that are doing research. We can start calling tomorrow. This booklet is put out by the Gay Men's Health Crisis, an organization of volunteers giving support to AIDS patients. They seem to know a lot and are very active.'' Her energy and enthusiasm are touching.

I call my mother, as promised, to tell her I've arrived safely and that Peter's condition is the same. She'll call tomorrow. I call David and Jonathan with the same news. All I can tell them is that I'll keep them informed daily in case Peter's condition becomes more critical and they need to come east. I call Maria. She's coming to New York tomorrow afternoon, should arrive around five o'clock.

Unable to resist fatigue any longer, I slide into my sleeping bag borrowed from the gay neighbors.

This will be my home now, whatever happens.

Wednesday, December 7

I wake early but stay in bed till my nephew, Lexi, leaves for school and David for his usual coffee with artist-friends. My niece and namesake, Barbara, is staying with friends.

I crawl out of the sleeping bag on the couch and slide quickly into layers of heavy clothing. The air in the loft is frigid. There are 1,700 square feet of refrigerated space, broken only by the makeshift walls David has erected to partition off a small bedroom for him and Louise in one corner, another for Lexi in the opposite corner. Barbara usually sleeps on the couch that I now occupy.

The bathoom—actually, just a toilet—is behind black plastic curtains. The only faucet, for cold water, is in the so-called kitchen, along with a two-burner electric hot plate. Hot water is supplied by a small automatic coffee-maker. Bathing must be either in the neighbors' bathtub—they have flaunted city restrictions and installed a gas water heater—or by going downstairs, out the door, and into the adjacent building, where there's a solitary shower left standing on the vacant first floor. It is all quite complicated, amusing, and completely lacking in privacy.

"Good morning," I greet Louise as she emerges from her bedroom.

"Good morning. How did you sleep?" she answers.

"Quite well, actually. I was exhausted," I tell her, bringing mugs of hot tea to the table. In the daytime, light streams into the immense loft through tall windows. We sit, huddled in blankets around the table, joking about the absurdities of housekeeping here. As we talk, I feel a heavy, gnawing anxiety growing inside me, building up pressure. I want desperately to go to the hospital, but visiting hours aren't until two o'clock.

At last, I get ready to leave. Louise lends me an aged, maroon coat, and I have long-forgotten mittens and a scarf from home. I feel like an enormous, maroon bear as I trudge down five flights of steps and into the street. It is freezing cold and I don't want to waste time walking, so I flag a taxi.

Outside Peter's door, I unlayer quickly. The hospital is stiflingly overheated. Mask, gown, gloves—I enter. A large, green metal cabinet hums busily next to the bed and I eye it apprehensively. It wasn't there last night. Peter's red face, eyes closed, is partially covered by the transparent green oxygen mask. The oxygen apparatus is noisier than last night. If he needs more oxygen today, the lung infection must be worse. Walter sits reading in the armchair near the window.

"What's that?" I whisper, pointing fearfully at the metal cabinet.

"That operates the cooling blanket to lower his temperature," Walter explains, also whispering.

"What's his temperature today?" I ask, alarmed. "How is he?"

"104.8, the last time they took it. The doctor should be by soon."

My anxiety increases. I sit rigidly on the edge of the straight chair at the foot of the bed. Peter is frighteningly still. He lies on his back, eyes closed, hands folded across his chest—deathlike. I watch uneasily, glancing often at his chest. It rises and falls almost imperceptibly.

The resident doctor beckons to us from the doorway. "I

want to talk to both of you," he begins. "Peter is not improving as we hoped and, frankly, we're not sure if he's going to make it. We need to discuss putting him on a respirator, in case his breathing gets even worse."

He looks only at Walter as he speaks and I resent the exclusion. Probably he feels safer talking to a colleague than to a potentially hysterical mother.

"What's a respirator?" I ask. There is much to learn.

"That's a device that takes over the breathing for the patient once its tube is inserted into the lungs." He is finally looking at me, hastily dispensing basic information. "At times, it can be useful if the patient has a good prognosis. But in this kind of case, where the prognosis is so bad, it can only prolong the inevitable, and is extremely uncomfortable. The patient cannot talk with the tube in.

"I think Peter should be in on this decision, if the need for the respirator arises," continues the young doctor. "It's only fair that we tell him the truth, tell him exactly what his chances are, and let him make the final decision. His chances aren't good with or without the respirator."

Shock, disbelief. I stare angrily at the young doctor in front of me. Where does he get the nerve to condemn my son to death without a fight? Hasn't he heard about hope? Does he really expect us to withhold any possible chance of survival from Peter?

Walter nods in agreement. I push down my horror and anger. I'll deal with them later. I must appear calm, even though I'd rather scream at them both, beat their smug, professional chests with raging fists and shriek, "Fix him, damnit! He wants to live! Can't you understand that?"

"Yes, he should have a part in the decision," I agree instead, my voice surprisingly level. "But I don't want you to present the choice to him as if he doesn't have a chance. I want you to present it in a hopeful, optimistic way. He's sure he's going to survive this. Last night, he spoke constantly of all he wants to do *when* he gets out of here, never *if*. He has hope, and you can't take that away from him. If it comes to using a respirator, tell him it's to help his breathing while he recovers the strength to do it alone. *Please* don't tell him he's going to die anyway.'' I struggle to keep anger out of my voice.

The young doctor looks at me superciliously, as if I were foolish to believe Peter will survive. I don't care what he thinks. This is my son, and I know it is not time for Peter to go.

''All right,'' he says reluctantly. ''We'll wait a little and see if we can get his fever down, see if his breathing improves at all, and then decide whether to tell him about the respirator.'' He smiles briefly, professionally, and leaves. We return to Peter's room.

''We could try giving him alcohol baths,'' suggests Walter, and he rings for the nurse. I look at him in surprised relief. He wants to fight!

''What do you think about giving him an alcohol bath?'' he asks the nurse when she enters.

''Well . . . I suppose it wouldn't hurt.'' She's skeptical, obviously considering it a pointless treatment.

''We're going to try it. Would you bring us a basin, alcohol, and more washcloths?''

The nurse returns with the supplies. We uncover Peter's motionless body—my God, it's so thin!—remove his gown and start swabbing his skin with alcohol. I can feel the fever burning my hands through the soaked cloths. The nurse returns every five minutes to take Peter's temperature. Peter's face remains impassive, unaware of our efforts, unaffected by the cool alcohol on his burning skin. I wonder if he's comatose.

Slowly, miraculously, the mercury starts creeping downward. Little by little, his face loses its crimson flush. We wash, wring, wash, taking turns and praying, hoping, our entire selves compressed into his; willing, wanting—and yes! It's coming down, 104 degrees, 103.5, 103, 102—it's down, we did it! We lay his gown loosely over him, cover him with the blanket. Walter looks at me, pleased and proud.

This crisis is over.

We read, glance at Peter, keep silent vigil, our thoughts pulling him back, pulling him away from the precipice.

Come on, Peter, stay with us.

"Hi!" Maria stands in the doorway, her long, honey-blond hair disheveled from her scarf. I've lost all sense of time and forgotten she would arrive at five o'clock. I jump up, startled, and go to the door.

"I'm so glad you're here," I greet her. "Wait, you can't come in like that. Look, you have to put all this awful stuff on before you can come in," I explain, tying the mask over her long, thick hair, tendrils catching in the strings. I tie a gown at the back of her neck while she struggles with the rubber gloves.

"How is he?" she asks anxiously.

"His fever was up to almost 105 degrees this afternoon, but we got it down," I tell her, glossing over the afternoon's fear and frenzy.

"Hi, Peter," she calls softly, nearing the bed.

Eyes still closed, Peter smiles faintly. He's back with us.

Sunday, December 11

Is he aware he has AIDS, or does he think he just has pneumonia? We've asked ourselves this question all week.

Peter talks only of his pneumonia, hasn't mentioned the word AIDS. He's in a fever-induced sleep most of the time, but when he's awake, he talks of all that he will do when he leaves the hospital. Few friends even know he's here and he apparently doesn't want them to know. He tells the few who have found out and visit him here that he has pneumonia and is going to California to recuperate for three months when he's discharged. He doesn't mention his rare type of pneumonia, nor AIDS, nor terminal illness.

It's possible, being so ill when admitted, that no one told him he has AIDS, planning to wait until he feels better and is more capable of understanding the implications. Or perhaps, feverish and heavily medicated, he doesn't remember being told. No nurse or doctor whom we ask seems to know. At moments, we think he does know and is blocking it out, denying.

Perhaps he knows and doesn't want us to know. Something tells me this is the problem. If so, surely he doesn't think that we'll reject him in disgust because of his homosexuality. He knows that that's no problem, for his father or for me. More likely, I'm sure he's aware that promiscuous homosexuals are considered the highest risk group for AIDS. Could he fear our moral judgment and rejection because we'll believe he's been promiscuous?

I don't think he's led an especially promiscuous life, though, at least not by late twentieth-century standards. As far as I know, he had one lover here for two or three years. Then he went to Los Angeles to study voice for 18 months. He met Frank when he returned to New York and, until recently, they've been together for two years. I suppose it is possible. Even so, I would never reject him, especially now.

Two nights ago, I left the hospital with Frank. Since he brought Peter to the hospital, I thought he might know what Peter was told on admission.

"I think they just said it was an AIDS-related pneumonia," he said.

"What do *you* think it is?" I asked, realizing from his perplexity that he must know little about AIDS. I've been reading everything I can find. Knowledge is my best defense against helplessness. But there's so little printed information—the borrowed pamphlet, a book I found at the bookstore, a few articles in "The New York Native," a gay biweekly newspaper that apparently has good AIDS coverage. That's all.

"I don't really know," he answered, puzzled.

"Frank, he *has* AIDS. This pneumonia is very rare, associated with low immunity, and it confirms his diagnosis. AIDS is the cause of all these past months of diarrhea, weight loss, fatigue, low fever—it's all called pre-AIDS."

"Oh," he looked surprised, shocked.

"This means you're at high risk, too, you know. I think you ought to get a checkup, make sure you're all right," I advised him with concern.

"Well . . . what are the early symptoms, how do you know if you have it?" he asked.

I was amazed at his naivete. How could these young men live in New York City, in the nation's largest gay community and the hotbed of AIDS, and not know more about it?

"It can take several forms, Frank. You can have all that Peter has had these past nine or ten months. You can also have night sweats, swollen glands, a fungal infection called *candida albicans,* or thrush, plus other infections—all these symptoms lasting a long time and with no logical explanation. Then, if blood studies indicate a situation that means your immunity is lowered, then you could well have AIDS.

"With nothing to fight with, all sorts of infections can take hold. These come from organisms that everybody carries but they're able to fight off. I don't know what they all are yet, except for PCP, or pneumocystis pneumonia, like Peter has now. It's from a protozoa in the lungs. Or Kaposi's sarcoma, a rare type of skin cancer that can go wild in AIDS patients. Both of these diseases confirm AIDS. Whatever, because of your relationship with Peter—AIDS is usually sexually transmitted, you know—you should go have a good checkup."

"Okay, I will," he promised, his black eyes wide, and we parted.

Maria and I trudge through the cold streets, carrying our usual bundles of fruit and home-cooked foods for Peter, requested magazines, and our own reading matter. He sleeps most of the day. Walter is already sitting in Peter's room when we arrive. He and Maria go to the small lounge outside the elevator, and I don gown, mask, and gloves to take my turn sitting with Peter.

Peter has been irritable and snappy the past two days. Instinct tells me that he knows he has AIDS, and his bad temper is a result of the conflict between wanting to tell us—and fearing to. I have resolved that I will open the subject today.

He's asleep. I gaze with sorrow and pain at his young face made gaunt and aged beyond his years by this horrifying disease. I already hate it passionately. All the statistics I've read now tell me that we probably face eventual defeat, death. That he will gradually accumulate more infections, his immunity will slide steadily downhill, and finally his system will be completely overcome.

That's what the experts say.

But I refuse to give up until Peter himself wants to. The fight will last as long as he wishes. In these last heart-breaking days, I have come to realize what it really means to be a mother, to fight for your child. Peter, all my children, are part of me—my body, my soul, my life. All else is nothing.

Twenty-six years ago, I lost my second son at birth, from a congenital diaphragmatic hernia that allowed his intestines to develop into his chest cavity and inhibited growth of the heart and lungs. I mourned never having touched him, known him. But I had no choice. Now I may lose Peter, too, and it will be so much harder—after all, I've known him twenty-eight years. It won't be without a fight.

Peter stirs, glances at me, looks away.

"You know, I don't just have pneumonia." The words explode, defensive and challenging. He stares straight ahead, waiting for my response. His guard is up, his armor on.

"Yes, I know," I tell him, sitting on the edge of his bed and grateful now for the cotton mask that hides my pain. He lies on his back with his knees up, the right leg crossed and propped on the left in an oddly casual position. I stroke his raised calf with my gloved hand. My God, I shudder, nothing but bone.

"Peter, I . . . we . . . know you have AIDS," my eyes fill but I *must* wait until later to cry.

Peter's green eyes, large and hollow, speak to me, sadly wordless, *I am going to die. Please, don't let me die!* And my eyes answer, *I am here. I will not leave you.* He seems to understand, and his eyes shine with tears, too.

"Does everyone know?" he asks finally, eyeing me with caution.

"Yes, Peter, everyone. Dad, David, Jonathan, Maria, your aunts and uncles—and nobody cares how you got it," I reassure him firmly. "All we want is for you to get well, that's all that matters. We all love you and are with you."

Peter raises his left arm toward me. I move closer, put my left hand on his, his right hand crosses and lies on top. I pat his hand, stroke it, and we sit quietly, all four hands joined for several minutes while he digests my words. Though tears sparkle in his eyes, his tension of the past days seems to dissolve. No, he will not be rejected, abandoned, cast out. Maybe everything will be all right.

Oh, Peter, why didn't you come to us sooner?

"It's going to be all right," I tell him. "We're all with you, *I'm* with you. This is a disease of ups and downs, but we'll get through them together.

"I'm not going to leave you, Peter," I promise.

He smiles faintly. His hands grasp mine tightly and I squeeze back. All is open, and we can go on. I pray fervently for the strength and wisdom to face the battles ahead. Contentedly, he drifts back to sleep, and I tiptoe out of the room to join Walter and Maria on the couch in the elevator lobby.

"He knows, he knew . . . ," the dam breaks and sobs overwhelm me. "We had a really wonderful talk." Walter touches my shoulder tentatively, and Maria, next to me, puts an arm around me and huddles close.

"Oh, Jesus, oh my God . . . ," I choke, wishing I could scream out my anguish. Fearing that Peter will die—whether tomorrow, in six months, a year—hurts as if he has already died. I started missing him seven days ago, with that early phone call. The ache of losing will never cease.

"Whassa matter?" I look up, see Anita the nurse, speaking to me in her loud, nasal, New York accent. What the hell does she think is the matter, I wonder angrily. She's seen AIDS patients. She knows what AIDS is all about. What does she think is the matter with the mother of one, for Christ's sake?

"I just had a talk with Peter, about his having AIDS," I tell her.

"Oh, don't worry about it, he's going to be fine," she says brusquely. "It doesn't mean he's going to die, y'know. Lots of 'em walk right out of here."

I look at her incredulously. Either she's stupid or she

thinks I am. I resent her callousness and ignore her as she turns and walks briskly away.

"He's known all along what he has," I tell Maria and Walter, calming down. "I feel better and I think he does, too. I've told him we're all with him. He knows. It was really good."

Fear, love, terror, mix and churn inside me. Will I be able to carry him through? I have to. I gave him life and now if he's to die, I'll be here for him. I have no choice. I made him a promise.

And I keep my promises.

3

Monday, December 12

Peter was tranquil today, after our talk. No more irritability. His dreadful secret is out, and nobody has abandoned him. Instead, he's been guaranteed the loving and unconditional support of his family. He knows he isn't fighting alone.

He slept most of the day, and we took turns sitting quietly with him, as usual. Maria returned to school in Baltimore this evening. She's going to take her finals early and be back on Thursday to stay through the holidays. I'm glad she'll be here. I need her. She knows that. We've been so close in the years since her brothers left home that we have an unspoken communication.

Today, the doctor started Peter on an experimental drug, pentamidine. He just completed a ten-day course of Septra®, the preferred drug for pneumocystis, and though he's not as critically ill, he's not shown the hoped-for improvement. His fever remains high, peaking at 103 degrees, and his chest X-rays show no recession of the densities in his lungs. Pentamidine will be administered once a day for ten days by injection into alternate thigh muscles. It is excruciatingly painful.

The days have developed into a routine now. In the huge loft on Wooster Street, cooking is difficult with the two-burner hot plate for five people. And then we often have guests for dinner at ten or eleven o'clock, after I return from the hospital. My brother, Sandy, has dinner with us when he comes in from Southampton every two or three days to see Peter. Walter has come for dinner several times, there are often others. It tasks our ingenuity to the limit but we have produced some fine dinners, we think. The problems in preparing food and the conviviality of finally consuming it provide much-needed humor and diversion from the grim truth just a few blocks away.

Louise unpacked her thirty-cup percolator, which we now use as a miniature water heater. Lexi leaves for school each morning, David for his morning coffee; then I get up and plug in the percolator. By the time I'm dressed, Louise is straggling out of their bedroom and we huddle over mugs of hot tea to get warm, chatting aimlessly, waking up.

The morning passes, but I still become increasingly impatient to get to the hospital and see how Peter is, and often it seems an eternity. The hospital has a number to call for information on a patient's status, but they only give me a meaningless "fair condition." Still, I call often.

I finally leave for the hospital by one o'clock. Unless the weather is too cold or I'm late, I walk through Greenwich Village on the way, taking a different route daily for distraction, shopping for Peter as I go—magazines, newspapers, special requests for food. He tries hard to eat the lukewarm, gray hospital food but he can't. "How do they expect seriously ill people, like cancer patients, to eat this stuff?" he asks in disgust, forgetting that his body has the same desperate need. So I bought some small pans and warm up whatever I've brought from home. We joke about setting up a catering service there for other patients.

Peter dozes most of the day but is awake in the evening, watching television till one or two in the morning. His late hours upset the nurses. They're unaware that, as a waiter of many years, he has always left work at one A.M., stayed up two or three more hours to unwind, and then slept until noon the next day. This schedule doesn't fit into the hospital's very easily.

Fortunately, the diarrhea of so many months seems to have been replaced by constipation. And a herpes lesion that developed at the base of his spine, the size of a quarter, is just beginning to disappear with treatment by topical acyclovir, a recently developed and effective experimental antiherpes drug. His mouth is spotted with white patches—this is thrush, or *candida albicans,* a fungal infection that, because of AIDS, can invade the entire system if not treated. He has to "swish and swallow" a vile-tasting antifungal medicine for this.

Usually, I leave the hospital at ten or eleven P.M., after helping Peter settle down for the night. We help him bathe and give him frequent backrubs and massage his calves and feet. His body aches painfully from being bedridden so long. I've devised a method for shampooing his hair easily. He hates to have dirty hair. So much of it has dropped out—his pillowcase is always covered with straight, brown hairs—that it takes no time to dry.

Maria, whom he has teasingly called "Sister Mary" since she was twelve and devoutly, righteously religious, is chief backrubber. He likes her strong musician's hands kneading his muscles, but I suspect that her touch, even through the rubber gloves, is what he really wants. He feels loved and cared for.

After the complicated dinner routine, everyone else goes to bed and Louise and I stay up late, huddled in layers of clothing around the oak table. We feel like two primitive women around their campfire, the single bulb hanging high over our heads and pushing the dark, cold shadows back a few feet.

Friday, December 16

I stand by the window, watching the dull, winter sunset and half-listening to Peter and Maria discuss music, his voice so soft, weak.

The pentamidine is ineffective so far. Peter's condition remains stable, neither better nor worse. His fever ranges between 101 and 103 degrees, and he still breathes with difficulty, using oxygen most of the time. I am anxious, hoping no new infection invades his weakened body. I have been reading everything I can find and am now aware of the myriad exotic bacteria, viruses, fungi, and parasitic diseases to which his lack of immunity now exposes him. My fears are justified.

Walter is back in Virginia for the weekend to be with his wife and elderly parents. Now that Maria is here on her Christmas vacation, I can count on her help and support.

"Would you like us to decorate your room for Christmas?" I ask Peter.

He has always loved this season: the aromatic pine tree, the gaudy decorations, the presents, special holiday foods. When he was little, he and I would turn out enormous batches of thin ginger cookies and decorate shaped sugar cookies. He always remembers this.

"Yes," he answers, with a small, pleased smile.

I leave Maria with him and depart. A block away, I buy a small pine tree, thinking that he'll appreciate its fragrance in the close air of his room. In a novelty store, I hear Christmas carols on the Muzak. Poignancy brings unexpected tears to my eyes. I cry a moment, there in the crowded store, remembering happy Christmases past, the children eager, excited, the family still united. The fear of future Christmases without Peter hurts deeply.

I miss him already. That damned music—the ancient, minor melodies of Christmas will always haunt me, their medieval melancholy and longing persisting even through the commerciality of their modern, electronic form. I know I will never hear their notes, year after year, without feeling the unbearable loss and pain of this instant. I wonder, as I dry my eyes quickly, if Peter realizes this might be his last Christmas, and I determine more than ever to fight that possibility.

I wander dispiritedly through the store, pushing through the anxious crowds and selecting strings of miniature electric lights, small, colored balls, tinsel—we always use too much tinsel!—candy canes, silver bells, and red velvet ribbon to make a door-hanging. I buy Christmas stockings for Peter, Maria, and David—he'll arrive Christmas morning—and small toys, gadgets, jokes. I spend too much money and don't care. All I want is for Peter to know that Christmas is still Christmas, even if he isn't strong enough to open his gifts.

I return to the hospital, take a deep breath, and force a smile before entering Peter's room. Louise is there with Maria now, and together we string the lights and decorate the tree. We tape Peter's Christmas cards in a design on one wall and festoon the other dull, green walls with yards of cellophane garlands; then hang candy canes, ornaments, and tinsel on them. I make a large bouquet of red, satin-tape roses and fasten them with a velvet bow to the door handle. Peter watches us with interest and contentment. We laugh and joke, denying the underlying sadness, and at last we plug in the lights and stand back to appraise the results. Too bright, too gaudy, definitely not classy—but Christmas! Peter is pleased.

When we leave, Peter, childlike, wants us to leave the blinking lights on. I know their gentle glow reminds him of Christmases past, of security, and of how much he's loved. That's what Christmas is for, after all.

Wednesday, December 21

"We're going to put him back on Septra," the resident doctor tells us. "We'll keep up the pentamidine, give him both at once, and see if that does the trick."

The pentamidine is still ineffective. Peter's fever refuses to abate. The chest X-rays are no better, and not enough oxygen reaches his lungs. He wears the green, plastic oxygen mask almost all the time.

I can see that they're only guessing. This is a shot in the dark, but there is no alternative. Septra and pentamidine are the only known drugs for PCP. If they don't work, Peter will not survive. The pentamidine shots have made his thighs unbearably sensitive. Now he will have to suffer ten more days of injections.

This has to work.

Thursday, December 22

Despite my intention to walk to the hospital today, the bone-chilling wind quickly persuades me to look for a taxi.

My southwestern thermostat cannot adjust to northeastern winter. I dread going to the hospital, hoping for an overnight miracle from the two drugs but fearing disappointment.

I tie the mask on quickly when I arrive, the ends tangling in my long hair as always. The cooling machine hums busily beside the bed. I detest its ominous placidity, its wordless reminder that fever is rampant. Peter's face is bright red again, his face and body impassively deathlike. Walter is already here.

"What's happening?" I ask fearfully. "Why is that thing on again?"

"His temperature went back up to 104 degrees," Walter tells me, whispering. "But it may be just a reaction to the Septra. The doctor said that can happen. They're hoping it's just that. If so, his fever should go down in 24 hours. If not . . ."

"I know."

We sit by the bed, keeping our silent vigil. I glance often at Peter's still face, hoping that our presence and positive thoughts will help him.

Get better, Peter, get better, get better. . . .

The day passes slowly. We take turns going downstairs to eat or sit in the elevator lobby and talk to ambulatory patients or other visitors. We stay until eleven P.M. Before leaving, I check with the nurses to be sure they have my number to call. It's good I checked; no one wrote my number on his chart.

It's been a bad day.

Friday, December 23

I race to the hospital, taking a taxi in my impatience. I called the hospital earlier to check on Peter but they merely spouted the usual "fair condition." I feel so helpless, so out of control, when I'm not in the hospital. What if they didn't call and there was a change for the worst? After all, they didn't even have my phone number on Peter's chart.

I mask, gown, glove, run anxiously into the room. Surprise, miracle! The cooling machine is tucked discreetly into a corner, and the fever is down. It was just a reaction to the Septra and I am ecstatic. His temperature is still above normal, but everything is relative, and we are learning fast to accept minor improvements as giant steps. The two-drug regimen will continue now, and once again my hopes rise.

Today, Louise and her family leave for Portland, Maine, to spend Christmas weekend with our mother there. She's been very ill with flu, yet she calls every night to learn about Peter. Walter leaves later this afternoon for Virginia, and Maria and I will be alone in the cold loft until Sunday, when my son, David, will join us. I wish Jonathan could come, too. It would mean so much to have all four children together for this special Christmas. But he only has the one day, Christmas, free from work.

I leave Maria and Walter with Peter so that I can do some last-minute shopping. The stores are full of surly, pushing crowds, and I am tempted to leave it until after Christmas, just postpone it all.

I really would rather not celebrate Christmas this year, my nerves and emotions are so frayed and my energy depleted. But traditions, or some semblance, must be maintained, especially when life itself is so uncertain. We create traditions in good times and they bind us in the bad.

Saturday, December 24

Christmas Eve. Peter is alert. His eyes are still fever-bright and he's weak, easily fatigued—but he's still with us. After these four frantically anxious weeks, we have much to be thankful for.

Maria and I stay with him all day, spelling each other. We are tired, and the hospital is unbearably overheated. But we don't want to leave Peter, nor does he want to be alone.

At midnight, we finally go. We turn out the overhead light but leave the tree glowing and blinking in Peter's darkened room. He seems content.

At one-thirty A.M., the phone rings. I reach for it, instantly apprehensive. *Oh God, no, not on Christmas.*

"Hi," Peter's frail voice. "I just wanted to be the first to wish you a Merry Christmas."

"You are the first—thank you! And let me be the first to wish you a Merry Christmas, too," I tell him cheerily, hiding my panic.

"And to tell you I love you."

"Oh, Peter . . . I love you, too." My throat thickens and my eyes sting with the sudden rush of tears.

"Good night, then."

"Good night, Peter. See you tomorrow."

Sunday, December 25

"Merry Christmas!" Maria and I greet each other, our words forming clouds of vapor in the frigid air. It was almost zero degrees last night, according to the radio.

David arrives at eleven o'clock. We have time to exchange gifts and open the traditional Christmas stockings full of trinkets and practical jokes before leaving for the hospital.

At one o'clock, we rush down the five flights of stairs and out into the street. The air is a wall of ice, so we run to hail a taxi.

"Who're you visiting in St. Vincent's?" asks our cabbie, a talkative, portly man of about sixty.

"My son is sick there," I tell him.

"Gee, that's too bad, awful to have to be in the hospital on Christmas Day," he sympathizes. "Gosh, I've had so much sickness, all sorts of surgery and stuff . . . it's a wonder I'm still here, got a lot to be thankful for. What's wrong with your son?"

"Oh . . . he has pneumonia," I half-lie.

"That's too bad. I hope he'll be okay soon," he says, turning the corner. "I'll tell ya, the people I really feel sorry for these days is those guys with this new disease, AIDS, that's just terrible. Well, guess that's one thing I won't ever get. Or that herpes all the kids are gettin' nowadays."

He guffaws as we pull up in front of the hospital. I squirm at his unwittingly appropriate remarks and turn to look at David and Maria in back as they mirror my response.

"Merry Christmas to you," I say, paying the fee.

"Thanks, same to you. Sure hope your son gets better real soon," he says merrily.

"He sure hit the nail on the head, didn't he?" I comment as we wait for the elevator.

Outside Peter's room, Maria and I don the familiar yellow gowns, mask, and gloves, and initiate David into the procedure. I enter, eye the square, green machine. Good, it's quiet today.

"Merry Christmas," we tell Peter. He's awake and waiting for us.

"Merry Christmas," he answers, smiling, happy to see us.

I present him with his Christmas stocking, stuffed with useless and nonsensical gifts. He's too weak to open everything at once, as I expected. At least we are together on this day and he feels our caring.

David has brought him a book, *Blue Highways*. Maria has spent two days making chocolate chip and peanut butter cookies for him, hoping to whet his appetite. She dashed back and forth to the neighbors' oven carrying sheets of cookies. Jonathan has telegrammed a lovely Christmas arrangement of pine sprays and cones, surprising and pleasing Peter.

Peter has deviously managed his Christmas shopping from his bed, asking each of us to buy something for another with the money he brought to the hospital. He planned what he wanted to give each of us, where to find it, and sent us separately on our errands.

Maria wordlessly shows me the card Peter has written to her: "Good person, sister, skier, percussionist, student, and now . . . No. 1 Nurse—Thanks for all your help. Love, Peter."

The afternoon passes quickly and Peter tires. I want to take David and Maria out for a special Christmas dinner while Peter sleeps. He insists on choosing a restaurant for us and calling for reservations. His nine years as a waiter have made him an expert on New York restaurants, but many places are closed today. Finally, he remembers a

restaurant around the corner, calls, and it's open. He
reserves a table, and requests that we bring him a bar-
becued short-rib dinner, their specialty. I hate to leave him
here alone, but my other two children deserve something
special, too.

We were away over two hours. The fireplace was warm
and welcoming in the restaurant, and we enjoyed the brief
respite from the hospital. Peter eats a small amount of the
short-ribs we've brought him with gusto. The rest is saved
in the refrigerator.

Tonight we are staying late. Nurses pop in and out of
the door to see his Christmas decorations. No other patient's room has been adorned, and they are impressed.
Peter seems pleased by their reactions, proud of what his
family has done for him.

It's been a good day for all of us.

Friday, December 30

Slowly but surely, Peter is getting better. X-rays show
his lungs are finally clearing. With more oxygen, his
breathing is vastly improved, and his fever floats at a
lower level, between 99 and 100 degrees. With less fever,
his appetite is improving.

We had a temporary fright two days ago. A laboratory
report indicated that Peter had Legionnaire's Disease and
he was started immediately on a course of erythromycin. I
cringed at the thought of yet another drug joining those
already barraging his system, but fortunately, someone—
God knows who—realized it was a laboratory error, and
the erythromycin was discontinued. We were relieved.

But also scared. Not only did this incident make me
realize acutely how vulnerable Peter is to any infection,
but my fears resurfaced about his care. How could they
make such a mistake? Walter had finally gotten his nerve
up, and both of us had talked to everyone even remotely
concerned with AIDS treatment or research. We were
informed that St. Vincent's was an excellent place for
Peter. I had no choice but to trust the experts. Still, I must

ask more questions, stay aware of what they're doing to my son.

With improved health and spirits, Peter's sense of humor is returning. Last night, as Walter, Maria, and I watched TV with Peter, a commercial flashed on the screen. A suburban matron stepped daintily out of her car and proudly announced, "I take Ayds, and I've lost thirty pounds."

"Well," we suddenly heard Peter in falsetto mimicry, "I have AIDS, and I've only lost twenty pounds."

We all laughed. This was our old Peter, back to ironic mimicry of the mundane.

Neither Peter nor anyone in his circle of friends was acquainted with, or even knew of, any AIDS patients. I believe this lack of personal contact with AIDS certainly accounts for part of his denial and delay in seeking medical help when the PCP first started. It seems that he really could not believe he had the disease, it hadn't touched his own world yet.

"Well," he now says dryly, "I always had to be the first kid on the block."

Now we know two other AIDS patients. One was his first next-door neighbor in the hospital who was hospitalized for four months with PCP and subsequent infections. He was discharged two weeks after Peter's admission. He's living alone, as his family, though not completely rejecting him, still is not very supportive, either. Though he and Peter were not able to get together for fear of infecting each other, they spoke by phone, room to room. He told Peter to be sure to contact the Gay Men's Health Crisis and ask to speak to a Bob Cecchi there, that he or another volunteer would counsel him either in person or by phone. Peter is anxious to speak to someone about AIDS and has been trying to reach this man. He has many questions.

The same room is now occupied by an airline steward, in for treatment of a second bout of PCP. I talk at length with his long-time lover and his mother while we sit in the lounge. I learned that this young man is his mother's only child, and my heart went out to her.

We can now begin making plans for Peter's departure from the hospital. He should be able to leave as soon as his temperature goes down to normal and stays there for two days. He is very weak. At 5'10", he weighs only 123 pounds and probably will never regain his former weight or strength. PCP can leave the system forever debilitated, and AIDS will keep the immune system irreversibly lowered. He will never work again and will be on full and permanent disability, though he will not receive any Social Security payments for six months. Luckily, this status will entitle him automatically to MediCal, as state-funded medical insurance is called in California.

Two weeks ago, I started the tedious, complicated paperwork required to establish his financial and medical needs. The New York Social Security office has a desk specifically to help AIDS patients and expedite their claims, and they have been extremely helpful.

Saturday, December 31

New Year's Eve. Tomorrow begins another year, and I am glad. 1983 was not a good year. A thief tried to break into my San Diego apartment when I was almost asleep one night, my car was stolen, and now, the immensity of Peter's illness. I know 1984 holds pain and uncertainty for Peter and me, but I'm not going to worry about that until it comes. One day at a time.

Peter is quite chipper today, as am I. I can already see that my spirits will be inextricably tied to his. When he feels well, so do I. And, conversely, when he is not well, my anxiety increases.

Ten-thirty P.M., and we gather in Peter's room. Walter was resting at his hotel, and Maria and I went to dinner so that Peter could sleep. David returned to Austin last week. The nurses have given us permission to stay late tonight. A friend of Peter's visited while we were gone and brought New Year's paraphernalia—colored curls of ribbon, noise-makers, whistles, and festive paper hats. We don the hats and festoon the Christmas garlands with pink, blue, yellow, and green ribbons, and watch TV, waiting for the ball to hit the top in Times Square and announce a new year. Peter is sitting up. I wonder if he feels the same bittersweet poignancy as I, that under our hopes for the new year lies the fearful certainty that he must fight to welcome another.

"Happy New Year!" we chorus, touching glasses all around.

And, Peter, may this year be good to you; may a cure be discovered, may you fulfill your goals, may you be as well as possible.

All my wishes are for him except for one—that I find the strength I will need to help him.

4

Monday, January 2

The telephone rings at noon in the loft. I answer, surprised to hear Peter's voice.

"Mom, I just finished talking to Bob Cecchi, remember? The volunteer at the Gay Men's Health Crisis that that other patient told me to call?" his voice is excited.

"Oh, good. I'm glad you finally got hold of him," I exclaim.

Peter's been trying to reach him for days. Bob, he tells me, has had diagnoses varying from AIDS to ARC (AIDS-Related Complex) to lymphadenopathy syndrome, apparently depending on his state of health. Though not having full-blown AIDS, he certainly could understand Peter's fears and anguish.

"He was so encouraging, so positive. He started by asking how I felt about a lot of things, and I told him I was a little worried about what might happen. So he asked me, 'Do you want to live?' and I said, 'Of course,' and he said, 'Then you will, you'll find a way.' It was really good to talk to him.

"Then I asked him about a lot of practical things, like being around children, animals, so on. He said to just use common sense. Don't go to movies or restaurants when they're crowded, stay away from animals, and for God's sake, keep away from kids—they're always sick with something!" he laughs.

"Sounds logical to me." I tell him. "How long has he been sick?"

"He was diagnosed a year and a half ago. He says he has his ups and downs. His immune status is checked every six months but doesn't seem to be at all relative to how he's feeling physically. He works over 60 hours a week as a volunteer at the crisis center," Peter says admiringly.

"That's encouraging, that would be a heavy schedule for anyone," I reply. How wonderful if Peter can do that well. "Does he have trouble coping?"

"He says it's been getting to him lately—there've been several deaths—and he's been told he should take a week or two off and rest. But he said that he feels AIDS has been a positive force for him, made him stop and think exactly what he wants, which he never bothered to do before. He says it forced him to re-evaluate his life, and now he feels he has something special to contribute and something to live for. I told him that's the way I've been feeling, too, and that I want to do some volunteer work in California. He said he thought I'd do just fine and wished me luck. He's such a sincere person," he finishes, his voice starting to sound breathless.

"I'm glad you got to talk to him, Peter."

From the new lift in his voice, I can tell that Bob's words were the best medicine yet. I thank the unknown Bob.

"Mom?"

"Yes?"

"I wish you'd call and talk to him, too," Peter requests. "I told him you would."

"Oh, yes. I'd like to very much. I was hoping to."

"Would you call him now, before you come over?" he asks anxiously.

"Of course."

"Okay, thanks. See you soon." Peter's voice has a fresh optimism in it.

*　　*　　*

"Did you talk to Bob?" Peter's first question as I enter his room.

"Yes, I did, right after we hung up," I tell him. "He really sounds nice. I didn't have many questions that you hadn't already asked, but it was nice. He's so enthusiastic, encouraging—must be a wonderful person."

"Thanks for calling him, I'm glad you did," Peter is still euphoric.

I'm delighted with Peter's excited eagerness to live, to make something good out of something so evil and negative.

I hope this will keep up a long, long time.

Wednesday, January 4

The pentamidine was stopped on Monday, after 22 days of painful injections into Peter's thigh muscles. Though he can get up now—he almost ran down the hall the first time, dragging his IV stand behind him—walking is difficult because of the pain. The doctors and nurses seem unaware of his extreme sensitivity, and Peter has to remind them of it whenever they come to examine him.

He is angry today at the intern who was on duty last night. Peter woke at two A.M., just as the intern was about to give him an injection in his left thigh.

"What do you have there?" Peter asked.

"What do you care?" the intern snapped back.

"I care very much, and I hope that's not pentamidine."

"What if it is?" the intern asked insolently.

"Because if it is, I'm not supposed to get it anymore," Peter replied. "I think you better check my chart and you'll see that it was terminated on Monday."

"Oh, no, the orders are still on your chart."

"I'm sure they're not," Peter insisted. "Go back and read them again, you'll see that I'm right."

The intern left the room and never returned. Obviously, he had not checked the chart carefully.

"I can see that I have to keep up with my medications and orders," Peter tells me, perturbed. "And what happens to people in comas, or people too senile to know

what's happening? Suppose they get the wrong medicine?
They have no way of defending themselves against error.''

I lamely attempt to reassure him, though I'm angry
myself. Peter is really disturbed about this incident and
doubly anxious to leave the hospital. Along with this fear
is that of picking up a new infection while hospitalized.
Yesterday, he spotted a cockroach crawling across the
floor. He's convinced the hospital isn't clean. He's probably right; the housekeeping is desultory, at best.

I must get him out of here soon.

Saturday, January 7

Peter is eager to start his new life in San Diego. He's
impatient to leave New York behind with its furious pace,
dirty streets, and thronging crowds. When friends call, he
still tells them that he just has pneumonia and is leaving to
recuperate for three months in California. He still wants no
one to know he has AIDS. He says he feels reborn and has
been thinking about his life with a new perspective and
hope.

"I've made a lot of mistakes, a lot of bad judgments,''
he speaks unexpectedly as I sit alone with him.

"Well, mistakes are to learn by.'' I look up. He wants
to talk.

"Yeah, but I made the same mistakes over and over,''
he insists.

"Well . . . it takes some of us longer to learn than
others. Besides, it's not the mistakes that matter, it's how
you cope with their results.''

"That's the trouble. I never learned from them,'' he
continues, unwilling to forgive himself. "I really made a
lot of mistakes.

"But don't go saying I'm self-destructive again,'' he
says belligerently, turning away, referring to my infer-
ences in the past that his life-course was exactly that.

"I suppose you've seen my drug history on my medical
charts.''

"No, I haven't . . . I haven't seen your charts. What

have you taken that you haven't told me about?'' I'm almost afraid to know, but I see that he wants to tell me.

"Oh, you know about the pot, the acid . . . angel dust a few times.''

And heroin?

"Have you ever taken anything by needle, Peter?'' I dread the answer.

"Yuh, I tried it twice, and I mainlined cocaine twice.'' I wince.

"I didn't like either one the first time, made me feel like I was on a roller coaster, really scary.''

"Then why did you take them again?''

"I just wanted to be sure I didn't like them,'' he said matter-of-factly.

Oh, God, I think. He could have gotten AIDS from sharing dirty needles.

"But I was always careful,'' he insists, as if reading my mind. "I always made sure the needles were clean and that I was in a safe place where I couldn't get hurt. The stuff was always available. I never bought it. People just had it at parties.

"I did get a little scared one time. I shot heroin at someone's house, and when I left I had absolutely no idea where I was. I was really dizzy and I don't know how I finally got home.''

I mourn silently. *Oh, Peter. How could you abuse yourself so? You, with your beautiful voice, so much talent, so much intelligence—and always throwing it away like dirtied tissue.*

I say nothing. Too late now for recriminations, it's all in the past. It doesn't matter anymore.

"I've been thinking a lot about it,'' he continues, "and I'd like to do some drug counseling with teenagers . . . keep kids from making the same mistakes I made. Could I do that in San Diego?''

"I'm sure there'll be a way to do it,'' I tell him enthusiastically. "We'll look into it when we get home.''

"And I'd like to write about my experiences with AIDS. Maybe it will help somebody,'' he says wistfully.

"We can leave my typewriter set up so you can write

whenever you want. You've always had a gift for writing, you know.''

''Do you still have the piano?'' Peter continues.

''Yes, I do.''

''I'd like to take lessons again. Do you think we could find a good teacher?''

''San Diego has two state universities, a symphony orchestra, several smaller musical groups. I'm sure we'll find someone.''

''What I'd like is someone who could also accompany me so I can get back to my singing. I've been too tired and low on energy to do anything but be a waiter for so long. And now I'll have the time to do it,'' he says pensively.

''Yes, you will. There's a good side to everything, and the good side to all this is that now you won't have to work and can do exactly what you want to do with your time.'' I encourage him, delighted he's thinking so constructively. I, too, have been thinking.

I don't want him to become an emotional invalid, preoccupied only with his illness. I know he faces gradual physical deterioration, and his lack of immunity bares his system to all sorts of exotic infections. But if he keeps his mind busy and sets himself small goals, perhaps his life will be satisfying and give him the direction he has always lacked. He's making a good start. I just hope the disease gives him time. With high hopes, an amazing recovery, and his talk with Bob Cecchi, Peter seems to feel invincible.

I can't think of a better way to start a new life.

Thursday, January 12

I can't believe it. We're on our way home to San Diego.

Everything has happened dizzyingly fast since Monday when we were told that Peter could leave today.

Suddenly we had dozens of details to take care of—plane tickets; having an oxygen tank awaiting him at home; portable tanks for use on the plane; a ride home from the airport; packing my clothes and enough of Peter's to last until his belongings arrive. Last weekend, Sandy, Frank, and I packed his few possessions, and I arranged to transport them west. The hospital social worker was a great help. She arranged a chair ambulance to the airport, found an oxygen supplier in San Diego, and contacted a social worker at UCSD Medical Center to arrange for Peter's continuing care at the Owen Clinic.

Irritating, last-minute complications arose over Peter's medical charts. The hospital wouldn't let us take them along and Peter's future doctor will have to send a written request for them. Ridiculous, I fumed. Too much delay. How do they expect us to inform that doctor right away of what has happened to Peter here, or to prove his disability in order to obtain county medical insurance, which we need till MediCal is approved? During the last hour, I had to hunt down the resident doctor and ask him to write a brief summary of Peter's illnesses and medications. He wasn't very pleasant about it.

At last we bundled Peter into a wheelchair, despite his protests—he wanted to walk—and outside to the waiting ambulance. Sooty ice covered the curb, and as Peter stood proudly to give Sandy and Maria a farewell hug, his feet flew up. I shrieked, thinking of six more weeks in the hospital, and we all lunged to grab him before he fell. We helped him into the front seat of the ambulance. Peter insisted on sitting in the front to see the last of his city. He appraised everything carefully, silently—saying goodbye to his home of many years. My only desire was to get him out of this abominable city, away from its dirt, crowds, and noise. Away from the frightening memories of the last six weeks.

The twinkling lights of San Diego lie directly beneath the plane, beaming us a warm welcome. Funny. I've been too concerned about Peter's comfort during the trip to worry about my fear of flying. We glide in low over Balboa Park and pull up moments later alongside the terminal. A wheelchair ordered for our arrival is lost, and we wait while someone goes to find it. Peter is quiet, tired. Finally I wheel him downstairs to the luggage carousel, where friends of mine, Tracy and her husband Ray, await us.

We arrive at my apartment, and my friends help us unload the car. Tracy is a close friend, and she and Ray are aware that Peter has AIDS. Though I know I can count on their support, they leave quickly. Tracy has a cold and fears giving it to Peter. Not ten hours out of the hospital, and we already fear contagion.

My neighbor hears our arrival and rushes over to welcome us. "*Ay, que mono tu hijo!*" she exclaims, admiring his good looks. She only knows that he's seriously ill. Peter answers in Spanish, we chat briefly, and she leaves, knowing we are tired. Peter looks about the apartment, acquainting himself with his new home while I make his bed and help him settle down.

We are home. The first round of our long fight is over.

Friday, January 20

We've been home a week now, seven busy days. The most urgent chore was ensuring medical coverage under San Diego County's Medical Aid to Indigents program— more red tape and endless requirements to fulfill. Treatment for Peter's many problems is outrageously expensive, more than his father or I can cope with. Thank God the St. Vincent's bill was paid by a New York fund for the medically indigent. Waiters are not insured by their employers, and Peter entered the hospital with just $90 to his name.

We also had to have Peter officially certified as permanently unemployable by the state of California. They seemed to have a problem realizing that AIDS is a permanent disability.

We were both anxious to find a doctor as soon as possible should problems arise soon. Owen Clinic, the clinic that I found out about for the treatment of homosexual health problems, seems to be the best place for Peter here. They've treated most of the local AIDS cases, and their doctors conduct AIDS research. The clinic is open on Tuesday and Thursday evenings in the outpatient department of UCSD Medical Center.

Peter's first appointment was last night. The examination went well. The doctor, an affable type, spent over an hour with Peter, examining him completely, taking blood for the lab, and sending him downstairs for a chest X-ray. He was young, blond, bearded, and wore sandals. Peter liked his unhurried but thorough manner.

"A California doctor," he laughed later. "He'd never survive in New York. They'd never let him take so much time with a patient, not to mention wear sandals."

The examination revealed that Peter has lost four pounds since we left New York and still has a low fever of 99.5 degrees. He told the doctor that he had occasional nausea, alternating diarrhea and constipation, hemorrhoids, and a persistent cough. He also mentioned casually that he often found himself losing his train of thought.

On examination, the doctor found Peter had thrush in his mouth again and that the suspected hemorrhoids were actually a reactivating herpes lesion in his rectum. He prescribed ketoconazole for the thrush and topical acyclovir for the herpes.

But the best medication was when the doctor told Peter that he looked amazingly well for having been so sick. That opinion was especially timely because Peter had seemed discouraged all day. Expecting his energy and strength to return as soon as he left the hospital, he's disappointed that he still feels weak and tired. But he left the clinic well-satisfied and confident of receiving good care and attention.

"I've had the worst craving for a double cheeseburger, vanilla milkshake, and French fries," he told me as we left the clinic. "Let's get them on the way to the drugstore, okay?"

"Yuk! Sounds awful to me, but sure, let's go!"

We ended up being out for five hours last night—the clinic, the drugstore, and the double cheeseburger orgy. Peter ate every crumb, drank every drop. He was exhausted when we arrived home but pleased with himself.

Peter's been staying up late to watch television and then sleeping until eleven or twelve in the morning. He fixes his own breakfast and lunch, a good sign. I must let him do as much for himself as he can, and remember my vow to keep him from feeling like an invalid. Living with a life-threatening disease is a new experience. Already, what we accept as "normal" is far from that.

Our normalcy evolves by itself, day by day.

Afternoons, we walk, lengthening the distance daily. A shopping center is a mile away, and after three or four days, we walked there and back, very slowly—a two-mile round trip. Peter went alone later, and I waited anxiously. He's still so weak and often seems confused.

It reminded me of when Peter, at seven years old, made his first trip downtown. We lived in a small, rural town in Virginia at the time. And though "downtown" was but a few blocks away, I worried by the window until he came into sight, striding nonchalantly back up the hill.

Peter returned from the shopping center as nonchalantly as when he was a small boy, but obviously pleased with his accomplishment. My worries were for naught. Since then, he has walked to and from the shopping center almost every day.

We've discussed moving to a more interesting neighborhood, perhaps near the hospital. Peter misses the New York atmosphere of interesting shops and throngs of people in the streets that my quiet neighborhood lacks. Besides, walking is his major source of exercise and entertainment, so it might be a good idea to move somewhere that offers him more opportunity to get out and see things, meet people, make friends. "As soon as I feel a little stronger," he tells me.

A few days ago, he touched my hand briefly and said, "Mom, I don't want you to feel hurt by what I'm going to say, but if I keep improving like I have been, I'd like to find my own apartment and live alone."

"Oh, Peter, I'm not at all hurt," I said. I have hoped that he would be able to live independently again. Better yet, that he would want to. "I think it'd be great."

He smiled, obviously relieved.

Tonight, Walter arrives for a two-day visit. I'm leaving in the morning to visit friends out-of-town, and he'll stay in the apartment with Peter. It's important, I know, to keep as much of my own life for as long as possible.

Monday, January 30

Today, I met a friend in Rancho California—an hour away. I felt uneasy about being away all day, leaving Peter alone, but I told myself that I need time apart from Peter, too. Peculiar how a cord seems to invisibly bind us. I don't know if it's good or not. He needs me, I need him, our emotional ups and downs irrevocably intertwine. Yet we try not to impose on each other's privacy and independence.

I spent the day enjoyably, painting, taking photographs, talking. I haven't had much time for my own interests. But by four o'clock, I was anxious. So I left for home.

The apartment was quiet when I arrived, already darkened by twilight but no lights were on. An uneasy feeling. Rushing to Peter's room; I found him in bed.

"Peter?" I called softly, uncertain if he was awake. He turned toward me, his face white and drawn. He looked depressed, sad, ill, and I reproached myself for not being here.

"How was your day?" I asked worriedly.

"Oh, not good," he answered almost apologetically. "I've been in bed most of the day. Had diarrhea the whole time."

My spirits fell. This would happen the one day I dared to leave. Everyone tells me I should get away, take care of myself, indulge my own needs. But the uneasiness I feel when away outweighs any enjoyment.

Today, I realized that we can count on nothing. A bad day can hit with no warning.

And nothing in my life is worth not being here when my son needs me.

Friday, February 3

We attended the first support group meeting of the San Diego AIDS Project tonight, the new group I found out about before leaving for New York. Peter felt well and was looking forward to it all day. His checkup last night was encouraging—weight up to 127 pounds, white and red blood cell counts up, and chest X-ray showing improved clearing of his lungs.

I was the only woman and nonhomosexual present. The men eyed me politely but curiously, wondering why I was there, until I introduced myself as Peter's mother.

The other participants were Charles, an ex-model whose extraordinary features were marred by the purplish blemishes of Kaposi's sarcoma; Jack, a slender, short blond who had PCP in December and now walks with a cane because of severe leg pains; Bill, who has had hepatitis B and lymphadenopathy (swollen glands), often considered pre-AIDS symptoms; Tom, whose lover John is hospitalized with PCP; Michael, who also has pre-AIDS symptoms; and Sam, a middle-aged homosexual with emphysema who has a deep interest in helping AIDS patients in any way possible.

Then there was Hiram, carrying his attache case. His black eyes shining with indignation as he told us about his lawsuit against his insurance company. All his correspondence and legal papers were in the case which, he told us, he always carries with him. Apparently, the insurers refuse to finance Hiram's medical care, insisting that he knew he had AIDS before taking out his insurance. Now Hiram, with his doctor's backing, is suing the company for $120,000.

After introducing ourselves and giving a brief AIDS autobiography, we discussed the format we should follow: whether to have joint weekly meetings both for patients and us parents, relatives, and friends who are called the "Worried Well"; separate meetings; or three meetings a month separately and one jointly. Feelings were mixed but not vehement. Peter said he would like to have me at the meetings. I was surprised—and touched, assuming he would want separate meetings for venting any negative feelings about living with his mother and depending on her again. We finally decided to have joint weekly meetings.

Bill brought up his frustrations about having so much spare time on his hands now that he's disabled. "I just don't know what to do all day long," he complained.

Peter chimed in, not so much frustrated about having spare time, but angry about his physical inability to use it constructively. He was unable, not unwilling, to pursue the many interests that he now had time for.

Later, we discussed a volunteer "buddy" system that was being started. A buddy would be assigned to each patient to help with housekeeping, errands, transportation, and most importantly, to offer companionship and support. They all knew they would need this. Why else were they here?

Peter's eyes lit up. He volunteered instantly for the training sessions that were being arranged, excited about the prospect of helping others in his own situation. I said a silent prayer that he would be able to do this. It was obviously important to him.

At one point, Hiram approached me. "I'm so glad you're here," he said enthusiastically.

"Thank you. I wanted to be."

"It's just so nice to have a mother here. I wish mine could be here, too," he said wistfully.

"Does she live in San Diego?" I would like to know another mother, someone with whom to share common pain and sorrow in the months to come.

"No, she lives in northern California. I wish she were closer. She comes down now and then, but not enough. Peter's lucky to have you with him."

"Well, after all, what's a mother for?" I asked him jokingly, and he laughed. I like Hiram. His brave fight with the giant insurance company and his childlike need for his mother are charmingly inconsistent.

The meeting lasted two hours, and Peter was tired when we left. But we both feel a camaraderie with these men, albeit forced upon us by the common thread of our suffering. Peter is especially happy about this first meeting.

I'm glad. He needs others to share this with. So do I.

Friday, February 17

We've been home just over a month now, and Peter does so little. He still sleeps long hours and is always,

always tired. His constant fatigue worries me. He barely has the energy to walk once a day, nap when he returns, eat, and watch television.

I've noticed that he seems to avoid anything relating to violence or suffering and changes the station quickly if they appear in a movie or on the news. Understandable. His own life bears enough of that. He chooses not to discuss it with me, but I'm sure he thinks about it.

Richard, the social worker who directs the Owen Clinic support group, has given him a book, *Getting Well Again*, by the Drs. Symington—a positive approach to life-threatening illnesses. Other than this book, his reading leans toward frothy magazines like *People* or *US*, or impersonal electronics or rock-music periodicals; nothing that takes much concentration. Yet he tries to remain positive about his plans for the future.

"I'd really like to get back to Santa Fe," he's said many times. He was in his teens when we lived there, and my uncle still has a sprawling adobe home atop one of the foothills of the Sangre de Cristo mountains. Since I sold our home there after my divorce, we all think of Uncle Park's house as the family homestead. Peter, especially, loves it, has visited there often since childhood. The house is built around a patio, rose-filled in the summer, and every window on the outer walls frames a panorama of the mountains.

"Well, maybe we could do that," I tell him, wondering if he'd have difficulty breathing in the 7000-foot altitude.

"I'd like to go up to the Ski Basin, see our old house, smell the piñon, and see some of those fantastic New Mexico sunsets," he says enthusiastically. "Maybe we could go this spring. I'll be better then, and the weather will be nice."

"That's a good idea, except then you couldn't smell the piñon burning at night," I remind him lightly.

"Hmm, well . . . I might have to do without that in the springtime, then. I'd like to get back to Hawaii, too. When I was there on vacation last year, I was too tired from work to visit any of the other islands. I'd like to see them the next time."

How wonderful if he can make at least one of these trips.

Tuesday, February 21

My new art agent just got my work accepted in several galleries in Arizona, New Mexico, and southern California. I have to pack and send several paintings off for consignment. One of the galleries, only 20 miles north, works through decorators and anticipates more commissions for me in the near future. I earn less from a decorator than by selling my own work commercially, but I won't have to pay framing costs and the increased volume will compensate. Oh well, I work fast, and the demand will motivate my work, which I need for my own distraction as well as the money. I'm pleased.

It does seem ironic, though, that I'm finally achieving some commercial success during what's bound to be the most discouraging and demanding period of my life. Well, somehow I'll do it. I've always felt life is a never-ending series of adjustments, and if one can stay flexible, it all works out.

Tuesday, February 28

"Isn't there a Neimann-Marcus store here?" Peter asked yesterday.

"Yes, it's in Fashion Valley, near here," I told him. "Want to go? I've never been there."

"Let's go, then," he said.

We left the house at seven P.M. The store was almost empty at that hour, and we walked slowly throughout. We found the gourmet foods department, and his interest perked up as we looked over the specialty offerings—elegant rich pastries and cakes, canned and bottled foods, spices, candies, and nuts.

"Ooh, that looks yummy," I pointed to a chocolate-chocolate chip cheesecake in the refrigerated section.

"Why don't we get it?" Peter suggested.

"Oh, no, not now. God, it costs ten dollars and it's tiny. Maybe another day, when there's a special occasion."

He seemed to disapprove of my thriftiness but said nothing. We walked outside and along the mall, then returned home.

That was stupid of me. We should have bought the cake and enjoyed it.

Life is too short for all of us.

5

Saturday, March 3

Today is my birthday, my fifty-first, and a male musician friend is here for dinner. We're going to a flamenco
nightclub that just opened afterward.

I really wanted to be alone with Peter tonight, but my
friend insisted on celebrating my day with me and I couldn't
avoid it tactfully. He knows Peter has AIDS and tries to be
supportive, but he doesn't really comprehend the situation.
He accuses me of being obsessive. I don't think I am. I
just don't have time for my personal life now. Peter is my
personal life. How can I get anyone to understand this?

Right now, I'm worried. Peter left at one o'clock, saying
he was going to the shopping center. It's five o'clock, and
he should have been back long ago. I can't seem to control
my overprotectiveness. He seems so fragile and weak and
walks so slowly, with an odd, flat-footed shuffle, his
shoulders hunched with tension. He looks confused and
bewildered, and I'm afraid. Afraid an impatient driver
won't stop when he's crossing the street. Afraid someone
will take advantage of his frail appearance and rob him or
beat him up. I am always apprehensive until he returns
from a walk.

I hear the key turn in the lock—thank God. "Oh,
good—you're back. Dinner's ready," I tell him, hoping
my anxiety is masked.

We sit at the table, my friend and I chatting. Peter is quiet. I know he's tired and would prefer a nap right now. We finish the first course and I clear the table.

"Just a minute," says Peter, going to his room and returning with a gold box and a card and placing them in front of me.

I open the card first. Inside, he's written, *To a tough Mama, xxxooxxx, Peter*. My eyes fill. I'm glad he thinks I'm so tough! What a lie I live.

"And what is this?" I ask, lifting the lid from the box. Inside is the chocolate-chocolate chip cheesecake we admired in Neimann-Marcus.

"How did you ever get this?" I exclaim, surprised and deeply touched.

"Well, how do you think? I went to Neimann-Marcus, obviously," he says nonchalantly.

"But . . . how did you get there?"

"I took the bus, of course."

"Thank you, Peter . . . this is great," I exclaim, and serve each of us a slice. It is lusciously rich and creamy.

"There must be 2000 calories in every bite, it's definitely the best birthday cake I've ever had, Peter."

It's a marvelous gift, but the most precious gift is his courage to venture out on his own—and his safe return.

We finish dinner, and I start to rinse the dishes. It's already ten o'clock. I'll leave the washing till tomorrow.

"Do you want to come with us, Peter? I'd like you to come." He looks so tired. I don't really want to leave him.

"No, you all go on," he says. "I'm kind of tired." He moves toward the sink, turns the faucet on, and reaches for the detergent.

"Leave the dishes, I'll do them in the morning," I say.

"No, I'd like to do them," he says firmly.

And I know that he wants to do this for me.

Tuesday, March 6

A neighbor joins me in the parking lot. "I was so surprised to see Peter out walking last Saturday. He must be feeling stronger," she tells me. "Where was he going?"

"Oh, you must have seen him on his way to Fashion Valley. He went there to get me a special birthday cake."

"Fashion Valley?" she says quizzically. "But I saw him headed the opposite direction."

"Where did you see him?"

"Oh, he was several blocks down Linda Vista Road, about opposite the school."

"How strange. He told me he took the bus, and that's way past the bus stop. I wonder if he walked all the way, or what. No wonder he was gone so long."

Well that explains his long absence Saturday afternoon. He must have turned right instead of left when leaving the apartment complex and gotten disoriented. Then was too embarrassed to admit his confusion to me when he returned so late, probably even frightened by it.

And I, too, am frightened.

Friday, March 9

Peter slides steadily downhill. Daily bouts of diarrhea and decreasing appetite weaken him, tire him despite determined efforts to eat. He sleeps longer, 16 hours or more a day, and is pale and gaunt.

He's embarrassed and self-conscious about his appearance, despite my half-lying reassurances that he looks fine. His hair is thin, and his thick, black eyelashes and brows are faded and sparse. His thinness upsets me every time I look at him. I shall never get used to it.

He seems very depressed, and I have difficulty persuading him to leave the house except for clinic appointments and the support meetings at the AIDS Project and at Owen Clinic.

The meetings at Owen Clinic are conducted in two groups, one for the patients and one for us, the Worried Well. We've been instructed not to discuss our separate meetings in order to respect the confidentiality of these often emotional sessions, so Peter and I rarely talk about what goes on in our groups. I like this. We do have different angers to vent.

Richard, the volunteer social worker, directs the patients' group. Richard is homosexual and diabetic, and his own chronic illness gives him an extra sensitivity to AIDS patients. Peter likes and respects him very much. My group is led by a medical social worker acquainted with bereavement through the loss of a brother with brain cancer, and an intensive-care nurse who has attended several terminal AIDS patients at her work. Both women are volunteers in the Owen Clinic. We discuss everything from bereavement, dealing with the loss we already feel for our dying loved ones, to how to cope with the day-to-day care that they need.

The Owen Clinic groups are different in character from those at the AIDS Project. Peter's group is strictly for AIDS patients, and mine is strictly for those of us involved in their daily care. Unfortunately, they only last an hour. On the other hand, the AIDS Project meetings are held in one large group for two hours, and include anyone, even those just seeking information. They therefore seem less professional, less helpful.

Peter seems to like the Owen Clinic group best. It deals more intensely with death and dying. He never talks to me about how he feels about dying. I'm glad he can do it with someone.

Saturday, March 10

Peter reads the book that Richard gave him, *Getting Well Again,* over and over. He says he gets hope from its philosophy of goal-setting, positive thinking, and visualization—a mental willing of the destruction of bad cells by good cells. I've read it, too, and find its positive yet realistic attitudes helpful whether one is sick or well.

Richard also gave Peter some meditation tapes to listen to. Their purpose is to teach, through meditation, the mind's power to heal and recuperate the body's illness. Stress, tension, and worry supposedly lower the body's immune system. Three times a day, Peter finds time to meditate and relax completely, usually in the red rocking chair or lying on his back in bed.

Sunday, March 11

As I feared, Peter was not capable of taking part in the buddy system at the AIDS Project. The training sessions alone required 30 hours of the volunteers' time. That was impossible for Peter, and he was terribly disappointed. "There's no way we AIDS patients can work that many hours. It's not fair," he raged.

Instead, he was assigned a buddy himself. He's taken Peter out several times—to the Palomar Observatory in early February, to dinner, and to the movies. Though he likes him, Peter isn't comfortable with him. His first excuse was that they didn't have anything in common, but later he told me that he doesn't trust him, feels he wants something from Peter.

His buddy is obviously an honest, sincere young man, and I find it very odd that Peter should feel this way. Peter has always been open and friendly with new acquaintances, and this distrust and suspicion is uncharacteristic. I don't know if this behavior is typical of chronically ill patients or if it indicates a personality change caused by something else. But what?

He anxiously sought a tactful way to end the relationship. Not wanting to hurt his volunteer's feelings, Peter told him that he didn't need him, that he could rely on his family. He suggested that the volunteer help a patient whose family is nonsupportive.

And so Peter grows increasingly reclusive. He doesn't want to "waste the energy" to make new friends. When old friends from New York call, he doesn't encourage them, doesn't tell them he has AIDS. He even refuses to return Frank's calls. He makes excuses to avoid leaving home. He speaks nostalgically of New York, but I believe he misses his freedom and independence, not the city itself.

I put myself in his situation daily and imagine his frustration and anger. At 28, he has abruptly lost his health, faces death, and must depend on his mother for nearly all his needs. He has no money until his Social

Security payments start in June. He has no transportation except for me, and he fears getting lost on the bus.

How peculiar that fear. He knew New York City and its complicated transportation system inside and out. Yet here, in this smaller city, he is afraid.

I am discouraged for him. He came to San Diego with so many plans and hopes. But the reality is that now he can do nothing.

He has tried. Recently, he arranged piano lessons and singing accompaniment with a music student at San Diego State University. He practiced only once after the first lesson, though, trying to play the first Hanon exercise and ''Fuer Elise''—music that should have been childishly simple for him to read. I heard his fingers stumble and hesitate, and I cringed, feeling his despair. And other than occasional humming in the shower, Peter does not sing anymore.

What worries me most, though, is his ''oldness.'' It reminds me of the symptoms of Alzheimer's Disease. He perches on a chair, his shoulders hunched, picking constantly at his moustache and chin and staring slack-mouthed into space. At times, he examines his arms minutely, saying he has some strange bumps on his skin. He's forgetful and hasn't been able to remember our telephone number even once. He forgets people's names and recent events—or mixes them up. In mid-sentence he forgets what he's saying, searches for words, then confuses them, using a word that sounds similar to the correct one. He loses his train of thought and angrily says, ''Oh, forget it!'' impatient with himself.

He is dull where he once was bright and observant, fluently expressive and ironically humorous. He concentrates on nothing more intellectually demanding than light comedy shows on television and popular magazines. The only serious reading matter is the Symingtons' book and Norman Cousins' *Anatomy of an Illness*. These are his Bibles, read and reread.

What does it all mean?

Monday, March 12

Peter asked me if I was baking ginger cookies today.

"No," I answered, startled. "Why?"

"Oh, I smelled ginger, and it made me think of when we used to make ginger cookies when I was little."

I felt uneasy. I haven't had a can of ginger in the house for years.

Tuesday, March 13

We sit in the dark, nearly empty theater at the matinee showing of *Terms of Endearment*. Our family advised us not to see it. The theme, of a mother losing her daughter to cancer, would be too painfully close to our situation. But we're both movie aficionados, and Peter brushed aside his distaste for films of suffering because this movie is an Oscar nominee.

In the movie, the daughter visits New York City for the first time during a remission of her disease. Her eyes widen excitedly as her taxi approaches the city. In front of her is the jagged, black silhouette of the immense city at dusk, thousands of small lights glittering in the windows of office buildings and apartments. I hear a gulp and soft sobbing next to me. I look at Peter through bluish light reflecting on his face.

"Oh, I miss it so much!" he exclaims, trying to hold back tears. My heart aches with sorrow for him, for what he was and what he now is. I choke back my own tears. Once again, I know he misses *living,* not New York. I am helpless to console him.

I would give everything if he could have it all back.

Wednesday, March 14

Peter enters the Owen Clinic waiting room, where I sit, anxious to hear the results of his checkup and how his support group meeting went. His face looks tense, but his voice is flatly emotionless—as it often is nowadays—as he tells me about his examination.

"They couldn't find anything wrong with my ears," he says, referring to the stopped up feeling that has been bothering him. "And nothing to explain my trouble swallowing. Could have been herpes in my throat but the endoscopy last week ruled that out. And everything else from that test was negative, too."

We had hoped the endoscopy—a procedure wherein a small tube is inserted through the mouth into the stomach and duodenum to inspect and biopsy the tissue—would reveal a cause for his continuing diarrhea.

"What about the bumps on your arms?"

"They looked at them but didn't say anything, I guess they don't know . . . or else just don't care," he said bitterly. "Sometimes I don't think it's worth going. I don't think they give a damn. They don't pay any attention to what I tell them, and I'm not even sure if they're listening to me."

"Oh, Peter, I'm sure they're listening," I reassure him hurriedly. "They're very concerned about you."

"Well, I don't know," he mutters as we leave his prescriptions order at the pharmacy downstairs. Noting a decongestant prescription, I wonder why he thought they weren't paying any attention to the complaint about his ears.

"Let's go somewhere for coffee," Peter suggests. "I don't want to go home yet."

"Okay, we'll go have dinner," I agree, hoping that he wants to share some of his anxieties.

We sit opposite each other at the Greek restaurant near the hospital. It's almost empty at this hour. Peter is agitated and worried.

"How did your support group go?" I ask. "Do you want to talk about what happened?" I don't usually ask him what they discuss, but I am certain something in tonight's session caused his anxiety.

"Yes," he answers. "I . . . well, what worries me is, what if something happened to you? What would I do? I'm beginning to realize that I can't take care of myself alone as I hoped. I'd have to depend on someone else. And I couldn't go to Dad's, in Virginia; he's four hours from the nearest medical center that would know how to treat me.''

"No, you couldn't, that's out of the question. But I don't think you need to worry. I'm planning on being here, like I told you in New York. Nothing's going to happen to me," I assure him, touching his hand on the table. But I mustn't minimize his worries, must present an alternate plan to ease him.

"But just in case—just in the *remote* case—that something should happen to me, you could go stay with David in Austin. The University of Texas is there . . . there must be good hospitals, and I know he would want to help you, Peter.''

"Okay." He seems relieved by my quick solution.

"I'll call him tommorrow to make sure, if you like.''

The waiter hovers nearby, and we read the menu, make our selections.

"I got a letter from Miriam and Seymour today," I say, changing the subject. We've known them since our days in Santa Fe. They live in San Francisco now.

"Oh, good, I really like them . . . what's their news?''

"They're excited about going to Greece in April. Aren't they lucky?''

"Will they be stopping to see us on the way?''

"Well . . . I don't know . . . I don't think so," I answer, puzzled. "They're in San Francisco, you know.''

"They could. They have to stop off here anyway.''

"No . . . I imagine they'll fly straight to New York and leave for Greece from there. San Diego isn't on the way.''

What is he thinking?

"Oh . . . oh . . . yes," he says, bewildered. "That's right, we're not in New York, I was thinking we were in New York." He speaks hurriedly, obviously hoping I won't see his confusion.

"No," I say, trying to hide my shock. "They might come down and see us after they get back.''

Oh, God. Something is dreadfully wrong in his brain, and I don't understand it. The inability to concentrate, the trouble speaking, remembering words, unable to play the piano . . . and now this. He didn't know where he was.

I must talk to his doctors. I'm so damned scared.

Saturday, March 17

Maria arrived tonight for a week's vacation. We went to the airport to meet her, then to a restaurant for dinner. Peter seemed glad to see her again, though he's so unemotional these days, I have difficulty guessing his feelings.

After we ordered our meals, she excused herself to make a phone call and was gone several minutes. Peter became quite agitated and disturbed.

"What's taking her so long?" he asked.

Why did he do this? I'm so worried about him, and I have an eerie sense of foreboding. I'm glad Maria is here, at least for a few days.

Wednesday, March 20

Another doctor appointment in Owen Clinic. Peter shuffles slowly in. We are late, as always. But after comparing notes with others in my support group, I have learned that AIDS patients are always late. They move so slowly, showering and dressing. They have difficulty organizing themselves to leave the house. I've noticed several who shuffle along like Peter. With black humor, I secretly call it the "AIDS Shuffle," as if it were a new dance step. I know they often dread clinic visits, fearing bad news or possible rehospitalization. I appreciate the secretary and nurses in the clinic never scolding them for arriving so late.

Peter sits dejectedly, head to the side, idly staring at the television on the wall. I have decided to speak to one of the doctors separately about my fears. As soon as Peter goes in for his checkup, I rush to the desk and ask if I can see either Dr. Hicks, the psychiatrist connected with the clinic, or Dr. Matthews, the physician who has been seeing Peter lately. Almost immediately, Dr. Matthews beckons to me and leads me down the hall. Dr. Hicks joins us.

"I didn't want Peter to know of my worries," I tell them hurriedly as we seat ourselves in the small office.

"He would be terribly frightened to know this, but I think he's losing his mental faculties. Maybe I'm wrong. But I'm very concerned. I'm glad I can see you both because I'm not sure if what's happening is physical or emotional . . . or both."

"Tell us what's happening," Dr. Matthews urges.

"Well, for several weeks now—four to six—Peter seems to be losing his memory. I didn't pay much attention at first. I mean, he's been through so much. But . . . well, he's always had an excellent memory, yet he can't remember our phone number. He forgets names, dates, things that have happened recently. He mixes words, uses the wrong one in the wrong place or one that sounds similar but is inappropriate. Last week he forgot we were in San Diego, thought we were in New York. And he forgets what he's trying to say, gets angry, and says, 'Forget it' in frustration. He can't seem to carry through on expressing a thought.

"Another strange thing—his mannerisms. They remind me of old people in rest homes. He sits hunched over, picking absent mindedly at his lips or moustache and staring into space. He walks with a shuffle, the foot flat and not heel-toe, like an old man. He just makes me think of an old man."

I stop for a moment. The old man that Peter has become saddens me so.

I continue. "I realize he's depressed and discouraged, and with reason, of course. But he's so flat, unemotional, reclusive. I can't get him to go out to meet people. When people invite him out, he makes excuses. I can't tell if it's an emotional depression, or if . . . *if* . . . maybe there's something going on inside his brain . . . an infection?" I say inquiringly, fearfully.

"Is there any history of depression in the family?" the psychiatrist asks.

"Not really. I was depressed for a few years after my divorce, but I think that was natural. I was adjusting to an extreme change in my life," I answer, skipping over the four years of anger, depression, and loneliness the divorce had caused. "But I got help, moved again, and things straightened out."

"I think we'll give him some neurological testing after his exam," they tell me, their faces concerned. I thank them, grateful that Peter will receive special attention.

I wait anxiously for Peter. At last, Dr. Matthews comes to the waiting room and tells me Peter has an appointment the next day in the Neurology Clinic at two P.M.

"Thank you," I say. "Do you see much brain involvement with AIDS?"

He looks down at me kindly, his brown eyes sad as always; "Yes, we do," he says simply.

Oh, my God. It never occurred to me, but there's no reason why infections can't invade his brain, too.

Wednesday, March 21

I'm up early this morning. Can't sleep with this gnawing anxiety. What will they find out today?

Peter seems to be asleep now, though I heard him in the bathroom several times earlier. More diarrhea. I die a little every time he has it.

I make coffee, take it outside to the patio, trying to think about the dinner party I'm catering tomorrow night. It's so hard to work now, but Maria is going to help me. She spent the night with Rachel, an old friend. She has my car, and I hope she'll be home soon. I worry when she leaves, anxious that something might happen to her, too. Living with AIDS makes you realize how fragile life is.

The telephone rings, and I jump to answer it so it won't wake Peter. It's the neurologist's secretary, asking me to bring Peter in as soon as possible. "Why do they want him in so quickly?" I ask, but the secretary doesn't know.

"I can't bring him now. I don't have a car till noon. We didn't think we'd need it."

"Can you have him here by twelve-thirty, then?"

"Yes, I'll try." I hang up the phone, my whole body tense. I try to convince myself that the earlier appointment is probably just a routine scheduling change.

The telephone rings again. This time I jump in fear. It's Maria.

"Hi, Mom. Now don't worry, nothing has happened . . ."

"My God, you can't do this to me!" I scream like a madwoman, the anger, fear, hysteria pouring out as I visualize her injured and bleeding.

"It's all right, Mom, it's all right. It's just that I parked the car in a no parking area last night, and they towed it away."

Relief. I try to calm myself. "I've got to have the car. You know Peter has to see the neurologist, and they just called. He has to be there earlier, at 12:30." I speak quickly, nervously.

"Don't worry. Rachel's mother is going to take me to get the car, and I'll be home right away."

I hang up the telephone, go peek at Peter. Still asleep.

I leave quietly and walk fast along the sidewalk. The foreboding I've had for several days is overwhelming. I feel sure something terrible is going to happen, and tears rise to my eyes, spill over.

Our life is fast becoming a nightmare. Thoughts and fears jostle, fall over each other, and I want to scream. God, I feel so alone! If only I could go somewhere and scream myself inside-out. I go back to the apartment.

Maria arrives. It's time to waken Peter, tell him about his new appointment time, and start him moving. He's grumpy, irritable. Is he frightened, too? I must stay calm for him. He must not know how frightened I am.

Peter shuffles into the living room, neatly dressed and hair combed. His face is white, haggard, he looks sadder than usual. I want so much to hug him tightly, drive away the obscene organisms destroying his mind and body. But I don't know if he wants me close. He's so remote now. I hesitate. He sits stiffly on one end of the couch, I on the other.

"Come sit next to me," Peter says softly, looking straight ahead.

I move quickly next to him and put my arm around his bony shoulders, holding him tight.

"Hold my hand," he whispers.

I take his hand, hold it firmly. Yes, he's fearful and apprehensive. I feel the tears coming and fight them back. I can't speak. I don't dare. We sit quietly for several minutes.

*   *   *

We've been waiting an hour and a half in the Neurology Clinic; Peter, Maria and I. I'm angry and impatient, wondering why we had to hurry so, just to sit and wait. I know others are sick, but Peter is among the very sickest.

I wish the doctors realized how sick he really is, how frustrating the continual waiting rooms, the waiting for help, any kind of help, always hoping one doctor will say, "Nothing to worry about. Just take this pill and call me in the morning."

At last a tall, moustached doctor in white jacket beckons and Peter rises slowly. Maria and I follow. Usually, he sees the doctors alone so that he won't feel like a small boy going to the doctor with his mommy. But today he wants us with him.

"Hi, Peter. I'm Dr. Rothrock. I'm going to give you a thorough neurological examination, and then I'll do a spinal tap on you, withdrawing a little spinal fluid which we'll send to the lab for analysis."

Maria and I watch as Dr. Rothrock tests Peter's muscular and neurological reflexes, his balance, his coordination. He examines his eyes minutely. He then tests Peter's thought processes by asking him to explain an allegory, tests his memory by asking him to repeat a series of numbers forward and backward. Peter does so quickly and correctly. Reciting the presidents backward, Peter lists the names so fast that the doctor tells him to stop at Kennedy. He then names three objects to be remembered in five minutes.

"Tell me, Peter, have you noticed any unusual smells recently?" the doctor asks.

"Well, I've noticed that some smells really bother me a lot, like broccoli and eggs. I can't stand them. And on the way over today I smelled burning rubber."

"Did you notice it, too?" The doctor turns to me.

"No, I didn't," I answer, surprised. I remember Peter's comment on the bad odor as we neared the hospital, and how I rolled my window down to see if I could smell it, too.

"Any other smells, Peter? Anything that might remind you of the past, for example?"

I sit upright. "Yes . . . he thought he smelled ginger the other day, said it made him think of ginger cookies when he was little." The doctor makes a note on his chart.

"How long ago was that?"

I look at Peter. He doesn't answer. "I think a few days . . . maybe a week or two ago, I'm not sure," I answer. Peter nods agreement.

We discuss Peter's memory loss, his problems in communicating thoughts and ideas, and Dr. Rothrock prepares the materials for the spinal tap.

Peter appears calm and Dr. Rothrock talks to him continuously, explaining the procedure. He's interested that Peter lived in Santa Fe, having skiied in Taos.

The spinal tap is completed. The fluid dripped slowly out of his spine into the waiting test tubes. The doctor instructs Peter to lie still for 30 or 40 minutes before sitting up and then leaves. Maria and I divert Peter with idle talk, and he, relieved that the procedure is over, is more talkative. Dr. Rothrock returns and appraises Peter.

"You can sit up now, slowly, on the edge of the table a few minutes to be sure you're not dizzy."

Peter sits up cautiously, still talking. He seems fine.

"Okay, I think you're all right, Peter. Go ahead and get dressed . . ."

"I think I'll lie down . . . I feel dizzy." Peter interrupts. He lies back and with no warning his whole body arms legs head torso start twitching and jerking uncontrollably and violently. My God it's a seizure! I think in horror as the doctor grabs his shoulders calls for help I grab his legs I am in shock and terror I can't believe my eyes it's an epileptic seizure Jesus Christ my poor baby I look at Maria paralyzed with shock her eyes white saucers her mouth wide open "Get up there, hold his shoulders down!" I scream at her and she moves quickly other people rush in a tall male nurse tries to hold him down and another tries to start an IV in his left arm my God! oh my God I moan his face is redpurple and twisting grimacing his lips pulled back his teeth bared like a rabid dog pinkish foam he's bitten his tongue No! Stop it! my heart breaks shattering splintering into thousands of pieces all over oh my God oh

Peter Peter but it's not Peter it's a wild tortured animal and I don't think I'll ever be the same.

The first needle tears out of his arm with another violent convulsion and there's blood all over the place oh Peter oh please get the IV started please poor nurse I hope she didn't get blood on her she could get infected she's struggling to get another IV going and they are yelling at someone to bring more Dilantin® and Valium® and hurry hurry he's going to need more I sob so scared and his face still writhing grimacing eyes staring widely at nothing and now he's screaming shrieking a poor animal. I say loudly as if he could hear, "Peter, it's all right, Mom's here, Peter, Peter, Mom's here, it's all right, they're fixing it they're fixing it it will be all right."

But I know it won't be all right, it'll never be the same.

I hold his knees down for dear life. Maria has his shoulders but I'm scared to grab his thighs. His thighs are still so sore I don't want to bruise them. He has the strength of fifteen men, yet he's a weak, emaciated boy. His screams farther apart now, deeper, gutteral, tearing me limb from limb, rising from some primeval depth, his body jerking fiercely.

The waves slower now, his eyes still glazed, unseeing, his face grimacing wildly. "Peter, Peter," I call to him. I don't know why because he can't hear me but maybe he can, maybe he can. People yell about the emergency room, they have emergency seizure equipment there till they can get him a room. Oh God, they're going to move him, how can they, he'll fall. A Guerney bed is brought in, everybody running and of course they can't move him, I knew they couldn't. It takes all of them to fight his wild body and finally lay it on the Guerney, strap it down with lengths of cloth. There are no restraining straps in the clinic and they tie him down, they tie my poor baby down like a ferocious animal. He doesn't want to hurt you, I want to tell them, but it's for his own safety. I'm so confused, it's a nightmare, a crazy insane nightmare—will we ever wake up?

The Guerney bed rolls out into the hall, the male nurse and another attendant push the IV stand, Maria and I run alongside. I talk to Peter, hoping he'll hear me and know

I'm here. He's still convulsing, his body jerking up off the bed as far as it can till the restraints force him down, protesting, and he is still crying out, moaning, screaming long gutteral shrieks that seem to rip through my flesh and to the very bone.

We're downstairs, off the elevator and in an examining alcove in the emergency room. Peter is hooked up to an EKG machine—why?—can something happen to his heart? I watch the electronic green line on the screen as it jumps erratically with every movement. I still talk to him, calm him, reassure him. An efficient, starched female doctor enters, tells me I must leave the room, I'm in the way. I don't want to, I want to stay with my son, why can't I? No, I must wait outside, there is a waiting room outside that door. Fat chance, I think angrily, I'm staying as close to him as possible and I'll be back inside as soon as I can.

Maria and I stand outside the door, in the way of everyone passing by, and I don't care. At least, through the window I can see him, know he's all right, even though he's alone. I see the restraints holding him down, how cruel, how brutal, they look so medieval. They must be angering him. He still struggles, though the electrical storm in his head must be fading. He twitches, rises up, fights the restraints, screams his terrifying animal shriek, and lies back down, babbling angrily, protesting defiantly in some strange language that only he knows. I feel torn, battered. I pray he won't remember what's happening. I look at Maria, her eyes still wide with the afternoon's horror. She will never be the same. She has aged 40 years today.

I stop the starchy doctor as she walks by and ask, "Can this possibly cause any permanent damage?"

"No," she answers brusquely. "It's the underlying disease that causes the damage." Supercilious. I know that, for heaven's sake. I don't like her.

We hover by the door, watching Peter through the window. I leave Maria on watch briefly while I go telephone Walter. He and his wife are due to arrive tomorrow for the weekend, and I'd better prepare them.

An hour passes. The convulsions lessen, reduced to an

occasional upward jerking and a growl exploding into a guttural shriek of protest and rage. I look both ways down the hall, the doctor is out of sight. "Come on, Maria, let's go in." We stand next to Peter and talk to him, stroke him, try to calm the remnants of turmoil boiling inside and hope that soon he will hear us.

Seven-thirty P.M. Peter's eyes are open but he doesn't see me. He tries to speak but utters only senseless syllables. He does not respond to my words but I keep talking, desperately hoping that he knows we are with him. More Dilantin was given an hour ago, and now his body just twitches every few minutes, like the aftershocks of an earthquake. The demons are slowly, reluctantly, leaving.

Nine P.M. Peter's room is finally ready and we follow the nurse and the Guerney upstairs to a ward with three other patients. A nurse will be in the room all night, watching for repeat seizures. This is an Intermediate Care ward.

"What is your name?" the nurse asks, starting to take his medical history and check his orientation.

"Peter," he answers. Good, he's coming back.

"Peter what?"

"V-O-M-L-E-H-N," he spells, loudly and distinctly. The nurse is taken aback but amused, and Maria and I laugh away some of the tension, knowing that he spells the name because people never understand it otherwise. He seems relaxed and good natured.

"Who's the lady standing on the other side of your bed?" asks the nurse, smiling.

"That's the lady who takes care of me," he answers, smugly playful. Yes, you're coming back, Peter. You're teasing her.

"What's her name?" she questions, unsure if he is teasing or skirting an answer he can't find.

"Barbara Peabody," he enunciates very clearly.

"What's the date today?" she continues interrogating him. No, that he can't answer, he looks puzzled. Nor does he know where he is, nor what has happened. We tell him he's in the hospital, in UCSD, and has had a seizure. He's stunned, has lost more than seven hours of his life.

I'm less worried now, seeing that he is slowly returning to normal. He's very drowsy—so much medication—and the intense physical and mental energy of the seizure have depleted his energy. We stay another hour to be sure he's settling down, then decide to leave. It is eleven-thirty.

"We're going now, Peter. Goodnight, see you tomorrow."

"Mmm," he mumbles, drugged. The nurse sits at her desk and I feel he will be well-supervised all night. Maria and I leave quietly.

"We've got to go shopping at one of the all-night groceries, Maria. I was going to get the food today for the catering job but . . . and there's no way we can cancel it now, it has to be done. I'll stay up cooking tonight, then get up and finish in the morning."

We rush down the store aisles, following the shopping list I made yesterday, take the groceries home and start washing, chopping, sauteing. Maria finally collapses. I work another hour, my hands busy while my exhausted mind runs back through the day, over and over.

It seems so ridiculously incongruous, cooking for a dinner party after the most horrifying day of my life.

Thursday, March 22

"What happened yesterday? They told me I had a seizure," Peter asks as I greet him in the morning. He has just been moved from the ward to a private room.

"Yes, you did, in the Neurology Clinic," I answer. "How do you feel today?"

"Oh, all right, sleepy. Still have a headache, and had diarrhea bad this morning," he tells me.

His voice is weak and I can barely hear his words.

"One of the doctors this morning told me that I might have gotten dehydrated from diarrhea yesterday morning and that that could have caused an electrolyte imbalance, and then the seizure."

"Oh, really? Well, maybe that explains it," I say, seeing that he wants to believe this. I don't. One morning's dehydration may explain the seizure, but not the previous weeks of memory loss, confusion, and disorientation.

"I'll have to keep myself well-hydrated so that doesn't happen again," he says pensively. "Ooh . . . I'm so stiff, and my throat and tongue hurt. I wonder why." He shifts position painfully.

"You're probably sore from the convulsions and fighting the restraints—it took five people to hold you down. You're pretty strong, you know," I tell him.

"Whew!" he exclaims.

"Yup, you really gave 'em a run for their money. And your throat is probably sore from yelling a bit."

I minimize yesterday's horrifying scenario, afraid he will be embarrassed to think he caused a scene—as indeed he did.

"I think you bit your tongue, too, that's why it hurts today. Just rest, you'll feel better tomorrow."

He dozes off, still sedated from the drugs. I go to the window, gaze at the view westward to the bay and the ocean beyond. He'll see some beautiful sunsets from here. He'll like that. I leave the room quietly.

Saturday, March 24

Peter was discharged from the hospital this afternoon. It's been a confusing, hectic, and frustrating week.

On Thursday, I went back and forth to the hospital, finished the catering preparations, and at five o'clock, Maria and I packed up the food and went to La Jolla to cater dinner for nine people. I could barely concentrate for worry and lack of sleep. Afterward, we went to the hospital for a few minutes to check on Peter and tell him goodnight. He'd had a headache all day and numerous tests were done to try and discover the cause of the seizure and neurological disorder that it evidences. Peter's father and stepmother arrived that day, too, and I alternated hospital visits with them.

I feel terribly depressed and discouraged. They've assured me the spinal tap didn't cause the seizure. So many tests, and nothing, no organism that can be attacked and destroyed. The spinal tap yielded a slightly elevated protein level which indicates an infection is present—but didn't identify it. The EEG, which records electrical activity in the brain, was normal. The CT scan, which photographs the brain, was normal. And all lab tests were normal. The final neurological tests demonstrated normal reflexes and reactions. Only short-term memory showed slight impairment.

Nothing. It's as if nothing happened. How can he be so sick and no cause be found? I used to breathe relief when his tests came back negative. Now I realize that negative is not good, that the infections elude detection while maliciously continuing to destroy Peter's body. I keep hoping for something—anything—to appear under the microscope, something that can be treated.

I sit alone in the darkness on the patio. The sky is clear and the neighborhood quiet. Everyone is asleep. My oldest son lies inside, asleep and sick, sick with a bewildering disease that has now invaded his brain. And Maria, my youngest child, also lies asleep, suffering in her own way. We are all hurt.

And nothing can be done.

Wednesday, March 28

Peter sits on the edge of the examining table, I on a straight chair next to the desk. We are in the Neurology Clinic, waiting for Dr. Rothrock. Always waiting. Maria returned to school in Baltimore early Sunday morning. I miss her already.

The four days since Peter left the hospital have been uneventful. Daily doses of Dilantin seem to be preventing another seizure, but we are constantly apprehensive. He still mixes words and has a low fever, between 99 and 100.5 degrees, and he has been lethargic and tired. From time to time, deep, body-shaking hiccoughs grasp him in short spells. They are painful but he doesn't complain.

He speaks so softly that I have to ask him to repeat himself often, which irritates him. "Maybe you should get a hearing test," he snaps. But I notice that the doctors, too, have to ask him to repeat words. When he tries to speak louder, he can't control his voice and it blares forth, and his laugh is awkwardly shrill. I'm unsure whether he's too weak to speak normally or if, for some reason, he's unable to coordinate his vocal chords. To avoid asking him to repeat himself constantly, I try to guess his meaning, and answer or laugh inappropriately. "That wasn't funny," he says angrily. His sudden, angry sarcasm hurts me though I know he's angry at his disease and himself, not me.

Dr. Rothrock finally enters. He examines Peter thoroughly—physical reflexes and reactions, simple commands, numbers and presidents backward and forward. We are getting used to the neurological litany. Peter answers alertly, his speech slightly slurred. As usual, the doctor names three objects to be remembered in five minutes: brown curtains, a pink lion, and a blue tree. The examination completed, we leave.

"Wait a minute," says Peter, halfway down the hall, and returns to the examining room.

"You didn't ask me what the three things were," he reminds Dr. Rothrock.

"Oh, I forgot. Well, what were they?" he asks, grinning.

"Brown curtains, a pink lion, and . . . mmm . . . a blue tree," Peter remembers triumphantly.

"I'm glad *you* remembered. Not only did I forget to ask, I forgot what they were," the doctor laughs.

We turn and walk slowly down the corridor.

"I think Dr. Rothrock should go see Dr. Rothrock." The old Peter smiles smugly, pleased that he's remembered something the neurologist himself forgot.

6

Tuesday, April 3

Owen Clinic again. This place is like our second home now. Every visit takes about four hours. Peter drags his feet literally and figuratively, and I have to drive slowly because he has an increasingly exaggerated fear of accidents—one of the many phobias he's developed, like leaving his bedroom door open all night. He insists that a closed door makes him feel shut off from the world. He puts his seat belt on carefully, feeling it gives him a magical protection, he told me.

The clinic personnel know us well by now, and Peter greets them like old friends. While waiting, the patients watch television or chat, discussing each other's progress and medications. Peter feels especially close to those who attend the weekly support group meetings with him. John, Ron, Jack, and Peter are regulars, and others attend sporadically.

We are finally called in. Peter is to have a follow-up spinal tap tonight. I know that he fears another seizure afterward. A neurology resident, Dr. Wong, comes in. He is very serious—Peter and I exchange a humorous glance—and obviously won't be diverting Peter with small talk. Peter lies on his right side, his shirt off.

As before, the spinal fluid drips out crystal clear. The procedure is soon over and two of the clinic's volunteer nurses enter, ostensibly to visit, but I'm sure they're here to help in case of a repeat episode. One is a male Navy nurse, the other the same intensive care nurse that runs my clinic support group, and Peter chats amiably with them as an hour passes. I slip out to find Dr. Wong. I have questions.

"Excuse me, may I speak with you a minute?" Dr. Wong looks up from his note-writing at the nurses' desk. "Is Peter apt to have another seizure even while taking Dilantin, or does that guarantee protection?"

"It should help prevent them," he answers, "but it's no guarantee. We'll be checking his Dilantin level periodically because it could need adjustment. The therapeutic range is very narrow so we have to be sure it's just right. Too little, he could have a seizure. Too much, he could have adverse reactions."

"Can he have a seizure while he's asleep?"

"Oh, yes, certainly."

"Then . . . it's never safe to leave him alone?"

"No," he replies. "It's not."

Oh, my God! How can I handle this? For some reason, I assumed he couldn't have a seizure when asleep. He's reclusive, so I know he won't allow a project volunteer to stay with him from time to time. I can't always take him along with me, either, and I don't want to hire a "baby-sitter." He would hate that. Somehow I'll manage. It seems I am housebound now. Thank God for my painting.

I go back to Peter's room. The nurses are still there. Peter sits up slowly. Waits. He puts his shirt on and stands up.

Nothing happens. We can go home.

Sunday, April 15

We are on a plateau now, lower than before but temporarily stable. I have learned not to look for improvement. My hopes that he will survive this have been dashed at every turn. There are no cures, no breakthroughs to rebuild his shattered immune system. We can only treat the infections that ravage his body. But they will win.

There will be no miracles.

My only hope now is that he'll have better days now and then. Peter still mentions trips to Santa Fe or Hawaii.

Two of Peter's friends from the AIDS Project, Tom and John, are planning a big party in June. They live with John's parents and have a large, shaded patio and pool. John has AIDS. Tom is his lover.

"D'you suppose you could help me with something?" Peter asked me yesterday.

"Sure, what is it?"

"Well," he answered slowly, carefully, "I'd like to do something for Tom and John's party, as a surprise."

"Yes?" I asked curiously. From his deliberate speech, I knew he had thought about this with much care.

"I wondered if you'd accompany me on the piano—we could take the little electric piano along—if I gave a short concert for everybody," he proposed.

"Oh, Peter, of course! I'd love to. That would be fun, and nobody there has heard you sing."

"Yeah," he agreed, feigning indifference. "I thought it might be a nice thing to do. I'll have to practice a bit, though. Better start soon, it's been so long since I've sung."

I am glad, not only that he has set himself a goal to work for and that he wants to share his gift, but also that he wants people to know, wants himself to know, that he is *not* a helpless invalid. He hasn't given in. I hope he'll have the strength to do it. The party isn't until June. It would be so important to him if he could accomplish this—important to me, too.

But my constant sense of foreboding hovers over me. Though I try to ignore it, it waits steadily for another crisis. Every morning at five A.M., it wakens me, and I can sleep no more. I get up, peek in at Peter—he's usually asleep. Early-morning diarrhea and a persistent cold with heavy nasal drainage and cough keep him from sleeping well. His left ear has felt stopped up for two or three weeks. No medicine alleviates the discomfort.

Every morning, I make coffee and go to the patio, leaving the glass door slightly ajar to listen and tiptoeing down the hall now and then to check on Peter, glancing through his always open door. I work on my watercolor paintings for a recent commission or on my new tapestry while the sun rises. My mind wanders, weaving its thoughts into the woolen threads or the daubs of paint. Other tenants pass by on their way to work, greeting me. *"Cómo está tu hijo?"* My Mexican neighbors always ask. How is your son?

No matter how many times a day I glance at Peter sleeping, I feel sorrow. I cannot get used to it. He lies on his back, hands folded across his chest, and I am instantly apprehensive—he looks as if he has died in his sleep and I check the rise and fall of his chest. Or he lies on his side, his outline skeletal against the wall. He sleeps shirtless, uncovered, and I see his bony shoulders, his ribs visible through the skin of his back, the sunken hollow between his rib cage and pelvis—there is no flesh to fill in the shallow gap. His thighs and calves, with no muscle or fat, meet grotesquely at knee or ankle. Sometimes, he puts a pillow between them for cushioning.

He's even more self-conscious now about his appearance, despite my attempts to bolster his self-image. But every time I look at him, the wasting tears at my heart. He is part of me, and though it indicates that his dying will be fast, his suffering over soon, I, too, die a little each day with him.

I can do nothing.

I buy too much food, grabbing anything off the grocery shelves that might appeal to his appetite—nutritious food, junk food, anything. He teases me, saying he hates to mention that he likes something because I'll go out and buy a truckload of it tomorrow. Though he has virtually no appetite, he tries to eat as much as possible, yet continues to waste away in front of my eyes. The diarrhea—the wretched, vicious diarrhea—is our greatest enemy. We are unarmed against its relentless destruction as it slowly, surely, sucks out his very life.

His voice is so soft. He tries to speak louder, and has a strange, unconscious habit of mumbling "hmmph!" every so often. It is a bemused, slightly skeptical sound, as if a voice only he can hear were telling him something interesting and incredible. Along with this is the occasional lip pursing that gives him an oddly philosophical air.

His neuromuscular coordination is so bad that he drops objects often. A shriek of profanity follows. Even though I should now expect it, I always jump, startled. It is one of the ways that he expresses his rage against his disease.

Oh, Peter. I am watching you die.

Thursday, April 19

Walter arrives tomorrow for Easter weekend. He and Peter are going to Laguna Beach together. At first, Peter was eager to go and carefully chose the hotel and made the reservations. But the last few days, he has seemed ambivalent about the trip. I think he's apprehensive about being so far from the hospital and his doctors.

I'm worried, too. He's been weaker, more easily tired, and extremely depressed this week. The diarrhea has increased in frequency and intensity, and I fear another seizure despite the Dilantin. But I think the change of scenery and company will be good for him. The only other time he's been away from me was three weeks ago, when he joined his father in Palm Springs for a medical conference.

That outing started well. Peter flew there rather than have me deliver him to Walter halfway. The short flight gave him a much-needed feeling of independence. When I left the airport, I hoped he'd remember to get off the plane in Palm Springs—his memory has been so bad recently.

Walter told me later that he sat in the sun by the pool but refused to go in the water beyond his knees. Another phobia. They drove back over the mountains in a rented car. Peter loves the mountains, but he became carsick and, overcome with nausea, missed all the splendid views of the green pines, boulder-strewn mountains, and vast deserts.

I must stop worrying about this weekend. Walter's a doctor, he'll take good care of him. The trip will be good.

My mind tells my instincts that they are working overtime.

Sunday, April 22

I was right. When will I learn to trust my instincts?

Walter called me on the way home from Laguna Beach this afternoon. He tried to prepare me for the news, fearing I'd be shocked and upset. But I already knew. When he and Peter got home, they confirmed my apprehensions. Peter suffered another seizure the first day in Laguna Beach.

Upset I was. The Dilantin did not protect him. Most frightening is the probability that this means the infection in his brain is spreading.

Walter had called Dr. Matthews and the Dilantin was increased to 400 milligrams a day. But who knows how long this will be effective? And what about the adverse reactions, side effects, the similarity of an overdose to his neurological symptoms? How will we tell one from the other? And Peter; will he become even more fearful and reclusive, more of an invalid?

But shocked I am not. Walter can't understand this. After five months of living with AIDS, twenty-four hours a day, seven days a week, I am becoming accustomed to crises. The only surprise anymore is the nature of each one. Fear, tension, horror—these are as routine to us who live with AIDS as coffee in the morning.

"How do you do it?" Walter asked me before he left.

I looked up in surprise. What a naive question. "I do it because I have to," I answered. "There's no choice so you find the strength."

My instincts tell me there will be more problems soon. This time, I will listen.

Tuesday, April 24

I sit on the dark patio, letting only the night see my tears. Peter is in the living room, watching "Saturday Night Live." The ribald, off-the-wall humor always makes him snicker. Ever since he read Norman Cousins' *Anatomy of an Illness*, in which the author touts laughter as signifi-

cant therapy in his own fight against death, Peter watches
as many comedies as possible.

"You'll probably live forever," he told me enviously
one day.

"Why do you say that?" I asked, puzzled.

"Because you're always laughing."

I am not laughing now. Tonight, on the news, Secretary
of Health and Human Services Margaret Heckler announced
that the virus responsible for causing AIDS has been isolated and that it would be only a matter of time—just
around the corner—before a vaccine and a cure followed.
The newscaster also announced that a definite cure for
AIDS was imminent.

I listened suspiciously, it was too good to be true. All
the experts, and I've talked to or read them all, have said a
cure is five to ten years distant, at least. I voiced my
doubts to Peter. This is just a first report, the news media
always exaggerate, wait and see. But Peter was almost
frenzied with optimism. How can I let my cruel skepticism
smash his hope? He's braver than I. I no longer have the
courage to hope for a cure.

Ecstatic, Peter placed a call to my mother in Maine,
knowing she'd rejoice with him. I listened to his weak but
happy voice relate the news and I cried inside, hating the
moment he finds out it's not true. Now, more relaxed than
he's been in months, he reclines on the couch, contentedly
watching his comedy show.

He has so much faith and hope. Now that he fights for
his life, he has the strength and determination he lacked in
earlier battles when life was taken for granted. He's sure
he'll survive, live, somehow, in any state, until a cure is
found and he regains his health. Every new crisis, the
suffering, are but hurdles to be leaped on the road back to
living again, and he tolerates almost everything without
complaint because of this hope. He denies the illness,
saying, "I don't really feel *sick*." But I don't argue.
Despite my tears and skepticism now, I suppose I don't
argue because I, too, have my private hopes for a miracle,

or at least that he'll get strong enough to go to Santa Fe or Hawaii . . . or just sing at the June party.

But the grimly accelerating statistics of death mock me. I won't deny him his hope. I'll keep pretending with him, though at times the strain is so hard, so tiring, like acting a part that is pure fiction. Oh, that it were.

The ultimate tragedy is that here, now, in twentieth-century America, I shall outlive my son.

Wednesday, April 25

Nine-thirty A.M. I sit in the hospital cafeteria, an untouched cup of coffee before me. Peter is having another endoscopy, another search for the cause of the diarrhea. Since the seizure last week, the diarrhea is worse and he's pale, listless, disheartened. Today, his spirits are better because of the news last night. I brace myself, not knowing if I can stand seeing his pain when it proves to be false.

I feel terribly discouraged, too, these days. All the tests—the test today—seem so futile. They are always, always negative. I have a sickening dread that at this rate he won't live beyond June.

I hurt so much for him. We are both so hurt, and I doubt sometimes if I can keep on. But I must. I promised. How can I ever forget the silent plea of Peter's eyes back in New York? As long as he wants to live, I will find the strength to *keep* him living. Once he decides its over, I'll have to find a different strength—the strength to help him die, to let him go, to say the right words, to touch him when he wants to be touched and not when he doesn't. And to accept my inevitable defeat. I cannot accept that yet.

But right now, today, I am weak, frail, discouraged, helpless, despairing, and alone. So alone. I feel the familiar burning as my eyes fill with tears. Damn, will I ever stop crying? I'm so tired of crying.

But I can't stop them, right here in the cafeteria, surrounded by white-coated doctors, nurses, lab technicians, secretaries—all chattering, drinking mid-morning coffee.

Please ignore me. Nobody ask me what's wrong or I'll get hysterical. And I mustn't. I have to go get Peter, his test should be through and he mustn't see me cry and know the depths of my despair and sadness.

It's noon now, Peter is sleeping, exhausted. I sit in the sun on the patio, willing the warm rays to soothe me. But it isn't working this time. I can't stop the despair, the crying. I need someone. Louise has offered repeatedly to come if I need her. Not yet, I kept saying. Now—now is the time.

I go in and pick up the telephone.

6:00 P.M. The cruel blow has struck. The telephone lines between AIDS patients, their families, friends, lovers, have been buzzing since last night. What have you heard? . . . Well, I heard . . . Who said that? . . . When did you hear that? . . . where did you read it? AIDS patients all over San Diego, and those who love them, are angry, bitter, and disillusioned.

The news was misleadingly reported. There is no cure for AIDS in the immediate future. The famous HTVL III virus is only *presumed* to be the AIDS virus. All AIDS patients alive today will be dead within three years—most within months.

Thursday, April 26

Peter has just come out of his Owen Clinic support group. He, like the others, looks dejected and beaten. The meeting boiled with the anger and resentment of the young men whose temporary hopes, so sadistically offered, are now cruelly ripped from them.

How could the press be so irresponsible? The telephone lines buzzed all night as we, the Worried Well, let forth our own anger. It was unfair, cruel, unjust, irresponsible, inhuman—a political move! Yes, it was a political gambit, the United States trying to take credit for isolating a virus that the French already isolated a year ago, calling it LAV. Everybody wants the Nobel Peace Prize, money, awards, fame. What of those who suffer for their gain—the thin, gaunt AIDS victim, innocently listening to a misleading newscast, renewing a hope given up months ago? Oh, how cruel and vicious, how unutterably cruel.

We, too, are suffering. The pain of watching our loved ones' vast disappointment is unbearable. We will write letters of anger and protest to the news media, to President Reagan, to Margaret Heckler.

But we don't, we don't have time. We are too busy taking care of the dying, trying to soothe and heal the wounds of bleeding disillusionment.

We don't have time to heal our own wounds.

Friday, April 27

It is comforting to have my sister here. We picked her up last night after the support group meeting. Peter insisted on going, though he was exhausted and confused. We won't be able to do much. Peter is too weak to be dragged about sightseeing, and I don't dare leave him alone. At least with Louise here, I can go grocery shopping without the usual haste. Everything has been so awful recently. Peter so weak and depressed. I, discouraged, frantic, and almost hysterical at the rapidity of his downhill slide. For a few days, I have someone to whom I can pour out my fears and anxieties. I have felt so alone, so weak, so helpless. Even the others in my support group cannot fill the void I am in.

Richard, the social worker who runs the Owen Clinic support group for the patients, is coming here tonight to talk to Peter. He offered Peter extra counseling, and I, in desperation, called him on my own this morning, asking if he could help me with Peter's depression. I took a chance of aggravating Peter by going behind his back. Fortunately, Peter didn't mind and was agreeable to the idea. He'll be here at five-thirty this evening, and the weekly AIDS Project support group is at seven.

I hear a knock on the door and open it. Richard stands there, smiling.

"Peter, do you want Louise and me to stay or go out while you talk to Richard?" I ask.

"I'd like you to stay," he answers. I bring a chair for Richard and he sits opposite Peter. Louise sits in the red rocking chair to Peter's right, and I on Peter's left, on the couch.

"Well, Peter, how are you feeling?" Richard asks kindly.

"Oh . . . pretty good," he answers. "Well . . . actually, I've been having a lot of diarrhea."

Richard presses further and Peter gives more details: Yes, he's been depressed, he confesses, and frustrated—so many things he wanted to do, no energy to do them.

"You know that depression comes from anger," Richard tells him. "When you're angry and don't let it out, you can get very depressed. Do you ever cry, Peter?"

"No!" Peter's voice has a slight tinge of indignation.

"It's not a sign of weakness to cry, you know. And you have good reason. You have a serious disease," Richard chides him gently.

"I don't want to cry," says Peter. "That would be giving in."

"Oh, Peter, that's not giving in. I wish you would cry." I can't resist breaking in. I wish so often that his anger and sadness would break through the unemotional barrier he has erected. I'm so tired of crying alone for both of us.

"Tell me what you're most angry about, Peter," urges Richard. "Are you angry at your disease?"

"No, not really."

"How can you not be angry at it? Wouldn't you like to say, 'I hate this fucking disease'?" Richard's voice gains vehemence.

"Yes," I agree wholeheartedly.

"I don't see why I should have to use that kind of language." Peter turns on me angrily. What? What's this sudden propriety? He's always used "that kind of language." He's evading the real issue of his anger at disease and dying. Well, at least he's showing an emotion, that's good, even if he gives it the wrong name.

"Well," Richard smiles, recognizing Peter's gambit.

"You don't have to use that kind of language, but you can say the same thing in other words."

"There's no point in being angry about it," Peter insists heatedly.

"How about anger at your doctors?" Richard changes tack. "Do you think they're taking good care of you, really paying attention to you?"

"I know they're awfully busy, they do the best they can," Peter says defensively.

"Yes, but aren't you angry that they can't help you more?" Richard prods. "I get angry with my doctors. As a matter of fact, I blew up at mine this week." Peter looks at him, surprised.

"Oh, I couldn't do that." Peter refuses to be baited.

"Tell me, Peter," Richard veers to the side. "What do you do on a typical day, besides sleep or hang around the house?"

"Oh, there are all sorts of activities going on here, there are all sorts of things to do," Peter waves his hand airily. I choke back laughter, don't dare look at Louise. He speaks as if this were a posh vacation resort.

"Well, maybe so, but what exactly do you do?" I think Richard also has to fight laughter. Peter certainly is the master of evasion. "Have you been playing this at all?" Richard taps the piano next to him. "Or doing any singing?"

"I've been practicing some singing, but the piano . . . well, it's been so long and it's awfully hard. It's very tiring." Peter doesn't mention that he's unable to coordinate his mind's message to his hands.

"I'm sure it is," Richard is sympathetic. "But couldn't you play a few minutes, rest, play some more?"

"Well, maybe I could," he agrees. But I know he won't. I've already suggested this to him.

"Tell me, who do you see, who do you talk to, besides your mom and the doctors?"

Peter shrugs, says nothing.

"So you've just been staying at home, seeing no one," summarizes Richard gently. "Peter, I'd like to make a contract with you. I'd like you to call somebody and go out once this week. How would you feel about that?"

Peter is quiet a few seconds. "All right," he agrees.

"That's a contract, then?"

"Yes," Peter answers.

"Okay." Richard looks at his watch. An hour has passed quickly. "Guess I'd better be going, I have an appointment. Are you going to your meeting tonight?"

"I don't know, I'm awfully tired," Peter answers.

And I know he is. This has been a grueling hour for him, with Richard hacking away at his carefully constructed defenses. I know he's perturbed and I won't push him to go if he'd rather not.

"Thank you for coming," I tell Richard gratefully, walking to the door with him.

"You're welcome. I was glad to help," he smiles.

I turn back to Peter. "What do you think? If you want to go to the meeting, we'll have to hurry, it's almost seven."

"Sure, let's go," he says, rising slowly.

Surprised, I say, "You don't have to, you know."

"No, I'd like to."

The usual format is to go around the group, each member giving a brief summary of the past week, what has happened, and how he feels about it. Peter is the last to speak.

"And, Peter, how has your week been?" asks Tom, who acts as facilitator.

"Well," he starts, shifting sideways in his chair and leaning his arm on the back. His face is haggard, the ceiling light throwing exaggerated shadows into his eye sockets and under his cheekbones. The exhaustion of emotion is evident. "I haven't had such a bad week, and I think I've coped with it pretty well . . . despite what *some* social workers seem to think," he remarks sarcastically.

I avoid looking at Louise. If our eyes should connect, I think we would giggle. Yes, Richard was indeed successful. He broke through the flat, impenetrable veneer of Peter's self-control and nicked the anger beneath.

Peter gives details of his week—more diarrhea, feeling

that the doctors don't listen to him. His voice flattens wearily as he finishes.

Saturday, April 28

Peter slept late today. I offered him breakfast, but he refused angrily. "I can do it myself."

He lashed out at me several times afterward and was clumsier than usual, dropping objects and cursing loudly each time.

Good, you're angry! I applauded him silently. Let it out, Peter, let it all out.

I can take it.

7

Tuesday, May 1

Louise and I wait with Peter for his checkup at Owen Clinic Tom and John are here, too. John has had a dry cough and extreme shortness of breath for several days but refused to call a doctor till his scheduled appointment tonight. Tom fears John has pneumocystis again. He's probably right, and it'll be the second time. I've heard that no one survives repeat pneumocystis.

I watch Peter closely. He's got severe rectal pain, but is unsure whether it's from diarrhea-caused hemorrhoids or another herpetic lesion. The involuntary facial movements continue—lip pursing, sudden eyebrow lifting, and a strange grimace that widens his eyes while simultaneously pulling his jaw open and down in the opposite direction.

And still the problem expressing thoughts. Before we left home for the clinic, Peter tried to explain a new theory about his diarrhea. His father sent him an article that says diarrhea is caused by malabsorption of fats, and Peter is convinced that he should be checked for that. Since he ingests so much fat (butter, cream, milk, cheese) in his attempt to gain weight, he thinks dairy products should be eliminated from his diet.

I feel he is grasping at straws, avoiding the truth: The diarrhea is caused by an intestinal infection that escapes diagnosis, and thus there is no way to isolate the organism and destroy it.

This afternoon, Peter tried to explain the theory to Louise and me. I couldn't understand it at first and said, laughing, "Wait a minute . . ." He angered immediately, thinking I was mocking him.

"You're just like the doctors," he said disgustedly. "You don't take anything I say seriously, or even listen to me."

"No, no, Peter, that's not true," I said quickly, regretting his misinterpretation. "I'm listening, I just can't understand . . . you'll have to explain it more slowly. I wasn't laughing at you, believe me," I tried to assure him. If he ever lost faith in me, whom would he trust?

"Oh, just forget it," he said.

"No. I want to understand, please go on," I insisted. But he couldn't resume the train of thought and gave up in confusion and disgust.

Last night, I was frightened to hear mumbling in my bathroom. I got up, saw Peter in the middle of the bathroom, bemusedly grunting "hmmph!" as he looked around, puzzled.

"How come you're in here?" I asked, alarmed.

"I don't know. I don't know how I got here," he answered, dazed and confused.

"Well, it's certainly all right. You can use this bathroom or I'll take you back to yours if you want," I offered.

"I want to go back to mine," he said, and I led him docilely back to his own bathroom and waited outside the door.

"Hmmph," he said when he came out. "I guess I must have been dreaming. These two men dressed in white woke me up and took me there . . . and just in time, too," he said ruefully. "I knew in my sleep that I needed to get up but just couldn't, and they led me in there. Don't know why they took me to your bathroom, though."

"Are they nice people?"

"Oh, yes, and very kind. They've appeared before. They lead me down this long path, very gently, and then we come to the bathroom."

"You mean, they're like guides?"

"Yes, that's it."

"That sounds nice, Peter," I tell him as he rearranges himself in bed and I start massaging his back. "Maybe they'll hang around to help you."

"Yes, I hope so," he answers sleepily. "They're always nice."

I went back to my bed and laid awake, thinking. Now we have hallucinations. What next? Well, maybe this isn't so bad. It's a comforting image. I've read that dying people often visualize guides who help them, lead them peacefully down a path or tunnel toward a bright light—death. I mustn't take this away from him.

But a chill passes through me. Does this mean that he foresees death as coming soon?

"Okay, Peter, come on in," beckons the nurse, interrupting my thoughts. He rises and follows her. I want to go with him. He forgets what the doctors have told him by the time he reaches the corridor. But I restrain myself. I watch his bent back as he shuffles along. Will I ever, ever stop missing his springy gait, his erect posture, his youth?

Louise and I wait, watching the televised news, but my mind is in the examining room. I both hope and fear that he will be admitted to the hospital tonight: hope, because I think he's declining too rapidly and needs help desperately; fear, because admission will verify my pessimistic foreboding.

"Dr. Matthews would like to see you," the nurse calls me. I follow her to the examining room where Peter sits on the edge of the table. The doctor's head is bent over his notes.

"I think we'll put Peter in the hospital tonight for more evaluation of his diarrhea," he tells me, raising his sad, brown eyes as I sit down. "We'd like to run more tests. He's down to 118 pounds. He's also got more herpes and we'll put him on acyclovir intravenously to clear that up."

I glance at Peter. He seems relieved so I nod in agreement. I guess he won't be going out this week, as he promised Richard.

"I've already called upstairs for a bed. You can wait outside till it's ready if you like," the doctor tells us.

We rejoin Louise in the waiting room. Tom wheels John near us and sits down. John's blue eyes are platter-wide with fear, and he's breathing oxygen from a small portable tank.

"What's happening?" I ask them.

"They took an X-ray, and they're going to put Johnny in. They think he has pneumocystis again," Tom tells us.

"Oh, no," I sympathize, dread and fear for John increasing the apprehension I feel for Peter.

"Well, at least you'll be neighbors," I say, attempting lightness. "And I hear Jack's in, too . . . more tests for his leg pains." We've known Jack since the first AIDS Project meeting and have often given him rides home.

We wait. Sam from the Aids Project brings a patient in, learns that none of us has had dinner, and runs out to bring back a large container of fried chicken. We eat, chuckling at the bizarreness of a picnic in the Owen Clinic waiting room.

At last, Peter's and John's rooms are ready. Peter refuses a wheelchair and we walk slowly upstairs, Tom pushing John along. Up the elevator to 10 East, into his room. John will be next door, and we see that Jack is two rooms down the hall from Peter. Most AIDS patients are housed on 10 East. The nurses there are knowledgeable and unafraid of contagion. As always, he has a private room to avoid exposure to another patient's peculiar opportunistic diseases, and vice versa.

"Whew," Peter relaxes gratefully on the bed, dressed in the hospital gown the nurse has brought. "I'm glad I'm here. I feel more secure," he tells Louise and me. "Now I know I'll get some help. They *have* to listen to me now."

Wednesday, May 2

Peter is resting quietly as Louise and I enter his room. I slept better last night knowing he was here.

He had a sigmoidoscopy earlier to look for any problems in the colon. We keep hoping to discover a reason for the diarrhea. He's receiving acyclovir every eight hours intravenously and continual saline infusion to alleviate the dehydration caused by the diarrhea. Louise and I sit in chairs in opposite corners.

"Mom, I've been thinking a lot since last night, there're some things I want to talk to you about," Peter says. His voice is soft. I rise quickly and sit on the side of his bed to hear better.

"Yes, Peter?"

"I . . . well . . . what I've been thinking is, if I pull through this, I see it as giving me a second chance, a chance to start all over again."

"That's a good way to look at it," I tell him, wondering where this will lead.

"And as soon as I get out of here, I want to really concentrate on my singing and get on with the piano," he continues, his face determined and anxious.

"Good, Peter, I think that would be good. I'll help you any way I can."

Oh, God, how it hurts, this crazy hope and faith he maintains. Or is it crazy? Has the brain infection warped his sense of reality? He lies sick, weak, wasted in front of me and speaks of new chances. It hurts. It hurts so much, knowing he has no chance at all—a few months, if we're lucky—and I feel the familiar sting of tears. No. Wait till later. I lay my hand on his.

"And I still want to do some writing," he adds, looking up at me. His eyes are bright with emotion and the force of his determination. His own tears are close to the surface. I feel a sudden anger. Damn! if only he could have another chance!

"I've been hoping you would. You have so much to say," I encourage him. But I know he can't do it. He can barely write his name legibly, cannot play a simple tune, cannot organize his thoughts.

"I was thinking, after I get my voice back in shape, maybe I could get into one of the local groups that do musical comedies," he goes on.

"Maybe you could. Like I told you before, there's a lot of theatrical activity here."

I want him to stop. Stop talking. Stop dreaming. It hurts me so much. But I can't. It's all he has left.

"I love you," I tell him simply. He nods, shifting his glance to the open window. I can barely stand it. I feel his body relaxing and remove my hand. His eyes close. I tiptoe back to my chair, sit unmoving. I can't even look at Louise. I'm afraid that if I move, the overwhelming pain, anger, and frustration inside me will explode and the room will flood with my tears.

At last, he's asleep. I nod to Louise to go, and we hurry downstairs, buy coffee, and go outside to the cafeteria patio. One sip of the hot, bitter coffee and my strength dissolves, washed away by the tears and pain that tumble out and onto the empty patio.

God, help me to go on.

Thursday, May 3

"I hope they don't fly in here," Peter says, standing by the window and watching two pigeons on the concrete ledge outside. The ledge is covered with white pigeon droppings. He has an obsessive fear of animals and the germs they could give him. He cringes when the neighbors' terrier bounds into our house for a minute and is afraid of the aviary around the patio at John's house. Though all the birds are caged, he insists that they get loose and are in the thickly-twined branches shading the patio, that their feather dust or droppings could fall on him.

"Maybe we should close the window," he suggests.

"I don't think they can get in, Peter, it only opens about five inches, and it gets so stuffy in here without air-conditioning."

"Well, I think they could," he says, eyeing the window suspiciously as he crawls back into bed. "Lower it a little bit."

"Okay, a little," I agree, narrowing the opening to three inches. He continues glancing apprehensively at the window, then dozes off.

Louise and I left Peter alone so we can go to my Owen Clinic support group. I need it tonight. I need the strength of the others to share my pain and tension. The weekly meetings both here and at the AIDS Project are slowly forming invisible bonds between us, the Worried Well, even though we meet just once weekly.

Everybody's patient seems to be "down" this week, and two others besides Peter are suffering constant diarrhea. We are tense and tired. Diarrhea is the main topic of conversation: how to pretend it doesn't bother us so the patient is unaware of our worry; how to clean it up and still retain the patient's dignity; how to get them to use adult diapers and Chux bedliners without embarrassment. The final concensus is that we should buy the diapers and Chux and leave them in a visible but unobtrusive place. Suddenly, the tension breaks, and we laugh, visualizing boxes of Pampers magically appearing in AIDS patients' closets throughout the city.

"If I'd only known all this was going to happen," says Tim, longtime roommate of Ron who has AIDS, "I would have carpeted the house in kitty-litter instead of pale beige." We all roar and guffaw with laughter, smothering our hysteria.

"My God!" exclaims my sister as we walk down the hall afterward. "I think what the hospital should provide is a screaming room for all of you, a place where you can all go scream your heads off. I don't know how you all live with it."

Yes, it probably should. But we carry our screaming rooms inside of us, day and night, week after week.

Friday, May 4

It is seven P.M., and I am sitting with Peter, watching the evening news.

Louise left this morning. I miss her already. With Peter in the hospital, we had a little time to ourselves, going out to eat, seeing San Diego between hospital visits. But the valuable time was spent on my little patio, talking and talking, exactly what I needed. The hours of talk, of letting out, had a restorative effect and somehow I know I can go on.

Peter had a liver biopsy this morning and is lying on his right side surrounded by sandbags to keep him immobile and to avoid bleeding. So far, no complications. He's quiet, seems depressed. The nutritionist visited earlier in the afternoon, informing him that he must try to eat 3000 calories a day and drink Sustacal shakes between meals. These are high-nutrition, nondairy cold drinks to help him regain weight and strength, about 250 calories per serving. He weighs five pounds less than when he left New York, nine less than in February.

We will have to wait a few more days for the results of the laboratory tests. The one for cytomegalovirus will take four to six weeks. Apparently, cytomegalovirus, or CMV, is an elusive, incurable virus, often not confirmed except by autopsy. But it is often responsible for many of the problems that Peter has, so they're looking for it now. Meanwhile, we can only hope that a curable cause of the diarrhea will be found.

Monday, May 7

I'm getting used to the hospital routine again. I try to sleep late, but without success. Even without Peter in the next room, I keep an ear open at night and wake early.

Walter flew in this week, and we take turns sitting with Peter. I run errands I can't do easily when Peter's home, and do some extra painting. As in New York, we give Peter back and foot massages. Since he's even thinner than then, he's more uncomfortable being in bed all day.

Now that he's been here a few days, Walter sees more clearly the constant strain we live with, the myriad infections and complications we fear.

Peter has recurrent thrush and herpes proctitis, and in AIDS, the fungus and the virus can invade other parts of the body at any time—lungs, intestines, eyes, brain— anywhere. He has undiagnosed, subacute encephalitis (inflamation of the brain); constant, undiagnosed diarrhea; increasing fatigue, loss of weight and energy; and an undiagnosed and uncomfortable ear congestion, nasal discharge, and heavy cough. He has also lost his previous immunities to such diseases as measles, chickenpox, and mumps. And, of course, he can always get pneumocystis again, lymph gland malignancies, various exotic parasitic diseases, and Kaposi's sarcoma.

His entire system is wide open for any invasive agent, as though it were a banquet table, awaiting the avaricious appetite of any and all fungi, bacteria, viruses, or parasites that may arrive, uninvited, for the feast.

"It's always something new, isn't it?" Walter asked wonderingly yesterday.

"Yes, that's what AIDS is all about," I said.

"I don't know how you stand it," he said admiringly.

"I don't know," I shrugged my shoulders. "You just do what you have to do," I said after a minute.

I don't like being thought of as some grand heroine. I'm just being a mother.

After 20 years together, does he really not realize that our children are the most important thing in my life?

This afternoon, Walter and I took Peter outside in the wheelchair. We stayed out over an hour, at sunset, and he seemed happy.

But it saddened me, reminding me of when he was a baby and we took him to the park in his stroller. Now he's 28 years old, and as helpless as the baby he was then.

Wednesday, May 9

I went to the Department of Motor Vehicles this afternoon and stood in line for a "handicapped" plaque for our car. Though I intend to make Peter walk as much as possible, I know there will be times when he won't be able, and we'll need this privilege.

But it's another surrender, another giving-in, and I placed the blue plastic sign in the windshield with sadness.

Thursday, May 10

The phone rings. Eleven-thirty. I have just collapsed into bed. I tense immediately.

"Barbara, I'm sorry to wake you." Walter's voice.

"That's okay, I wasn't asleep. What is it?" Fear. Something's wrong. I left the hospital at ten. Walter was with Peter and he seemed ready to sleep.

"I just wanted to let you know, Jack died about an hour ago."

"Oh, no . . ." I sit up quickly. "They've been expecting it for days, thank God his family came. He had so much pain. Does Peter know? Should I go over?"

"No, I think it's all right. He doesn't know. I just left his room and they told me in the hall. Peter was falling asleep, so he won't know till tomorrow, or I'd stay. I'm calling from downstairs right now, on my way back to the hotel."

"I'll be there early in the morning, then, to be with him when he finds out," I tell him.

Jack is the first AIDS patient we've known to die. I weep in the night for him. He suffered such excruciating, debilitating pain in his legs. Everyone thought he was exaggerating, seeking attention. One night, going down in the elevator after clinic, he slumped to the floor and curled up, fetus-like, in pain. He could barely walk.

I wept, too, for his other pain—the pain of his mother's rejection. He envied Peter's having his mother with him and needed his own desperately. But she, a Bible-toting fundamentalist, insisted that he repent of his sin of homosexuality so that he would be saved—and again loved. What a hypocrite. If the essence of Christianity is unconditional love, how can these fervent disciples of Christ make their love conditional, especially to their own sons?

His family arrived yesterday. Jack held back his dying till his mother arrived. So little, so late. He needed them much sooner.

The phone rings again.

"Mom?"

"Yes, what is it?" I stiffen. Has he found out?

"Mom, Jack just died."

"Oh, I'm so sorry," I feign ignorance. "How did you find out?"

"Someone came in here. I was almost asleep, and they told me he just died." His voice sounds calm.

Damn. Who was so stupid as to go in his room, knowing he's sick and seeing him asleep, and give him the devastating news, then walk out and leave him alone with it?

"Peter, would you like me to come over?" I want to be with him. This is his first death. But I'm so tired. I don't want to get up, dress, drive, unless he needs me.

"No, it's okay, I'm all right," he answers. "You know, Jack really gave up when he was diagnosed in January. Remember, when anyone asked him how he was, he'd answer, 'I'm dying?' He just had the wrong attitude, he wanted to give up."

"I know, he did. Look, I'll come over if you want me to."

"No, go to sleep, I'm all right. I'll see you tomorrow."

I hang up the telephone, feeling guilty. But I'm so tired.

Friday, May 11

"How's Peter today?" I ask the nurse outside his door.

"He says he feels pretty good, but he's very quiet, seems depressed to me," she answers sympathetically. "He's got a little temperature, too, around 100 degrees."

I go inside. Lunch sits untouched on the table. Peter is dozing. I sit down quietly.

"You know, about Jack. . . ." Peter's eyes open. Good. I want to know how he feels.

"He just didn't have the right attitude all along. He was sure he was going to die, was completely negative. He didn't have any hope at all. I used to get angry at him," he says. "I'd sit across the table from him in our group and he'd be going on and on about all his aches and pains. I wanted to ask him what Bob Cecchi asked me in New York, do you remember?"

"Yes, he asked you if you wanted to live," I answer.

"Yeah . . . well, I always wanted to ask Jack that."

"You never did?"

"No. I don't know why not," he says, pensively.

"Well, I think you're right, he didn't want to live. But I also think that he really was in a lot of pain. That wasn't fake. He insisted that the doctors weren't listening to his complaints. I think he was right. He was in excruciating pain and they didn't believe him because they didn't know what they were seeing. They didn't know what to do or what it was," I tell him.

I shall never forget little Jack, moaning and writhing in pain, his blue eyes wide and terrified. So thin, limping along in his faded bluejeans and white sneakers. And always that frantic, silent plea for help in his eyes.

"Well, maybe so," accedes Peter. "But I still think he had the wrong attitude."

"You're right on that," I agree. He wants to believe that a positive attitude will conquer all. Who am I to deny it?

Surviving AIDS is the first long-term goal Peter has ever followed through on. Even though he will probably lose, his determination grows daily and I do all I can to bolster his hopes. His character is growing, taking root, and he's finally proud of himself.

Indeed, sometimes his faith is so strong, I find myself believing he will succeed.

Saturday, May 12

"They took me down to the ENT Clinic already," Peter tells me as I enter his room. He's been complaining of congestion, pain and ringing in his left ear, and intermittent headaches, and is positive that the doctors are ignoring his complaint though they've examined his ear many times. They cleaned out his ears and drained his sinuses and will send the fluid to the lab for testing.

"Hi, Peter," Dr. McCutchan enters the room. I like him. He sees Peter often at Owen Clinic and I can tell he cares. "I'm covering for Dr. Matthews this weekend. How are you feeling?" he asks solicitously, smiling slightly beneath his salt-and-pepper beard.

"Fine," Peter replies automatically. Liar, I thought.

"Well, looks like we have some news for you, finally."

I breathe an inner sigh of relief. Thank God, they've found something!

"We've isolated a mycobacterium. We're a little puzzled because we can't identify the type, but it's similar to what other AIDS patients are showing, something called 'mycobacterium avium intracellulare,' or MAI, a tuberculosis like organism. We found it in your bone marrow and your liver. The cells need longer to culture out completely, but on the basis of what we have now, we're going to start you on treatment for that," he finishes.

"Is this the cause of his diarrhea?" I ask.

"Probably," he answers, nodding.

"Can it . . . can it also be the cause of his brain infection?" I hesitate to ask. A solution to that would be too much to hope for.

"Well, I really don't know," he admits, stroking his beard pensively. "But there's no reason to deny the possibility."

I remain calm externally despite an unaccustomed optimism inside me. Is it too much to hope for? How wonderful if the treatment cures his brain infection, too!

"We'll be giving you isoniazid, or INH; it's used for regular tuberculosis. Plus pyridoxine; ethambutol; ansamycin; Pyrazinamide®; daily injections of streptomycin; and rifampin, till a drug called clofazimine arrives—we have to order it from the leprosarium in Carville, Louisiana. It's used for leprosy and has had some success with MAI. I have to warn you, you'll have to sign for this drug, as well as several others. It's experimental. But this one will darken your pigment, anywhere from red to purple, but probably well-tanned, and it doesn't go away later. Also, your urine or sweat will turn red, so don't be alarmed by that. It should come before you go home on Monday."

I am stunned by the endless list of drugs. He's already taking clotrimazole for thrush, Dilantin for seizure control, and Tylenol® with codeine for diarrhea. Enough diseases are attacking him already. Now what will all the drugs cause in their attempt to fight the diseases? I am glad we finally have a result from all the endless testing, but which will be worse ultimately—the disease or the cure?

"What about side effects of all these medications?" I ask the doctor.

"We'll have to wait and see. He won't have to take all these medicines for more than a short while. We'll be testing to see which ones are working and eliminate those that aren't."

The doctor leaves. Peter seems unmoved by the news, lies quietly on his back. His temperature is up to 101 degrees and he has little appetite.

But I feel a small, rare elation. It's been so long since anything good happened—a slow, steady slide downhill since soon after we came home in January. What an upside-down world, when positive test results can be called good. But then, everything is relative, and now we have a little hope—dare we? Maybe he'll get some strength and energy back, have some good time, weeks, maybe months.

Just a few, please.

Sunday, May 13

Today is Mother's Day. When I arrived at the hospital this morning, Peter had a lush, green plant with a pink plastic "Happy Mother's Day" sign sticking up between the leaves. Obviously, he delegated Walter to buy it for him. There was also a card, with a rabbit family on the cover—mother bunny and her two children strolling in the woodlands. One of the baby bunnies is saying, "Mommy, do you know what I think?" Inside, Peter scrawled unevenly, "Now let *me* know what I think!"

Whatever does this mean? I thanked him profusely for the plant and the card, meaning to ask him later about the significance of his words. But with hospital confusion, I forgot, and I sit here now, wondering what he meant.

Is he feeling so unsure of his mental powers that he wants me to guide him more, tell him what to think? Or does he feel I'm running his life, that he's not in control anymore—just what I've been trying not to do? Or is he referring to that bond we now share, wherein I seem to know what he's thinking without his telling me. It's all so difficult.

All meanings are possible. I don't know.

Tuesday, May 15

Peter came home today. We couldn't leave the hospital until late afternoon, waiting for his medications to arrive from the pharmacy. The drugs arrived in two big, brown grocery bags. I've never seen so many medicines intended for just one person.

I'm on the patio now, it's midnight. Peter was tired and went to bed early. He wants so desperately to live. Please, please, I tell the night, let him have some good time, let these medications work. And fast—before something else happens.

Thursday, May 17

We're waiting at Owen Clinic, as usual, for Peter's checkup. At least we didn't have to make a special trip for his streptomycin shot today.

The streptomycin injections—that's all that gets Peter out of the house now. I was given the option of learning to give them myself or taking him to the clinic every afternoon and having a visiting nurse administer them on weekends. I don't like to give injections and decided on the daily trip and weekend nurse routine. After two days, I decided I'd try to conquer my squeamishness and learn to give the shots myself, until it occurred to me that the daily clinic trips were a way to get Peter out of the house. It's worth the drive. Once he's up, dressed, and out, it's easy to persuade him to go magazine buying or window shopping, and thus get some exercise and a taste of the world outside our door.

The nurse calls us into the examining room.

"Well, Peter, you seem to be holding your own," comments Dr. Matthews after examining him. The nurse has given him his streptomycin shot and we're almost ready to leave.

"Are you getting any exercise, Peter?" the doctor asks.

"Oh, yes," Peter answers. "I do situps in the morning,

about twenty-five, twenty jumping jacks, some pushups, and leg bends.''

I look at him, astonished. He can hardly get himself into the bathroom! I glance at Dr. Matthews, his face is impassive. I sense he doesn't really believe him.

All he has to do is look at him and know it's not possible.

Tuesday, May 22

Three A.M. I can't sleep. Anxiety and apprehension almost stifle me. Peter is agitated and can't settle down long enough to sleep. Some invisible force won't allow him to stay still more than five minutes. I gave him backrubs to relax him. They didn't work, but he seemed to like them, like my touching him and talking to him quietly. He's been in and out of the bathroom—diarrhea. I jump up and listen through our open doors. I am an infant's mother again, with every sense heightened to respond to the least sound and movement.

I watched him closely yesterday. He was restless, his cheek muscles grimacing involuntarily, his eyebrows lifting, his jaw pulling downward in the opposite direction, wrinkling his forehead. He raised his hands slowly, gracefully, as if underwater. His words were garbled, sentences unfinished. I thought of calling the neurologist but decided to wait. Maybe it would pass. Despite the 400 milligrams of Dilantin, I am terrified of another seizure and that I won't be able to manage it alone.

Ten A.M. The entire apartment is charged with electricity. Neither of us has slept all night. I finally called Dr. Rothrock at the Neurology Clinic a short time ago and we have an appointment with him at five P.M. He assured me that the Dilantin will prevent another seizure. I think he sees me as a hysterical mother with an overactive imagination. But *I* am here, *I* am with Peter, and *I* think he's wrong.

I sit on the couch, looking at, but not reading, a magazine. Peter walks slowly, unsteadily, into the kitchen, takes yogurt from the refrigerator, gets a spoon, and sits at the table without speaking. He eats a few spoonfuls slowly, returns the yogurt to the refrigerator, and goes slowly back to his room. I stay seated but listening. All right, he's back in bed.

I hear Peter's toilet flush. He's up. I tiptoe to the hallway to listen. He doesn't like me to be oversolicitous, nor do I like to hover, so my ears have learned to hear around corners. He's back in bed. I sit down again. Quiet. He's up, walking around his room. I stand, listen, sit again. Up, listen, down. The morning passes slowly, my foreboding intensifies. I can't eat.

One P.M. I go to Peter's room. His eyes are closed but he's not asleep. "Peter?" I call softly.

"Hmm?" he answers.

"We have an appointment at five with Dr. Rothrock."

"Okay," he murmurs. Strange that he doesn't question it. I return to the living room.

One-thirty P.M. I hear Peter's shower running and station myself outside his bathroom door. Sounds all right. I go next door to my room, pretend to be busy there while he dresses. I peek in. He has his trousers on, his shirt buttoned crookedly. I laid his clothes out last night, fearing he might not be able to make decisions today—and fearing a quick trip to the hospital.

"Want some help?" I ask at the doorway.

"Do you know where my sneakers are?" he asks, puzzled.

"I think you took them off in the bathroom last night, let me look," I answer, pretending they must be lost, though I know they're on the bathroom floor and ordinarily he would know that. I put them on the floor in front of the bed, gently guide him to sit down. Awkwardly, he tries to slip his feet into them, tries to tie the shoelaces, but his fingers won't cooperate.

"Want some help with that?" I ask. He nods. He must know he's not well, too, or he would rebuff me angrily. "I can do it myself," he usually says.

I kneel on the floor and straighten his socks. They're crooked, the heel pocket on the top of the foot. I tie the shoelaces, stand up. He stands, too, peers curiously around the room as if for the first time, picks something up, examines it, puts it down, mumbles senseless syllables. I follow him, waiting, watching, ready to grab him if he starts an involuntary movement, but he moves slowly, fluidly, as if his limbs were not connected to his torso. I talk to him slowly, calmly, continuously asking questions he has to answer to see if he's still with me. He wanders around the room, out into the hall.

"Let's sit on the couch, Peter," I guide him slowly to the couch, help seat him. He's completely underwater—submerged—away from this world, his head turning, twisting at an odd angle on his thin neck, his eyes unseeing.

"Let's watch some TV, Peter," I suggest in an unnaturally loud voice as if he can't hear me. I turn on the television. A black-and-white rerun of "I Love Lucy" is on. Good, that's simple and familiar, maybe he can connect to that. I sit next to him, close, watching him covertly.

"Oh, that's a good show," he says, childlike. He appears to be watching it.

Good, Peter, good. Stay with it, stay with me, stay with me . . .

The minutes pass like hours. He looks at the TV, his face grimaces, he laughs, is silent. His head twists slowly to the left down slowly up in a circle his eyes seem to see something—"Mom, I'm seeing those black worms, bright lights . . ."

"Lie down, lie down quickly, Peter," I command loudly. He leans back, I guide him, and he starts convulsing before he's all the way down.

Oh God! I have him curled around behind me his back against the sofa I twist I grab his knees tightly with my right hand change quickly I cannot turn completely around grab his knees with my left hand push my body against his grab his hands with my right hand and pin them down to the cushion his shoulders his legs his arms are all jerking violently oh Barbara hold on hold on tight and he'll be all right Jesus Christ my poor baby my poor poor baby and finally it slows gradually slows, the convulsions are farther apart and irregular and we did it, I did it, I was able to do it. Oh thank God it's all right and he isn't hurt. We did it!

We sit quietly for several minutes. I relax my hold but don't let go completely in case it happens again. Spasms still clutch him, his eyes are open, blankly unseeing.

"It's all right, Peter, it's all right, it's all right, I'm here, Peter, Mom's here, it's all right . . . ," I repeat and repeat, wanting to reassure him, hoping he can hear me. We wait, he's calming down, he wants to get loose, get up. No, he's still not here, I must keep him down as long as I can.

He struggles, fights to get up, can't stand being restrained. I finally have to let him up, he staggers, almost falls, heads for the hallway staggering bouncing off the walls won't stop won't let me hold him fights me off angrily and I follow right behind him ready to grab him. I have to call the doctor, how am I going to get to the phone, I can't leave him alone, he's staggering, falling all over the place, oh God, I didn't expect this.

"Sit down, Peter, please sit down," I tell him firmly. I seat him on the bed but he stands immediately, I can't get him to say in one place. He wanders, stumbles, into the bathroom, out, he doesn't know what he's doing, talking pure gibberish, I have no idea what he's saying.

"Peter, stay in one place," I yell at him but he doesn't hear me. I have to get to the telephone, it's around the corner in my room, I have to take a chance, I don't know what to do, I have to get him to the hospital.

"Hello, hello . . . this is Barbara Peabody, Peter Vom Lehn's mother, Dr. Rothrock told me to call if Peter had a seizure, he just had one, I have to talk to Dr. Rothrock," the words tumble out. I'm standing by the door of my room, as far as the cord reaches, watching Peter. He's up again and staggering. For God's sake! Let me speak to the doctor you stupid bitch!

"He's with a patient right now, he can't be disturbed," says the secretary.

"Listen, I talked to him this morning, he told me to call if Peter had a seizure, what should I do?" My voice rises in hysteria and frustration. "I don't know what to do!"

"Well, I don't know, I can't tell you," she replies unemotionally and I'm trembling with helplessness and panic. No one told me what I should do if this happened. How can I get him to the hospital alone?

"Tell him I'm taking Peter to the emergency room, tell him please to meet us there, please!" I speak fast, I can't wait, hang up the phone. Peter is about to fall over the chair, I rush to catch him just in time.

"Come on, Peter, we have to go to the hospital, come . . . this way," I guide him down the hall but he's weaving, bumping into the walls, staggering. I don't know how I'm going to do it but I've got to get him there. I unlock the door, guide him out, he's lurching from side to side, I'm so afraid he might hurt himself on the cement wall, he rushes along, zigzagging, lurching, I can hardly keep up with him. He doesn't know where he is, where he's going, I keep grabbing at him but he's bigger than I am.

We're beside the car, I hold him while I unlock the door, open it. "Come on, Peter, get in the car, come on, back up," but he's staring at the sky, now tries to keep walking, confused, looks at the car, puzzled, speaks gibberish, I don't know what he's trying to say. Oh, God, I want to cry, the pity burns and burns, but I don't have time to cry. I guide him, push him gently into the seat, place his feet inside on the floor, he keeps trying to get out again. I get the seat belt on him, I don't know how, I close the door quickly. "It's all right, Peter, it's all right," I yell, dashing to my side of the car and jumping in. He's fighting his seat belt, wants to loosen it. "No, Peter, leave it on, leave it on," I say, starting the ignition.

I want to speed to the hospital but I can't, he's fighting angrily, fighting everything, wants to get everything off, can't stand being constrained. I drive slowly so I can keep one hand on him, keep him from opening the seat belt buckle, thank God for seat belts. He wants his shoes off, he has one shoe off, the other, I let him take them off. He's trying to unbutton his shirt, he can't get it off because of the seat belt so he attacks that again, I pull his hands away and he unbuttons his pants wants to get them off they're strangling him, again the seat belt is in the way and he's moaning, groaning, crying incoherently, pulling at the seat belt again but his fingers don't work right, he shrieks loudly, frustrated, angry at the restraints so he turns, unlocks the door and I reach behind him lock it again and he's reaching for the door handle, my God, we're on the freeway and I'm watching the road and taking his hand off the door handle, oh God, let us get there soon, we're on the off-ramp, good, we're close and he's crying, sobbing with frustration and speaking gibberish, senseless syllables, and I know what he's saying, he wants to escape, he wants to be free and this crazy electrical jumble in his head doesn't work right, the wiring is all screwed up. "No, Peter!" I yell as he reaches again for the handle talking to him as to the child he used to be, the child he is right now, going for a drive with his mommy, oh Jesus! oh my poor baby that you are now.

There's the hospital thank God, we turn in, I jump out leaving the door open and run to his side before he can get out. He's fighting with the seat belt again and I snap it open, help him out, he doesn't know where his feet should go. I guide him into the emergency room, yell, "He's had a seizure, please get me Dr. Rothrock, I already called," and an orderly brings a wheelchair. We try to seat him, hold him, wheel him to an alcove and get him up on the bed, now we wait for the doctor. I can't sit, he keeps trying to get off the bed. I stand next to it, keep talking, trying to soothe, he quiets, then tries again to rise. My hand is on his arm as much to feel his muscles tense as to soothe, and I push him gently back, over and over, put his legs back on the table, talk, talk, talk, oh I'm so damned tired, drained, if I could just sit down but there's no one to watch him for me.

A nurse comes in, starts to take his history. I wish I had his history and medications on a cassette tape, I could just play it off to her. I assemble my mind, tell her what happened, list his medications. I keep them in a small notebook with me at all times because we've found that one doctor doesn't always know what another has prescribed. She questions Peter, his answers are unintelligible, he doesn't know where he is. Oh, God, I'm so tired.

A doctor, a young woman, enters, asks the same questions as the nurse, she's a neurology intern. I repeat the answers, my eyes always on Peter. She tests his reflexes, asks him more questions he can't answer. She leaves. We wait. Peter keeps trying to get off the bed. I push him down. He lies still, moaning, his eyes still blank and empty.

Minutes, hours—still no Dr. Rothrock. I can't leave Peter alone to investigate. Where is he? I'm so tired, so frustrated. I see a footstool, pull it close to the bed and sit down, but just for a moment, Peter tries to get up again and I have to talk, calm, push him back down. Why doesn't someone come, why isn't his bed ready upstairs?

We are so alone.

Four-thirty P.M. A resident enters, pushing aside the curtains. Thank God, we are climbing the hierarchy. He asks the same questions, takes notes. Please, just hurry, finish, take us upstairs and let him rest.

"Sit up, Peter," the young doctor commands. Peter doesn't understand. We pull him upright. He's confused, disoriented, wants to lie back down. We hold him up. The doctor tests his reflexes. More questions. Peter is irritated, angry at being pushed, forced to think when his mind can't think, doesn't work right.

"All right, now sit on the edge of the table," instructs the doctor. Peter doesn't understand, starts to lie back.

"No, Peter, around this way . . . there," I say, helping him to sit up again and moving his legs for him.

"Now, clench your fist and I'm going to try to lower your hand. Don't let me." The doctor grabs Peter's hand and lowers it with no resistance.

"No, Peter, you have to try to keep it up," he says, annoyed. "Let's try it again." Once more, Peter offers no resistance.

"Come on, Peter, try harder," impatience tinges the doctor's voice. He pulls on Peter's fist, Peter tries weakly to resist, unsure of what he's supposed to do. The doctor repeats the test on the other arm, then tests his knees, feet, and ankles for reflexes. The knees and ankles jump extraordinarily high at the hammer's taps.

"Now lie down again," the doctor orders. I help Peter to turn and lie back. Peter twitches in annoyance and tries to push the doctor's hand away as he palpates Peter's abdomen.

"Now look, Peter, you're going to have to cooperate. I don't have all the time in the world, you know," the doctor reprimands brusquely.

I sense Peter's angry frustration at the physician's impatience and his own incapacity. I'm angry, too, at his impatience and intolerance. For heaven's sake, isn't he aware he's had a seizure, he's totally out of this world? What kind of doctor are you, anyway?

"Now listen to me, Peter . . . Peter, are you listening to me?" Peter is trying to concentrate, trying so hard to think, but the doctor's abruptness bewilders and agitates him. My God, he doesn't even know who or where he is, what do you expect of him? I try hard to control myself, not to say anything. I don't want to upset Peter more, but I want to berate this rude doctor for his cruel insensitivity. Why doesn't he realize that if he were kind, slow, patient, he could finish the exam faster than by antagonizing and confusing Peter even further?

"Where are you, Peter?"

Gibberish.

"What is the date today?"

Nothing.

"Who is the president?"

Peter looks at him blankly.

"Can you remember these three objects?" The doctor names them. No, he doesn't even know what the doctor is talking about.

Oh Christ, leave him alone, hurry up and go, go away. As if hearing my silent pleas, the young doctor writes his notes hurriedly, finally leaves. Where the hell is Dr. Rothrock? He knows Peter and deals with him well, but why can't he see the seriousness of his illness? Doesn't he believe what I tell him?

Five-thirty P.M. Dr. Rothrock arrives and I exhale relief.

"Peter, do you know what has happened?" he asks, his tone gentle. Peter looks at him vaguely.

"You've had another seizure, Peter. You're in the emergency room at UCSD," he tells him kindly, trying to reorient him. "We're waiting for a bed for you upstairs. We're going to do some more tests and try to see what's causing this. Now, let me take a look at you."

He glances quickly at the resident's notes and examines Peter briefly. I am grateful for his quiet calm and see that Peter is responding to it. At least someone here knows how to treat a confused, post-seizure patient. If only he had come sooner.

All the doctors are gone, nurses come and go, and we wait and wait. I leave the cubicle once and look down the hall. Peter is up right away, ready to stagger off, and I rush back, lay him down again. His speech is still unintelligible and though he weakly resists, he's cooperative.

Nine P.M.

"Your room's ready, Peter, let's take you up," a nurse finally enters and starts wheeling his bed briskly down the hall. I follow, carrying his clothes. His sneakers are still in the car.

Peter moves from the Guerney bed to his own and lies back, exhausted. I pull a straight chair near and sit by his side while the nurse takes yet another history. He still cannot concentrate and I give the answers. Dr. Monaco, the impatient doctor from the emergency room, enters and informs us he will be doing a spinal tap. I sign the permission. I don't like this man, but I have no choice but to let him treat Peter.

The nurse wheels in a small cart with the lumbar puncture kit on top, and the doctor begins the procedure. Peter still twitches slightly but the needle is inserted and fluid drips slowly out, clear and unclouded. Dr. Monaco leaves with the tubes of fluid and Peter turns onto his back and lies quietly, his eyes closed.

I sit with my hand on his to comfort him with my touch but also to be aware of unusual movement. Some deep instinct won't allow me to relax yet. His hand twitches at moments and I watch him constantly. Yes! I knew it! Peter's hand jumps suddenly. I leap from the chair and grab his shoulders as the convulsions start. Oh, God, no. But yes we are off and running and I scream, "Nurse! Nurse! Help, seizure!" I don't want to wake or alarm other patients but I scream again "Nurse! Nurse! Seizure!" and I'm sitting on the bed almost on top of Peter, pushing his shoulders into the pillow my elbows pushing on his chest so he can't raise up please help please come quickly where are you? I don't know how long I can hold him down alone a nurse runs in pushes the buzzer and another comes bringing the IV tray it is the IV nurse thank God she puts gloves on quickly readies the needle and tries to insert it it's in good but no it's out and he's bleeding like before and his face is blue grimacing he's the wild animal again oh God stop it stop it soon please I can't stand it I'm glad he's on a bed it'd be so dangerous oh no now they bring restraints and they put them on him my poor wild animal son oh Peter—"Peter, Peter, Peter, it's all right, Mom's here, it's all right, it'll be over soon, Peter, Peter" I keep saying and I think he hears me he's starting to slow down the outrageous demon is leaving giving him back to us thank God yes, it's stopping, the violent waves are turning to shudders not as regular oh God how much of this are we going to have to bear oh my poor poor baby and now he's tied down, he's trapped and fighting it, he rises up "Peter, lie down, lie down," he hears me!

Every time he rises up, I say, "Peter, Peter," and he answers, he actually answers! "What?" he says though his eyes stay closed. "Lie down, Peter, lie down," and miracle, he lies down, thank God he can hear me. I release his shoulders, his arms are strapped down, and he can only twist from side to side and rise up occasionally, but it is just coming in slow, irregular waves now. Every time I call, "Peter," he answers, and I tell him to lie down, I'm here, and he obeys.

I hear the nurse say he will get ten milligrams of Valium, fifty milligrams of Dilantin through the IV, and ten more milligrams of Valium during the night. I sink back into the chair, emptied, drained. When will this hell of horrors end? I hold his hand again and look at his face, still red from the exertion, but he sleeps soundly, drunken with sedation. Again, he twitches slightly now and then but I feel certain the storms are over for today.

Oh, Peter, how much of this will we go through, how much can we stand? My eyes burn with the tears I haven't had time to release all day—no time for crying. And now I don't have the strength to cry.

Wednesday, May 23

I sit in the chair by the window in Peter's room, watching him sleep. I was too tense to sleep when I finally got home at midnight last night. I stayed to be sure Peter was all right. I feared he was oversedated at first. His heart rate slowed considerably and the nurse called the intern, but it adjusted itself.

A day of horror, horror, horror—that's the word that runs continually through my mind, over and over. How much more can he take? Why doesn't he want to give up? It's all so horrible. His legs hurt too much from the injections to walk, the streptomycin injection sites adding pain to the remnants of the pentamidine pain. And he's so weak, so wasted. The diarrhea continues to wash his strength out, and the brain infection—he can't express a complete thought, use the right words, or even remember words.

He wanders in and out of another world and he knows it. How frustrating, how horrible to be losing your mind. And yet, he wants to go on. The sicker he is, the more determined to survive. Where does he get this inner source of strength and courage?

I look out the window and watch the traffic below. All you people out there, I muse, rushing about your business. Do you have any idea of what this disease called AIDS really is? Do you have the slightest inkling of what its victims are suffering? Do you know of the horror? Assuredly not, and I envy you.

Some I hate—you who think it's exactly what homosexuals deserve, that they're perverted and abnormal anyway. But what if it were your son, brother, friend, father? What then?

I know already. Most of you will abandon them, leave them to die alone, terrified and despised. First, you can't accept their homosexuality, and next, you can't face dying and death.

I look at Peter sleeping, his face pale and lined. No one deserves this, no one.

I turn. Dr. Monaco has entered the room with two other residents. "Good morning, Peter," he says. Peter moves, wakes up, doesn't recognize the young physician.

"Who are you?" he asks.

"I'm Dr. Monaco, I saw you yesterday in the emergency room," he answers. "You had a seizure at home, then another one here last night."

Dr. Monaco begins the questions. Peter knows his own name and that he's in UCSD Medical Center. He knows it's May but not which day. He identifies objects—a cuff, a tie, a nose—with difficulty, using either an invented word or one that sounds similar to the correct one. Eventually, he adjusts and corrects the mistakes with help. He can recite six digits forward and four backward, but can only remember Presidents Reagan and Carter, unlike his usual rapid-fire backward listing of the presidents. His hearing and vision appear normal, but his tongue falls to the left when instructed to stick it out. The doctor comments that the tongue has wasting on the left side. Whatever does that mean? There is continuing left ear and left sinus infection. Could there be some bizarre connection?

Peter is cooperative during the examination but eyes the doctor with hostility and is not as friendly as usual. After the troupe leaves, Peter turns to me.

"Who were they?" he asks.

"They were neurology residents," I tell him.

"And that one who was leaning against the wall just now, who's he?" he asks with pronounced disgust. "I don't like him."

"That was Dr. Monaco. He took care of you in the emergency room yesterday." I wondered if he'd remember him. It's interesting that he doesn't recognize him by physical appearance but seems to by his emotional reaction, a primitive awareness that this man is not to be trusted, he may mistreat him again.

"What'd you say his name was?" he asks again.

"Monaco," I answer.

"Oh, I thought it was Nayroc. Well, I'm going to call him Dr. Nayroc. It's an ugly name and that's what he deserves."

"Okay, Dr. Nayroc it'll be," I agree, laughing, glad for this small trace of Peter's characteristic humor.

"Come on, Peter," the nurse and I assist him to a wheelchair. Time for a CT scan, another cross-sectional, photographic look into his brain to see if any lesion, tumor, or signs of hemorrhage can be detected. I walk alongside the wheelchair, looking down at his bent, knobby head, the sparse hair, the tendons in sharp relief on the back of his head. For the thousandth time, his thinness jolts me painfully.

"I'm going to the cafeteria while you're in there, Peter. Be back in half an hour, okay?" The CT scan should take about 40 minutes. I have time to relax.

I return in half an hour, surprised to see Peter already in the hall, a nurse ready to take him back upstairs. He sits hunched, looks dejected.

"They couldn't do the scan," the nurse tells me.

"Why not?"

"He panicked, they couldn't keep his head still to get good photographs, he kept moving," she answers.

The claustrophobia. Damn, I should have warned them about that. And with the drugs and his post-seizure state, of course he panicked. I feel guilty for leaving him.

The technician joins us. "He just went crazy, was screaming and fighting, couldn't seem to stand being inside the machine, said he couldn't stand being tied down."

"No, he really hates it," I tell him, wishing they wouldn't talk about him in front of him. I know he's embarrassed.

"We'll try it in a couple of days when he feels better," the technician returns to his cubicle.

"Oh, no, they're not going to put me in that thing

again," Peter says with emphatic anger. "I told them I couldn't stand it and they insisted on doing it anyway."

"It's okay, Peter, don't worry about it," I pat his bony shoulder as the nurse wheels him back to the elevator.

Thursday, May 24

Midafternoon, and we decide to take a short walk down the hall. Peter, though still very tired, is more alert and his words are clearer.

Awkwardly, Peter tries to slide his feet into his slippers. I lean over and help, then hold his bathrobe open for him. He's unusually interested in the other patients and peeks curiously into their rooms as we pass by.

"Oh, I wonder who that is? I wonder what's wrong with him?" he remarks, starting to enter a private room.

"Come on, Peter, I don't think we should go in," I lead him gently out. He shuffles along, I hold his thin arm and he doesn't object. He reminds me of a tall, floppy grasshopper as he ambles happily along, making odd, peering motions as we walk. He is childlike, with small boy's innocent curiosity, and makes little jokes and comments about the nurses and other patients as we pass them in the hall, chuckling to himself, amused at his own humor.

His observations are bizarrely comical, and I giggle, too. But my laughter thinly curtains a new sorrow—is he going to remain in this infantile state? It's now 48 hours since the last seizure and he still is not normal. He's a child, happy in a child's world. Is this from so much medication, or is there more brain damage?

Who knows, I think wearily. Maybe this is a blessing in disguise. I look up at him ambling happily along the corridor, "hmmphing," peering inquisitively, chuckling. Anxiety and fear are gone from his face. His green eyes are wide and innocent behind his thick lenses. He mixes words and pauses, cocks his head, laughs at his errors. Oh God, let him stay like this—why not?—protect him from the present and future horrors.

Insulate him comfortably in childishness.

Saturday, May 26

Home again. It seems that all we do now is pack, go to the hospital, unpack, pack, and come home again and unpack. We're both tired of this routine. Peter is tired of being punched, poked, prodded, injected, and awakened at night. And I, though I can sleep better without listening for every slight sound, am tired of the back-and-forth to the hospital.

The childlike behavior is gone, as if it never happened. The doctors searched for every possible neurological problem, but with no results.

A CT scan was finally done last night. It revealed no gross abnormalities. There is no lesion, no atrophy, no tumor mass, no hemorrhage—nothing out of the normal range of size or shape. An EEG also showed nothing significant.

His clinical symptoms do not fit any easy diagnosis. As soon as one symptom makes a diagnosis feasible, a lab result, CT scan, or some other test denies it.

The most probable diagnosis is "sub-acute encephalitis," possibly caused by CMV. However, CMV has not shown up in any of Peter's lab tests, which is not necessarily significant since the virus can take four to six weeks to grow in culture and is so elusive it may never appear.

The neurologist assumes the problem lies in the temporal lobe, based on the characteristics of Peter's behavior and neurological symptoms. But with nothing abnormal in either the EEG or CT scan, it is all presumption. And without knowing where the infection is focused, a biopsy cannot be done.

Peter is now taking 600 milligrams of Dilantin a day to prevent another seizure. Possible side effects are so similar to the neurological symptoms the drug treats that I don't know how we will know which is which.

It's like a nightmare. I wish it were. Bad dreams eventually dissolve.

Monday, May 28

The AIDS Project has moved recently into a large, old hospital building on Vauclain Point, a promontory near the hospital. The support meetings have reorganized, too. Now patients and Worried Well meet separately for three weeks, and have a joint meeting the fourth week.

Tonight, Ramona, a professional masseuse, is speaking to the monthly joint meeting, demonstrating the value of massage and acupressure in the alleviation of tension and stress, the everyday companions of everyone in this room tonight. Peter sits on my right, hunched over. He is anxious to learn more tonight, as stress is considered a factor in lowering the immune system.

On my left sits a small, thin, old-young man with enormous, puffy, purple-brown spots on his face. A dark, woolen cap with visor is pushed down on his head, despite the heat, and long wisps of dull hair jut out at odd angles. His brown eyes dart around the room and he has a strange, demented mien. I've never seen him before at these meetings. His disfigured face is my first introduction to advanced Kaposi's sarcoma.

"But I have somewhat limited energy. What do you suggest I do for a lighter type of exercise?" Peter asks. Ramona has just been emphasizing the importance of good nutrition and exercise.

"Why don't you do some pushups, lift weights, stuff like that?" interrupts the strange creature next to me before Ramona can answer. Peter looks at him incredulously. I almost ask if he knows what pneumocystis is, and its effects, but I bite my tongue, trying not to be the smother-mother, jumping in to save her boy from the school bully. I see others are bristling, resentful of the man's attack on Peter and ready to defend him.

"You know, you have to push yourself, you have to make yourself do these things. You can't just sit around doing nothing," the man continues critically.

"I don't plan to," responds Peter calmly. "I do as much as I can, but I'm not able to do as much as some people."

Why isn't he furious with this jerk?

The little creature looks at Peter sneeringly. I'd like to punch him out, but this is Peter's fight. Peter ignores him, as if he didn't exist, asking Ramona other questions and listening intently.

I look around the room and see sympathetic faces, silently applauding Peter. And Peter, impervious to the man's gnat-like attacks, defends himself with a quiet dignity and pride I have never seen.

You got class, kid. I'm proud of you.

Wednesday, May 30

We went to the medical supply store today to buy a cane. Peter is weak and unsteady and needs it as much for balance as for support. I thought MediCal would pay for it, but they only pay if it is purchased with a doctor's prescription, and costs more than $35. Then it takes three to four weeks to get approval.

"That's ridiculous," I told the salesclerk. "You have canes here from $4.75 up. Why would MediCal only pay for the most expensive? No wonder government insurance plans are in trouble with that kind of philosophy."

"That's their rule," she said.

We bought the $4.75 cane. Peter seems rather pleased with it. I think he imagines it gives him a certain dramatic sophistication.

But to me, it's another step down. Observing other patients, I see a pattern to the progress of AIDS. First the handicapped plaque for the car, next the cane, then the wheelchair, and finally the hospital bed at home. I hate giving in to these signposts.

I hate it.

8

Sunday, June 3

My fingers have been crossed night and day and I hardly dare to hope. What is happening? Peter has felt vastly better the last two or three days. He, too, is amazed and delighted at this sudden change, and we wonder what has caused this improvement. Could the MAI drugs be working so soon? We must enjoy it while we can.

Maria is coming today for three weeks' vacation before spending two months at the Aspen Summer Music Festival. Sandy is arriving from New York an hour later for a three-day visit. Peter wants to go to the airport with me, but we realize that though four adults can fit in a Datsun, four adults with six pieces of luggage cannot. I am sorry not to take Peter along. Going to meet visitors makes him feel normal.

Wednesday, June 6

Seven A.M. Peter joins Maria and me in the kitchen. His face is haggard and tired again, and my spirits slump. I've just returned from taking Sandy to the airport. He and Peter had three good days together, with Peter well enough to play host and enjoy his company. But by last night, I could see Peter beginning to tire, words slipping from his grasp, and I know now that the brief interlude of hope is over.

Now, I watch as he takes his pills slowly with water, eats some yogurt, then opens the sliding patio door and peers out at the hazy, June morning. Leaving the door open, he turns and sits on the couch, gazing vacantly into space.

I know without asking that the electrical jumbling is starting again in his brain. I see his upper cheek twitch, his eyebrows lift involuntarily. He sits rigidly, his body curved tensely. I see that he's apprehensive, fearful of another seizure, but I know he won't talk about it. He seems to have a superstitious feeling, as if the reality of words, of spoken fears, makes him vulnerable. I often wish he would speak of his fears, but he has a right to build his defenses as he wishes, and I respect that.

"I think I'll go back to bed for awhile." Peter stands slowly, walks down the hall.

"Maria," I speak softly, "I think something is starting again, I know the signs." I try not to frighten her. "Don't worry. I'll call Dr. Rothrock in awhile, but I don't want to take him to the hospital if possible. He's so terrified of the restraints and I'm not going to subject him to that. I've already handled it once alone, and I'm not scared of seizures anymore, and you can help me, too."

"Okay Mom. I can help, don't worry," she reassures me.

"If anything does happen, it won't be for awhile. It takes time to build up. But, whether today or some other day, the important thing is to get him down, on the floor or the couch, so he won't injure himself. Once down, get him on his side, grab his legs and arms, curve him around your own body and you can hold on better. Even if he has one, with 600 milligrams of Dilantin it shouldn't be too bad, I think."

I send Maria for groceries, then call Dr. Rothrock. He's with a patient, the secretary tells me; will return my call.

Peter comes back in the kitchen, turns on a classical radio station, listens a minute, turns it off, and goes back to his room. I wash dirty dishes. Maria returns with groceries and we store them away. I peek at Peter, lying on his back, hands folded across his chest. That position makes me so uneasy, chills me eerily.

Noon. Dr. Rothrock has not returned my call. I call the clinic. Yes, he's free for a minute.

"I'm a little worried," I start. "Peter is restless, really agitated, mixing his words up a lot. Do you think he could have another seizure?"

"No, he shouldn't. All the Dilantin he's taking should block it, and his Dilantin level was perfect last time we checked it," he answers, then pauses. "But then, that's what I said before."

"I know, that's what I'm remembering," I say. "Do you want to check him today, or what should I do?"

"No, there's no use. Just keep watching him, and if he has a seizure, bring him in. I want an EEG taken right after a seizure."

All right. That sounds easy. Just wait and watch. Watch and wait. Okay.

Oh, Dr. Rothrock—all you doctors—if you only knew how hard it is, how Peter suffers with fear, anxiety, complete helplessness before a seizure, feeling his brain scrambling, the jabs and sparks of the wires as they short-circuit, feeling the gradual loss of control over his muscles and speech. And I watch and wait, hearing the words jumble more and more, the mindless wandering around the apartment, the pursing mouth and grimaces, the underwater movements, the slow but steady slide into dementia as my heart burns and breaks again into a thousand pieces.

Damn. What hurts most in this insane and wretched disease is not the physical deterioration, the diarrhea and the various lesser infections. These are bad enough. But this, the obscene wasting of his brain—this is what hurts so deeply.

And I can do nothing—calming words, soothing massages, repeating that I'm here and he's not alone—not enough. Even my presence doesn't really help. He walks alone in his dementia, unhearing and unseeing.

Ten P.M. The storm has been moving in all day, slowly clouding and darkening the landscape of Peter's brain. He can't sit still more than two minutes. His face grimaces strongly now, his tongue lolls out without control. His head and hands move, arc, curve, in their slow, underwater fashion. He stands, goes to his room, picks something up and puts it down again, speaks words that make no sense, his private language of dementia. I give him food; no interest. I follow after him, guide him when he staggers. Surprisingly, he doesn't complain. He either doesn't realize I'm behind him or is glad I am. My every sense, every nerve, is wide open. He sits next to me and I feel his smallest muscle move. He hallucinates, sees strange objects, but so far, no white lights or worm shapes. Maria helps, following him around. She's so good with her big brother, so strong.

One A.M. Maria collapses, exhausted.

"Come lie down a bit, Peter," I guide him to his bed, help him to lie down. He has little command over his arms and legs, as if they were someone else's. With help, he turns on his left side, facing me.

"Would you like a backrub?" I ask. Yes, he nods, his eyes staring blankly ahead. His right hand claws constantly at the sheet, his bony fingers scraping, scratching, clutching rhythmically at the cloth beneath him. The skin of his face grimaces incessantly, pulling and stretching his mouth into a bizarre, humorless grin, baring his teeth and wrinkling his cheeks, as if manipulated by an invisible, diabolic hand. He has had no control of his tongue for over two hours, and it lolls constantly out the left side of his mouth, smothering his words. It annoys him. He keeps trying to push it back in his mouth with his hand. He tries to talk to me. All I hear are muffled, senseless sounds, but my inner ear hears him.

"I know, Peter, I know, it's very frustrating," I sympathize, rubbing his back, his arms. "It's all right, it'll go away in a little while, we just have to wait it out, it's all right."

I rub his scalp and he closes his eyes, gives a soft moan of pleasure. I keep rubbing, combing my fingers gently through his sparse hair, watching his drawn face as the invisible fingers twist, pull, jerk the muscles spasmodically. I can feel it myself. I feel the skin stretch, relax, stretch, feel the tongue fill the mouth and fall out, and feel the frustrating anger he cannot express as his right hand claws ceaselessly at the sheet.

"Peter," I speak again. "It's all right. It's all right. I'm here with you. And so is everybody else, we all love you," I assure him.

He raises his head suddenly, looks straight at me for a second. "Of course," he enunciates clearly, almost scornfully. "I know that."

I want to laugh with relief, glad he knows he's not alone and amused at his brief return to reality. "Well, I just wanted to be sure you knew," I say, giving him a gentle tweak on the arm.

"Fmmph," he answers, his tongue lolling wildly. I talk on and on, quietly, slowly. I know he can't understand what I'm saying, but hope the sound of my voice will calm the demons inside. I don't know what else to do.

Three A.M.
"Peter, let's try to sleep a little while," I tell him. My eyes are burning with fatigue. Just ten minutes of sleep would keep me going. I push him gently toward the wall. He seems a little quieter, his hand not clutching, but slowly, rhythmically, smoothing the sheet. Maybe he can sleep now. Maybe the storm is passing over.

"I'm going to sleep in here, to be with you," I tell him as I lie down on top of the other bed. I'm afraid to get under the covers, afraid I might fall deeply asleep. The light is on in the bathroom, the door partly closed, and the dim ray of light falls on the carpet. My eyes close.

Suddenly, I hear a clicking, sit upright—plastic—the pills! I jump up, run in the bathroom. Peter is shaking his pill vials, looking at them, then dumping them all down the toilet. My God, has he taken any?

"Do you want some help, Peter?" I ask, quickly scooping up the remaining brown vials on the counter.

"Yes, take these—you take them, I'm afraid I might take them wrong." His words are woolly but I can understand them.

"All right, I'll take care of them, don't worry." What a

relief. I've been trying for quite a while to think of a tactful way of gaining complete control of his medications.

"Did you take any pills now?" He shakes his head. I run to the kitchen with the plastic vials, dump them on the table, and rush back. He hasn't moved.

"Okay, Peter, that's all taken care of. Let's go back to bed." I guide him and he walks docilely, like a child.

"How about another backrub?" I ask. He nods. His body is tense, rigid. His face still grimaces and his right hand starts gently smoothing the sheet again, but the rhythmical movements are not as frenzied as before.

"Now try to relax, think of something nice, something pleasant. Think of Hawaii," I suggest, oiling my hands and rubbing his back as smoothly as I can. His eyes close but his body remains stiff. I can feel the rib bones clearly through his flesh. I think he's quiet. I go back to my bed.

Scritch-scratch, scritch-scratch, shoosh-shoosh. What's that? I jump up, puzzled. Oh, God, he's in the bathroom again. I push the door open, peer inside. Peter is bent over the toilet, scrubbing, scrubbing with the toilet brush.

"Peter, what are you doing?" I ask gently.

"Mssshtobb," he mumbles.

"Come on, let's go back to bed, I think it's clean enough now." I take the brush from his hands and turn him, walk him slowly back to the bed. He totters. I don't know how he got into the bathroom both times without falling. He lies down obediently and I massage him again. He tries to speak, but his lolling tongue impedes the words. I pretend to know what he's saying, answer ambiguously, keep soothing, calming. Finally, I think—I hope— he's sleeping. I crawl back to the other bed. I am unutterably tired.

Six A.M. Up to the bathroom. Diarrhea. I stand outside the bathroom, ready to rush in. No, it's all right. I help him back to bed.

Seven A.M. The sun is rising. Peter sleeps. Wait, one more bout of diarrhea, back to bed, and he's really asleep. I think the worst is over, and no real seizure. The

Dilantin barely controlled an outright breakthrough, but what agony, what torture these past hours have given Peter.

Nevertheless, we managed to get through it, all alone—no doctors, no hospitals, no restraints.

All alone.

Friday, June 8

I find myself wishing that, when this is all over and however it may turn out, I can go somewhere alone—a deserted beach, an empty house, a hilltop—and scream my head off for a week. There is nowhere I can do it now. I can cry, but there's no place to scream, and the stifled screams of hurt and frustration reverberate through my skull. After that, I want to cry for another week, just as loudly as I want. Then I want to sleep for a month.

I have my crying on automatic timer. I leave the house, get in the car, and images of Peter fill my eyes. I see his body, a bag of bones on his bed, feel my frustration and helplessness—that's all it takes, and I cry for the five-minute trip to the grocery store, check my tears at the door, and cry again on the way home.

Meanwhile, I carry my screaming room inside me. It has no doors.

Saturday, June 9

We are on the way to Peter's first professional massage appointment. He's been looking forward to this all week, hoping for relief from his constant tension. I helped him to dress. He was very confused about what to wear and how to put it on. He staggered and lurched down the walk to the car, holding his cane but not knowing how to use it. I guided his arm.

"Oh, there's that guy again," Peter exclaims. We are in the middle lane headed east on Interstate 8. "There, look . . . we're just passing him, in the blue sports car."

I glance around quickly. I see a blue sports car but don't recognize the driver. "What guy?" I ask.

"Remember, that one at the project with the bad Kaposi's, the one who gave me a hard time at the meeting?"

"Oh, yes. That didn't look like him, though. Are you sure?"

"Oh, yes, that was him," he answers. "I know it was."

I know it wasn't. The driver of the blue sports car was young, healthy, and unfamiliar. Peter often thinks he sees people he knows.

"Did you like the massage, did it help you?" I ask Peter on the way home.

"Yeah, it was really nice," he comments, "except I feel dizzy and my stomach is upset. I think . . . I think I'm seeing double, too. See that little red Fiat in front? I'm seeing two of them, it feels weird. How many minutes till we get home?"

I step on the accelerator, rush to help him out of the car when we get home, fumble with keys, guide him into my bathroom, the closest, and he vomits profusely.

"Wow, just in time," I tell him, dabbing his face with cool water and helping him to his feet. "Are you all right, do you feel any better?"

"Yes, a little. I just want to go to bed," he answers feebly. I help him to his room, settle him on his bed, and he sighs with relief.

I leave him dozing and rush to the telephone to call Dr. Rothrock. He returns the page immediately from a public telephone. I hear traffic in the background and he explains he's out jogging.

"Hmmm . . .," he responds after I summarize the day, "he's already on such a high dosage of Dilantin, it's unlikely he could have a seizure,"—familiar words—"but I think I'll lower it and add Tegretol®, which is more specific for the temporal lobe. Would have given it to him before but it can affect the liver, and he already has tuberculosis there. I think he's probably on too high a dose of Dilantin, especially with the nausea, vomiting, and double vision. That usually distinguishes an overdose from a seizure. Let's see how he does on this, and let me know if there are any problems," he concludes.

I hope he's right, that today's problems are due to an overdose and not something new developing. Peter's antiseizure medication will now change from 800 milligrams of Dilantin daily to 600, plus 200 milligrams of Tegretol. It seems like a frightening amount of drugs to be pouring into his system, but there is no choice.

Tuesday, June 12

No matter how wretched Peter feels, he always insists on going to his support group meetings at Owen Clinic. Tonight, he's with his group, and mine is meeting with Dr. McCutchan. We've prepared various medical questions for him to answer. At this moment, he's discussing CMV, or cytomegalovirus, the incurable virus assumed to be infecting Peter's brain.

"There is a new drug just coming out for CMV, a derivative of acyclovir called DHPG," he tells us. "It has had very promising results in the lab. Now we have to test it on humans."

"How soon will it be available?" I ask anxiously.

"About two months, more or less," he answers. "And you can be sure Peter will be among the first to get it."

Thank God. I'm afraid of hoping—not unrealistically for an AIDS cure, but for something to stop the CMV before the dementia captures him completely. Yet small grains of hope pop in my head and I hardly hear the rest of the discussion.

"How was your meeting?" I ask Peter as I join him in the hall.

"Oh, fine. I gave them a little demonstration number," he says airily.

"What do you mean?" I ask.

"Oh, had a little seizure at the beginning, just a small one, didn't amount to much. Richard grabbed me. Actually, I just got rigid, blacked out for a few seconds," he says, as if it were nothing to worry about.

Thursday, June 14

Since the seizure-like episode last week, Maria and I have been taking turns sleeping in the extra bed in Peter's room. I don't dare leave him alone at night, afraid he'll fall from the continuing dizziness and injure himself. And he gets up several times in the night with diarrhea.

He must have another herpes lesion reactivating, too. His drawn-out groans of pain from the bathroom are almost too much to bear. Peter tolerates pain well, never has complained, so I know it must be excruciating. I'm sure the neighbors can hear his cries. I wonder if they think we run a torture chamber down here. The diarrhea seems to hit with dependable regularity, any time from two A.M. until about seven or eight A.M. and in two to four bouts of repeated, multiple attacks. He hardly sleeps at all. I don't know how he bears it.

There is incontinence now, too. The diarrhea literally explodes. He valiantly tries to clean it all up himself, embarrassed to call for help, but sometimes he's too exhausted and leaves his underwear soaking in the sink. He tried using adult diapers, but the plastic covering is hot and uncomfortable. I bought several pairs of underwear the other day and told him to consider them disposable. He shouldn't have to be bothered with embarrassment at this point.

Last night, though, I tried again to get him to accept my help. I heard his scream of pain and anger, and ran to the bathroom door.

"Peter, can I help you?" I asked.

"No, it's all right."

"Look, Peter, I've had years and years of experience in cleaning up that stuff—all four of you kids, you know. I can do it a lot faster than you can," I offered tentatively.

"Okay, come in," he said. Good, this time I hit the right button. He sat on the toilet, unable to even stand without stepping in the foul, ochre liquid at his feet. I took a deep breath, put rubber gloves on quickly to protect myself from infection, and cleaned it all up fast, in a matter-of-fact manner. With a wet towel, I cleaned the floor around his feet, turned the shower on and adjusted the water temperature, then guided him into the stall.

"There, now just wash up and you'll be ready for bed," I told him, and grabbed his underpants from the floor, rinsed them like diapers in the toilet, then soaked them in the basin with water and bleach. While Peter bathed, I wet a rag with bleach and quickly cleaned the toilet, the walls, the floor, the corner of the bath rug, cursing silently, scrubbing vehemently as my tears of angry frustration dripped into the bleach on the linoleum. This wretched, cruel diarrhea. I hate it so much and the humiliation, the debasement, it causes. Damn damn damn damn! Angrily, I rinsed out the underpants and hung them on a rack, stripped off the rubber gloves and threw them in the wastebasket.

"Okay, here's your towel," I called, forcing a smile to my voice. I enfolded him in the big towel as he stepped out of the shower and rubbed him dry quickly.

"How about a short backrub?" I offered.

"Yes, please, I'd like that," he answered, exhausted.

I oiled my hands and rubbed, massaging the stiff, tense muscles. Little by little, he relaxed.

"Good night, Mr. Peter. Have a good sleep." I went back to the other bed.

My God, I am so tired. I don't think I'll ever feel rested again.

Friday, June 15

Maria does so much for Peter. She insisted he go to the motor vehicles department to get his new license today, which he needs for identification. He fought going, saying he was tired. When they finished battling the crowd and waiting in line, he growled sarcastically, "Well, now you've done your public duty." Maria was hurt, not understanding that it's humilating for him, the big brother used to being in charge, to now be cared for by his sister, nine years younger. Though we try to maintain his autonomy, he's as helpless as a child.

And he knows it.

Monday, June 18

We Worried Well sit in a circle outside the AIDS Project. The patients are meeting inside. The sun has just set, and the night is cool and refreshing. We are seven people, all united by AIDS. None of us would have met without this common bond. We are from all walks of life, regions, religions, professions. Some are families of patients, some are lovers, some are just concerned friends. Some have already lost their loved ones, others are still fighting, at different stages. Judy, who nursed her brother for a year before he died five months ago, is telling Maria she must be sure to tell Peter all she feels for him now, before it's too late and she's left with regret for things not spoken.

Peter appears at the door, shuffles to an empty chair next to me, and sits, his cane in front of him. The conversation shifts quickly to the latest movies in town.

"This is all you talk about, the movies?" asks Peter humorously.

"Why, yes, Peter. That's actually what we get together for," I tell him. "Is your group through?"

"Oh, no," he says in disgust. "They were all smoking and I couldn't breathe so I decided to come out here with you all."

"Okay, welcome," I tell him. But it strikes me as curious that he left the group. I know he hates the smell of smoke. But something tells me that perhaps the discussion turned to something he didn't want to face. Death? Dying?

I won't ask. He would talk about it if he wanted to. I won't invade his privacy, his dignity.

Tuesday, June 19

This morning, I talked with John on the telephone. "I know you're not supposed to tell what goes on in your meetings, John, but I want to know—did you talk about death last night?"

He told me that they did indeed talk very seriously about death. A new patient had joined them and wanted to know how they were all dealing with it. Apparently, Peter acted very uneasy during the discussion, said nothing. Finally, he stood and walked out.

They weren't smoking.

Maria took Peter to see *Star Trek III* today. Since the recent outbreak of herpes, Peter takes his "doughnut"—a red, rubber, inflated ring—with him everywhere. Otherwise, he cannot sit for very long. According to Maria, he arranged it on his seat in the theater and was about to sit down when he looked up expectantly to the right. After a second, he sat. "Oh, I guess they're not there," he told Maria. Puzzled, she looked to his right. The whole row was empty except for them.

"That was so strange," he told her, bewildered, as they ate pizza afterward. "I could have sworn two people were going to sit next to me in the theater. I thought they followed me into the aisle, but when I looked around, no one was there. Hmmph," he said in his characteristic way.

Wednesday, June 20

Since the first AIDS Project meeting, when many patients expressed their frustration at having too much spare time, I've wanted to give art classes to these men. I hoped that this would not only give them something to do, but perhaps provide an emotional outlet as well. Peter thought it was a great idea, too, but because of the past months of uncertainty over where the project would finally locate, I've been unable to do so. Now that the group is settled in their new location near the hospital, I began my art classes today.

I had three students: Peter, John, and Michael. None has ever painted before. I wanted to start with some simple drawing exercises to teach the basic rules of composition and color. I set up an uncomplicated still-life outside on the lawn, and we sat on the grass in the sun.

John and Michael did two or three drawings apiece, learning the concepts of negative space and complimentary colors. Peter did only one drawing. The lines were wispy and hesitant but the color choices were sufficiently varied. He did not fill in the objects with solid color. I don't think he enjoyed it very much. He seemed tired from sitting up and concentrating so long, and not pleased with his work, despite my compliments. I know it's difficult for him to coordinate mind-to-hand messages. I wish I could have started earlier because I fear it's too late to help him in this way.

The class will meet every Wednesday afternoon. John and Michael seem enthusiastic, and I'm glad to have an opportunity to help other patients constructively, to do for them what I am unable to do for Peter.

Friday, June 22

My mother is arriving at ten this morning from San Francisco, where she's been visiting my sister Charlotte. She'll be here a week. I'm sure Peter will be back in the hospital during her stay. He can't go on much longer without treatment. He's had diarrhea ten times this morning, and with every episode, the rectal herpes lesions become more aggravated. His screams tear through me, yet he refuses my help, and refuses to let me call the doctor for fear he might be readmitted to the hospital. I can't stand it much longer.

Maria is leaving on Sunday for Aspen. She's torn between staying, knowing Peter could die this summer, and following her career needs. We've agreed that I'll call her home if the situation becomes worse.

It's really just as well she's not staying. The apartment is small for three people when one is chronically ill, and Peter has admitted to me that her energy tires him out. That's probably true. But I think it's also true that he's painfully envious of her energy and youth, knowing he will never regain his own.

Sunday, June 24

Maria woke Peter up to say goodbye this morning before leaving for the airport. I heard her voice from the hall, trying to make the farewell sound normal. They both spoke hesitantly, using usual goodbye words that veiled the unspoken awareness that they might not see each other again.

I hated to see her leave. I'm so afraid I will need her before the summer is over. I hugged her and we both cried. Even at the gate, I almost called her back, almost said, "Don't go, I need you."

But I let her go, wishing she were older. At nineteen, I can't ask her to take more on her shoulders than she already has.

My mother and I are in the living room, talking quietly. An agonizing scream tears the air apart and I stiffen. I glance quickly at my mother. She says nothing but mirrors my anguish. I run back to Peter's room and listen at the bathroom door. Another shriek, and my hands claw my face in pain. The shriek subsides into deep, drawn-out groans. I try to still myself to speak.

"Peter, are you all right?"

"Yeah, at least I made it," he moans, attempting lightness. I wait until he's back in bed, then return to the living room.

"Barbie, this can't go on, you've got to call the doctor," my mother says as I sit down again on the rocking chair. She's been listening to Peter's pain for two days now. "You just can't go on like this, you won't last."

"I know, but he doesn't want to go back in the hospital again so soon, and I know how he feels. Besides, he has an appointment tomorrow in the CRC. He can tell Dr. McCutchan about it then."

"What's the CRC?"

"That's the Clinical Research Center, where they draw blood and do exams on the volunteers for Dr. McCutchan's AIDS research studies."

"What are the studies for?"

"One is to collect data to try to determine who's a likely candidate for AIDS, so they can predict better earlier," I explain, glad of the distraction. "The other is, more or less, to try to find out what processes make AIDS patients'

immunity keep descending so that they're increasingly
prone to infection and disease." I pause. "Well, that's
rather an oversimplification."

"How often are they tested?"

"About every three months, I think. They're also testing their blood for its immune status, their T-cell ratio, and
such, and do skin tests to see if they react to certain
viruses and funguses. Peter doesn't have any reactions.
He's lost all immunity to anything, including all the childhood diseases he's had."

"Oh . . ." she says, surprised.

"Let's get some lunch," I suggest, standing. I'm unable
to sit still very long anymore. My nerves are tuned so high
I can never rest completely and sleep only a few hours at
night.

"Today is the famous party at John and Tom's, the one
I told you about. I wonder if Peter will want to go later. I'll
ask him when he wakes up."

"Oh, dear. Do you think he should go?" my mother
asks, worried.

"Yes, of course he should. It's so hard to get him out,
and it's good for him. It doesn't matter if he gets tired. He
can always sleep later, and being out is worth his getting
tired."

Late night. Peter and mother have gone to bed and I'm
alone, trying to unwind before going to bed myself.

Surprisingly, Peter wanted to go to the party. We arrived very late, of course, but there were still many people
there. As with all AIDS functions, party interaction is
slowed down, rather like a film played at half speed. In an
odd way, it's quite enjoyable—people take time to genu-
inely enjoy the company of others without the frenzy
modern parties often have.

I took along the lightweight chaise lounge I bought
recently for Peter to lie on outside, knowing he would not
be able to sit upright for long. I remembered his hopes to
sing today. But so much has happened to him since the
idea occurred to him in May, so much more strength has
drained out. He hasn't even been able to practice. Peter

and another patient laid side-by-side on their lounge chairs, and the two entertained regally from their thrones.

Once again, all the guests were united by AIDS. If they weren't patients, they were patients' lovers, friends, or project volunteers. Only five relatives were present, including mother and I.

I enjoyed the gathering except for one brief moment, when I glanced at the faces around me. How many of these young men will be here this time next year, I wondered?

And how will we fill the empty gaps they leave?

Monday, June 25

"I think I'll ask Dr. McCutchan to take a look at my rear while I'm there," Peter tells me as we drive toward the hospital for his appointment in CRC. He sits, oddly tall, on his "doughnut," and my mother is in the back seat.

"That's a good idea," I say, glad that he intends to do what I already determined to do. I cannot bear any more of his pain.

We park and Peter hobbles slowly along beside us, finally sinking gratefully into a chair in the CRC waiting room. Another patient and friend has an appointment today, too, and we talk with him.

"Hi, Peter, how are you today?" Dr. McCutchan enters.

"Not so good," Peter admits in understatement. "I wonder if you'd take a look at me first."

"Sure, come on down the hall, we'll find a room." Dr. McCutchan leads the way.

"I think we'll put Peter in the hospital for a few days, give him some acyclovir for his herpes again, and reevaluate this diarrhea," Dr. McCutchian informs me when they return.

Peter looks at me, a relieved look on his face.

We head for the tenth floor of the hospital, to be admitted right away. "Mom, would you mind bringing up one of your paintings tomorrow, to decorate my room?"

"Fine," I agree.

Please take good care of him, I plead silently. Find something you can fix, please, in a hurry.

Tuesday, June 26

Peter is depressed, looking sad. We are in the hospital. An X-ray of his chest was taken this morning, but the results were unclear because he couldn't breathe deeply enough to expand his lungs. The doctors aren't sure if there's increased density there or not, and another X-ray will be taken. He's already on blood and enteric isolation, as is usual for AIDS patients. No one is allowed to touch his bodily fluids, for fear of contagion. He's also on respiratory isolation and he doesn't like this. It means everyone visiting him has to wear masks. But I think the main reason he doesn't like it is because he fears that he might have pneumocystis pneumonia again. He's denying it, saying that the "dumb" technician told him to take a deep breath and didn't wait. I'm scared, too. He might not survive another bout of PCP.

He had more episodes of diarrhea during the night with incontinence each time. He's so embarrassed and humiliated when the nurses have to clean up the floor, the bathroom, change the bed linens. I try to assure him that it's nothing to them, they're used to it, but my pain for him breaks my heart. The nurses have brought a portable commode, hoping he can get to that faster.

I have an ever-growing admiration for his nurses. Peter is but one of many AIDS patients with this problem, but they go about their chores very matter-of-factly and treat him with respect and affection. They come and go constantly, asking how he feels and encouraging him to talk about his feelings. He seems to feel their concern for him too. When he was admitted yesterday, he went first to the nursing station and announced, "Well, here I am again," and several of the girls ran to him, said they were glad to see him, and asked what he was in for this time. He feels very comfortable in their care.

Ron, another AIDS patient, is in the room next door. He's been here a week for more evaluation of his continu-

ing diarrhea. He also has a deep, frightening cough. At first, we thought there was a large, older man down the hall. We could not believe when we found out it was Ron that anyone so thin and emaciated could cough so deeply. It frightens Peter, as it does me. Ron is even thinner and weaker than Peter, white against his sheets and his body barely discernible under the covers. I feel he has not got long to live. His wracking cough echoes constantly through the hall, chilling me with eerie foreboding. It is like a warning trumpet, and I know Peter has the same presentiment.

After all, it could be he.

Wednesday, June 27

"Hi, Peter, how are you feeling today?" asks Dr. Andia, his intern. She had cared for AIDS patients while a medical student in Texas, but Peter is special. He's her first AIDS patient here, and they've established a special bond in the past two days that they've known each other.

"Had diarrhea about five times last night again, and the herpes seems to be hurting even more, for some reason," he answers, discouraged.

"That will take a few days to clear up, I'm afraid. But the second X-ray still shows density and we feel sure enough that it's pneumocystis to start you on the Septra immediately and try to get it before it gets worse. We'll give you some oxygen, too, to help your breathing," she adds.

Peter doesn't answer. His face is calm, impassive, but I see the fear in his eyes. He wants to live so desperately and it's just one barrier after another and another and another, endlessly. Except for early June, when Sandy was here, he hasn't had any good days.

The doctor leaves and I stand by Peter, touching his arm.

"Bad news, huh?" He nods silently, looking out the window. He knows—I know—that if he looks at me he'll cry. I wish so much he'd let himself, but know that he won't.

"I'm glad at least they caught it early this time. It won't be as bad as in New York. And look at how well John is doing. He's had it twice now." I try to convince myself as well as him.

I sit quietly with Peter as the day wears on. And that now-familiar feeling of heaviness, a truly physical pressure, fills my insides, growing, growing, increasing with each passing moment, crowding everything out, and it won't let me go. What I'd like most is to find my lonely beach and scream and cry.

But I can't. It's not time.

Thursday, June 28

Peter asked me to make a sign for him to hang on his door today. The sign is to say, "Please do not come in. I'm meditating."

Despite how poorly he feels; despite hospital procedures; despite testing schedules—Peter insists on his time alone.

Friday, June 29

"Well, my God, look at you! Up and dressed so early, great!" I exclaim. Mother and I have stopped at the hospital on the way to the airport, so she can say goodbye to Peter. Peter is sitting in his chair, completely dressed and hair neatly brushed, waiting for us.

"Of course I am. You don't think I'm going to say goodbye to Nanna dressed in that thing, do you?" He points disdainfully to the hospital gown thrown on the bed. My eyes sting and I turn away quickly. This is his final gift to his grandmother, the memory of him dressed, neat, and proud.

"Oh, Peter, I appreciate it so much! You look very nice. You must have gotten up early today," she tells him affectionately. "It's wonderful to see you looking so well." She accepts her gift graciously.

Peter tells his grandmother that he thinks he should

study computer programming, maybe he could find some part-time work he can do at home.

"That sounds like a good idea, Peter," she tells him enthusiastically, falling into his fantasy. They discuss where and how he could study, the value of computer skills nowadays.

It is time to leave.

"I'll walk you downstairs," offers Peter, the gracious host. "I've already told the nurses."

"All right, let's go," I say.

We walk slowly down the hall, Peter pushing his IV stand along beside him, chatting. I am surprised and thankful that he has mustered the strength to do this. I know he'll sleep the rest of the day, but he'll feel very satisfied with his success, proud of his small accomplishment.

We arrive at the emergency room exit. The car is outside. Peter bends to kiss his grandmother.

"Well . . . goodbye, Nanna. Thanks for coming, I'm sorry I had to be in the hospital during your visit," he says, smiling affectionately.

"Goodbye Peter. Don't worry about that. I'm just glad to have seen you. Now think hard about getting well," she tells him, and gives him a tender hug.

He turns, walks slowly down the hall, turns again to wave goodbye. We take a few hesitant steps and I turn to watch him walking away, pushing his IV stand along and peering about. I fight the urge to go with him, to make sure he gets back upstairs safely. The first-floor corridors of the hospital zig and zag like a maze and I'm afraid he'll get confused.

"Don't you think you should go with him?" my mother asks anxiously, worried by the same thought.

"I want to, but he'd be offended. He has to do it for himself. I'll just keep my fingers crossed," I answer. I watch as he reaches the first corner, turns in the right direction. "Well, he made the first turn right."

"Was that all right for Peter to do all that?" my mother asks.

"Yes, it's fine, it's wonderful! He proved to himself he

could, and he wanted to do it for you," I tell her. "It was very important to him."

For us, all is relative. What is small to others is immense to us, and what is terribly important to others doesn't matter at all anymore. We live day to day, our joys existing on a miniature scale: a beautiful flower, a colorful sunset like those we shared in Santa Fe, a trip down the hall with his grandmother. We no longer look for the fields of flowers, but appreciate the single bloom we hold today, in our hands, for minutes, or hours.

Saturday, June 30

"Oh, by the way," Peter tells his father on the telephone, "I hope you're not coming out so often because you think I'm about to kick off," he emphasizes the last two words. "Because I'm *not*. I plan to be around a long time."

I nearly fall from the chair in surprised amusement, visualizing Walter on the other end, gulping and at a loss for an answer. He's planning to come next week, a week earlier than previously planned. I know he's worried about Peter's condition and hospitalization. Fear that Peter is, indeed, about to kick off is exactly why he comes so often, and Peter is well aware of it.

A few days earlier, though, Peter expressed anger at Walter's frequent visits.

"If it's because he has guilt feelings about the past, then he should get over that. I told him a long time ago that that was all in the past and forgotten."

"Well, he's German, you know. They always like to hang on to their guilt complexes for a long time," I told him lightly, not wanting to say that whatever guilt Walter feels as a parent is intensified—cannot be forgotten—by the severity of Peter's illness.

"I just wish he wouldn't come as often, it's always so exhausting," he said tiredly.

"You know, you don't have to entertain him, Peter. He's coming to see you, not San Diego," I said.

"I just feel like I have to provide something to justify

his long trip and the expense, but it really tires me out,'' he answered. ''And he always acts like I'm such a hero, telling me how brave and heroic I am.'' His brows lower in anger and irritation. ''I'm not being a hero, for Christ's sake, I'm just trying to live. There's nothing heroic or brave about that, and it really makes me mad. If anyone's heroic around here, it's you, getting up to clean up my messes in the middle of the night.'' He rubs his brow, agitated.

''And the other thing is, he always wants to kiss and hug me. You know, everybody's always talking so much about hugging and touching, and I just don't always want to be hugged and touched, only when I want to be. It's too tiring.''

I have tried to explain to Walter that he should space his visits farther apart because Peter does *not* want to think he's dying. His entire coping mechanism is based on hope and denial, and they certainly have kept him alive longer than meek acceptance and self-pity would have. And it's his right—his life, his death. Peter must handle it as he wishes and we must accede to him, respecting his autonomy and dignity. Walter says that it's very difficult for him, being so far away, and that he feels helpless. That's understandable.

But Peter's rights are more important.

9

Sunday, July 1

The night is dark and quiet as I sit on the patio. Breezes from the ocean have subdued the heat of the day. I need these little nighttime pauses to collect my thoughts and feelings, to gird myself for the next day. They are more restorative than sleep itself.

Today was long. Peter's room was hot and he was wheezing and short of breath, especially while talking. He used the oxygen often. I talked little and avoided asking questions he'd have to answer. At least his weight is back up to 122 pounds and he's been eating well.

A letter came from Maria a couple of days ago, written on the plane to Denver, and I sit now, rereading it. The love and concern she feels for Peter and me is deeply touching, and I feel her near, though she's hundreds of miles away.

She feels her three weeks here were too short, and that she was torn between going to Aspen and staying here with us. "In my mind, I know that Aspen is the best thing for me . . . but the rest of me is aching to be there with you."

She admires my strength, is proud of all I've done, not just with Peter, but also with the support and art groups, my own art, and "just keeping your own self together," for so many months now. "After only three weeks, I feel drained and tired," she writes. She realizes that though the family comes to visit, the bulk of the work and responsibility is on me, and suggests I start thinking of getting outside help, fearing that I will get overtired and sick.

She also suggests that I think about what I'll do after Peter is gone, and that I consider staying with her in Aspen if it happens this summer, citing the beautiful scenery there as a positive change.

I have, indeed, thought about what I'll do afterward. Going away to a quiet, lonely place—maybe my long, empty beach where I can cry, scream, whatever—is my first wish, a place where I can just let out the repressed frenzy and hysteria of these past months. I appreciate her loving thoughtfulness. Maybe I will go to Aspen. She ends sending Peter her love. "Damnit," she writes, "I had a dream he was coming with me!"

I fold the letter, put it back in its envelope. This is Maria, my 19-year-old daughter, with the wisdom, perspicacity, and ability to express love that many supposedly mature people would envy.

I am so lucky that Peter and I have so much support from all the family.

Monday, July 2

"I'm so afraid my lungs are going all rotten again," Peter told me today.

"Yes, I can feel your tension," I said, rubbing his back, feeling his rigid muscles. I was glad he could speak of his fears. Maybe talking would help banish them.

"I've *got* to relax," he said after awhile, his eyes open, fists clenched.

Tuesday, July 3

Peter and I are watching the evening news. The air in his hospital room is hot and close, pervaded by the sick-sweet smell of diarrhea. Now and then he dozes off, then revives suddenly to comment on the broadcast. Though he seems alert, one nurse told me that last night, someone found him wandering around the hall and had to take him back to bed.

I came in at nine A.M. today, in time for his return from a bronchoscopy. Peter was a little frightened about having this procedure done again. A tube is inserted into the lungs to take a biopsy of the tissue. Last night, he asked that a film strip on the procedure be run on the hospital's closed TV, and we watched it together. This preparative education about the procedure, the small dosage of Valium that he insisted on, and the doctor's continual reassurance rid him of his anxiety, and the tube went down smoothly and painlessly.

I knew the reason for his fear. In New York, the tube was jammed down his throat with no explanation or medication, and was extremely uncomfortable and frightening. He said that it felt like a bottle brush being scrubbed up and down inside his chest. "Why didn't they prepare me for it in New York?" he asked with irritation this morning.

Wednesday, July 4

"Next time you go out, do you suppose you could bring me some books? I'm really tired of these magazines," Peter asked me this morning.

"Sure, I'd be glad to. Got anything special in mind?"

"I'd like to read those books Shirley MacLaine wrote, her autobiographies. She did a lot of study on reincarnation and it might be interesting. Or any biographies, whatever."

"Okay, I'll look for them this afternoon."

What a surprise. Other than *Getting Well Again*, he hasn't been able to concentrate on anything heavier than light magazines. Is it possible that his brain infection is going away? His speech seems less confused, his memory better . . . Can I hope, with caution?

Friday, July 6

Walter is here. He arrived last night. I took advantage of the respite to go to the beach with friends today. We stopped by the hospital first for a few minutes. My friends are Spanish speaking, and I was amazed that Peter conversed animatedly in Spanish. I don't think he could have done that two or three weeks ago. Something paradoxical is happening. Peter is still so sick—weakness, fatigue, short breath, low fever, diarrhea—and yet daily he becomes more mentally alert and efficient.

Fat-absorption tests were completed yesterday, and all dairy products and fats have been cut from his diet in hopes of alleviating the diarrhea. He is indignant that these tests were not done before, as he requested. He feels the doctors ignored him. And now he's sure the new diet will help. It's easier for him to believe this than that the diarrhea is caused by an organism that cannot be traced or treated.

I enjoyed the afternoon at the beach, barbecuing chicken and watching the moon rise, but could not relax completely. I cannot seem to break the bonds of worry even for a few hours.

Monday, July 9

Click-click-click. Phyllis stands at the foot of Peter's bed. She is the nurse-practitioner who has worked under Dr. McCutchan since April, assisting him with the collection of data on his AIDS research groups and attending patients, both in Owen Clinic and in the hospital. Her feet go at 60 miles per hour and her brain at the speed of light. And yet her disposition is always cheerful and loving, her speech dotted with exclamation marks.

"Have I got good news for you today!" she greets us at noon. "I talked to Dr. McCutchan earlier—you know he's back east—and it seems that DHPG, the new drug for CMV he told you about, is finally being started on an experimental basis, and he wants you on it as soon as possible!"

I almost faint. This is incredibly good news, the first flicker of hope in so long.

"How soon can he start taking it?" I ask anxiously.

"Hopefully, if we can fulfill the preliminaries, he might even be able to start it next week. You might just stay in the hospital and have it right away . . . if you don't mind, Peter!" She beams at him.

"That's okay with me," he says, smiling.

"All right. I'll be talking with Dr. Spector, he's the CMV specialist here and in charge of administering the drug, and then we'll let you know."

"Oh, my God, that's fantastic!" I exclaim. "I thought it was going to be at least another month before it would be available."

"I know, we didn't expect it so soon, either. Dr. McCutchan was really delighted." She smiles widely. "And how are you feeling today, Peter?"

"A little better, I guess. I think the diarrhea may be a bit better."

"Good. And how is your vision?"

"I can see fine. It's just that now and then the room looks sort of cloudy—or smoky—it's hard to describe. I can see everything, it's just like there is a film over it all," he tells her.

"Okay, Peter. I'll be in to see you tomorrow." She turns and clicks out, and we hear her step into Ron's room next door.

"How long have you been seeing things cloudy?" I ask Peter, feeling my apprehension grow. This is the first I've heard of cloudy vision.

"I don't know. Not too long. It's just now and then, anyway," he tells me. "It's nothing bad, but it is annoying."

Oh, God, no. I've heard of blindness from AIDS-related infections—a one-time visitor to our support group told of her son's blindness caused by herpes in the eye, and of his despair. After that, he lost his will to live. No, please. Don't give us that, too.

Wednesday, July 11

Walter came to the hospital at ten this morning, so I decided to wait until noon to go in. The nurse woke Peter at two-thirty to take him to the Opthalmology Clinic, and I'm alone in his room.

A few days ago, I bought a book of crosswords, thinking they would be a quick distraction in the hospital, something to pick up and put down at random, and not

requiring the concentration I need—and lack—to read books.
I find the puzzles strangely comforting, simple and mechanical, and I think of Mme. Du Farge knitting steadily in front
of the guillotine. There is a macabre similarity, except that
I care deeply about the victims parading slowly past my eyes.

We were told yesterday that a protocol must be followed
before the new drug can be administered. Retinal photographs must be taken before treatment can begin to docu-
ment the CMV retinitis that is believed to be causing
Peter's cloudy vision. Several fuzzy, white spots—called
white cotton-wool spots—have been seen on Peter's right
retina since last March, though till now he hasn't complained of vision problems. A series of photographs will
be taken after the treatment, too, for comparison. Supposedly, once the photographs are taken, the DBPG treatments can be started.

Soon is not fast enough for me. Despite Peter's recent
mental acuity, I am terrified of the brain infection spreading. And now, with the threat of blindness from CMV
retinitis, my impatience has multiplied.

Friday, July 13

I've been up since six A.M., painting on the patio. I was
commissioned to paint eleven watercolors by the end of July,
and I want to finish them before Peter comes home, which
will be either on Monday, or ten days later if they give
him the DHPG next week. The telephone rings.

"Hi, Mom?" Peter's voice.

"Who else?" I answer in good humor. "How are you
doing today?"

"Oh, pretty good." He hesitates. "I wanted to tell you
something. I mean . . . well, it was going to be a surprise,
but I think I ought to go ahead and tell you."

"Well, you know I love surprises. Why don't you wait
and surprise me?"

"No, I want to tell you now. See, I wanted to get you a
dishwasher when I got my first Social Security check, and
it was going to be a surprise for Mother's Day, but I was
in the hospital then."

"Oh, Peter . . ." The damn tears sting. I sniff them back. "Oh, that's so nice!" I almost blurt that he shouldn't spend his money on me, but I don't. This is something he wants very much to do, something he *can* do.

"We had it all planned. Tracy was going to help me pick it out, and we were going to have it delivered on Mother's Day. And I told her, nothing second-hand or used. I want a brand new one, *with* guarantee."

I laugh. Tracy is always boasting of her good bargains on used merchandise, and it's a joke between us.

"So," he goes on, "I want you to shop around and find out what you want and go get it, get exactly what you want."

"Well, look, Peter," I tell him. "Why don't I pick up a *Consumers' Guide* and bring it to the hospital, and then you can research it there and tell me what's best, just as if you shopped for it, and then we can get it when you get out."

"Okay, that would be fine." His voice is getting wheezy.

"This is really a surprise! And I appreciate it, Peter. Thank you. It's a very thoughtful gift." I am anxious to hang up before he hears me cry.

"Well, I just thought I should do my share of the housework," he says offhandedly.

"Okay, I'll see you shortly. Bye."

I hang up and burst into tears.

Saturday, July 14

Tired as he always is, Peter still insists on washing, shaving, and combing his hair carefully. If I were as constantly fatigued as he is, I don't think I'd bother. My appearance would be the least important part of my life.

I think I know why he's so determined to be well-groomed. When he was first admitted in June, he overheard gossip that the doctors thought Ron was giving up because he didn't care how he looked anymore. Once scrupulously meticulous about his appearance, Ron now lies passively in bed all day, his hair rumpled, and a ragged beard covers his usually clean-shaven chin and cheeks. I've visited him briefly now and then, shocked at his appearance, and do indeed wonder if he has lost his will to live.

But Peter—sick, tired, wasted—still insists on living, and now stands bent at the sink, washing, shaving, combing. He asks me to trim his moustache now and then. There is no way he's going to have anyone saying he's lost his will to live.

Not Peter Vom Lehn.

Sunday, July 15

Walter left early this morning. Today is his fifty-third birthday, and he'll be spending it crossing the country.

Peter is well enough either to be discharged tomorrow or start the new drug for CMV. I can hardly believe it. When he was admitted three weeks ago, I didn't think he'd leave the hospital alive. But then, in May, I feared he wouldn't survive through June. Ironically, he was admitted for treatment of diarrhea and herpes and neither has improved very much. But during the course of their treatment, he developed—and survived—a second bout of pneumocystis pneumonia.

The real miracle, though, is the vast improvement in his mental state. His words are not as confused. His memory is much better (at last, he remembers our phone number). He is oriented to his environment, and he's been reading books voraciously, as if to make up for lost time. His reading speed, always fast, is undiminished and, more importantly, he seems to digest and remember the material. I can't bring him new books fast enough.

"I finished Shirley MacLaine's other book last night," he tells me. He is quite talkative today.

"How did you like it?"

"Her theories on reincarnation are interesting. She studied it intensively, went anywhere in the world she could to investigate, and knows a lot about it."

"What do you think about it?" I ask, hoping this might lead into his own feelings about death.

"Oh," he twists, turning on his side to face me. "She's

very convincing, she believes in it completely. But . . . I don't know. I've never thought much about it, and I can't say that it really interests me that much. It's not that important to me," he pauses, thinking. "Anyway, I don't want to think or talk about death and dying while I'm living." He pauses again. "I can't see much point in it. When—*if*—it comes time to die, then we'll gather everyone around and talk about it." He lies back. The subject is closed.

Now I have it, his message is clear. We are not going to discuss death, but concentrate on living, on surviving. When—if—the dying approaches, I am to summon the family and he will talk about it then. Then and not before. Giving word is giving in.

Peter rolls over onto his back. He has given his message, and I have heard it.

Monday, July 16

"They're letting me go home today," Peter announces as I enter his room shortly before eleven.

"What?" I ask, surprised. "I thought they were going to keep you in to start the new drug."

"No, now they say I can't start it now. There's some big deal about protocol or something," he says disgustedly.

I feel his disappointment and sit quietly, thinking. "I don't understand this. I'm going to call that doctor and see what's going on," I say angrily as I pick up the phone and try to locate Dr. Spector, the CMV specialist. Finally, I get through.

"We thought Peter was going to be started on the DHPG for his CMV infection, and instead they say he's being discharged today."

"No, we can't start it until we complete the protocol." Dr. Spector explains, calm, detached.

"What exactly does that entail, and who requires it—the drug company, the hospital, or who?"

"The drug company won't let us use the drug without it. It's not even as far as what they call the experimental stage, and Peter would be one of the very first to receive it. To qualify, we have to have a complete set of photographs of his eye, both before and after treatment, a psychological evaluation of his mental status to demonstrate mental deterioration, and/or he has to be on a 'compassionate plea' basis; that is, in immediate danger of dying,'' he explains.

I boil with anger and frustration. For God's sake, I want to scream, what does all that matter? My son may go blind and crazy without this one chance.

''Well . . . I want you to know that we want very much for him to try it. Time is of the essence,'' I enunciate, trying to keep my voice from breaking. Don't antagonize the doctor. Don't frighten Peter, I tell myself.

But time is so important. These young men's lives are measured by the day, not by the week, month, or year. The bucket tilts, the drops spill out faster and faster, and no one is righting the bucket and stopping the flow.

''Yes, I understand. You can be sure Peter will be put on the drug as soon as we can do it. We'll notify you,'' Dr. Spector concludes calmly, ''All right. Thank you very much,'' I hang up the telephone.

Now that the treatment will not begin soon, Peter is eager to leave the hospital. But everything seems to be conspiring against his departure, and the multiple delays make him impatient. Time is so important to him. His list of prescriptions was sent down to the pharmacy this morning and still have not been returned. And he requested a last word with his intern. He wants her to recheck the herpetic lesion, apprehensive that it is reactivating.

At six P.M., the medications still have not arrived, but his intern finally appears. She examines Peter, assures him everything is fine, but he remains unconvinced. I wonder —he does not complain without cause and is usually right about his symptoms.

At eight o'clock, the pharmacist finally appears, carrying two big, brown grocery bags of medicines. He explains them and Peter understands completely. He will still be on 600 milligrams of Dilantin and 200 of Tegretol daily as anti-seizure treatment. Two drugs to treat the tuberculosis-like MAI have been eliminated as ineffective, but he will still take ansamcycin, clofazimine, isoniazid, and pyridoxine. Chlotrimazole lozenges are for the oral thrush. Metamucil®, Lomotil, and Tylenol with codeine are for diarrhea control, and AlternaGEL® is for the abdominal cramps and pain he has had recently. Multivitamins with iron are for nutrition, as is the low-fat diet of 2,800 calories daily, devoid of all dairy products except yogurt. That will tax my culinary imagination, as milk and cheese have been his main sources of calories until now.

Peter seats himself in the wheelchair and I grab the brown bags. I feel as if we are carrying an entire pharmacy home with us.

Tuesday, July 17

Peter slept soundly last night, glad to be home and grateful that no one woke him up to take his vital signs, weigh him, or ask him how he felt. Previously, he has felt secure in the hospital, receiving care for his acute problems. But this time, both Dr. McCutchan and Dr. Matthews were away most of the three weeks at medical conferences, and he felt insecure being cared for by interns and residents.

Today he was eager to go out and get the dishwasher for me. We decided on the brand we wanted while he was in the hospital, studying the *Consumers' Guide* carefully. I made calls to check prices, and we went to an appliance store, trying to decide on the color. At last, we chose white.

"What's the resale value on these?" Peter asked the salesman, then turned to me. "That's in case we should move somewhere there's already a built-in dishwasher."

"Oh, it's excellent, probably next year you could get two-thirds of what you're paying," the salesman assured Peter.

I felt a familiar twinge of poignancy at Peter's talk of our moving, selling the dishwasher—his plans for the future.

"I think we'll take this one," he said authoritatively, pointing to the white machine.

"Good choice, you won't be sorry," the salesman said. "Come over here and we'll fill out the papers.

Peter sat next to the desk, leaning on his cane. I wondered what the salesman thought of him. Did he wonder why he uses a cane, is so thin, have any idea of his real age?

"What name should I put the guarantee in?" the salesman asked Peter.

"I'm paying for it, but I'm giving it to my mother," Peter answered proudly. "Better put it in her name."

We left, all arrangements completed, and spent ten minutes in a nearby bookstore before going home. Peter slumped onto the couch, pleased with his purchase. His satisfaction touches me.

Later, Walter called, anxious to know how Peter's first day home was.

"Oh, just fine," answered Peter. "We ran all over town today and got Mom's dishwasher. I'm really exhausted tonight from so much running around, but it was worth it."

I listened, startled. We spent an hour in one store—not exactly "running all over town." His exaggeration and bravado amused me. Actually, that small foray was a monumental excursion.

All is, indeed, relative.

Sunday, July 22

Charlotte flew down from San Francisco today for a short visit. She's been planning to come for several weeks, but waited until Peter was relatively stable, as he seems to be now. She'll leave tomorrow.

Peter's been anxious to ask her how she dealt with polio, which she had as a child. He wants to know how she kept her spirits up and recovered the strength to walk again after being completely bedridden and paralyzed for two years.

I told both her and my mother of his desire some time ago. But Charlotte doesn't really know how she did it, nor where she found her strength. She is puzzled about what to say, knowing how important her words will be.

"Just lie!" Both my mother and I exclaimed separately. "Make it up, as long as it's positive."

I already told Peter that undoubtedly, his grandmother's own strong will and determination kept Charlotte alive the first crucial days, and later conquered all barriers, not just to convalescence but to a normal life. She simply refused to accept that Charlotte would never walk, would be a "cripple"—much as I have hoped that Peter will not see himself as an invalid. I've told him of her insistence on Charlotte's daily exercise routine to rebuild her muscles, laying her each day on an old, gray Army blanket (which I'll never forget) on the dining room table and working the muscles for her.

"My mother just refused to believe she'd never walk again—Charlotte never had a choice," I told him.

Charlotte and Peter just went up to the pool together. Peter carrying his lightweight chaise lounge. I stayed in the apartment with the excuse that I have to start dinner, but hoping that, alone, they can talk about this. I watch them walk up the path, Peter thin and pale in swim trunks, and his aunt following with her pronounced limp—which she still ignores completely. No, I think, she has never seen herself as "different." Her own children don't know all she suffered—because she never saw it as suffering.

Wednesday, July 25

Peter's vision in his right eye is rapidly getting worse. He has begun wearing a black eyepatch to avoid the frustrating distraction of its faulty vision. We are increasingly impatient for him to start on the DHPG. Already, that eye is virtually useless, but he says he can bear that as long as the infection doesn't spread to the other eye and he becomes totally blind. How well we can accommodate our thinking when we have to. It's like the glass of water: is it half-empty or half-full?

I wonder why more AIDS patients aren't committing suicide, as some have. This is a disease of generally young men who have previously been healthy and vital. It is a humiliating debasement of mind and body. But hope springs eternal, as is said, and where there's life, there's hope, though little remains of life as they've known it. It must be the same thing that kept the Jews alive in Nazi concentration camps—that faint, tiny spark of hope and faith called the human spirit.

There is more similarity than the will to survive. AIDS patients are over 70% homosexual right now. And like the Jews, they are a persecuted, vilified group. Homosexuals are ridiculed, discriminated against, and condemned. Instead of being jeered at as kikes and Christ killers, they are called queers, fruits, faggots, fairies, sissies, and are considered an abomination of nature and God's law. But they come from all societies, all cultures, all races, all religions, all walks of life, socially and professionally. I believe they are born, not created homosexual—some sort of chemical or hormonal imbalance before birth, perhaps. Who knows, and what does it matter? They are human beings.

AIDS is considered by many to be a well-deserved punishment for differing from the norm. "AIDS is God's pest control," read the placard I saw once in a demonstration. These people, guised as sincere Christians, think that AIDS is the "final solution," just as the gas chambers were for the Jews.

There is another similarity: the face of the AIDS victim—and "victim" is the favored nomenclature of the press. The body itself is gaunt, knobby, emaciated, and it hunches over and shuffles along, weak from malnourishment. And the face—the face is prematurely aged. Men of 30 appear years older, the skin stretched tight over cheek and jawbone, wrinkling dryly and painfully when they smile. The hair is thin and has lost its sheen. The eyes are torturous, sunk deep into their bone-ridged hollows, the eyelashes and brows sparse, and their sparseness accentuating the eyes, giving faint parentheses to the message, "Why me?" —and to the eternal plea for help, for life. And though they hate to be called it, they *are* victims. Not of their chosen lifestyle, but of society's prejudice, its unwillingness to help them, to answer their plea.

My son has an AIDS face.

And now he is starting to go blind, the right retina half-covered with viral debris. He is accommodating, using his left eye more and turning his head slightly to utilize its vision. I watch him covertly. I see him misjudge space and bump into furniture, drop dishes, stub his toes, followed by the usual, sudden scream of rage. But he still denies patiently, as with every other loss. First we deny, then we bargain, then we accept. Okay, one eye is gone, leave me the other. All right, both gone, I'll use my sense of touch . . .

Friday, July 17

We had a clinic appointment last night. Dr. McCutchan is anxious to start the new drug and told us that another patient showed improvement at first. He declines to say what happened afterward and we don't ask.

Every day, we are more impatient and frustrated by the delays and red tape. First, one doctor is out of town, then another, and of course no one works on weekends (two more days lost). Dr. Spector says we have to meet "protocol specifications"; "compassionate plea" if in imminent danger of dying—and I wonder, what the hell do they think AIDS is?

Since Peter may yet have a few weeks or even months, we have to prove CMV cells are in his blood cultures. Yet it takes four to six weeks to show up—if it shows up. The latest requirement is a three-hour neuropsychological evaluation of his mental and motor skills, This, like the retinal photographs, must be done both before and after the treatment.

I think I can handle complete blindness. What frightens me about not treating the diseased retina is the possibility of the infection spreading from there to the brain. His seizure disorder is already assumed to be caused by CMV. What more do they want? If this isn't a compassionate plea, what is? I wonder how they would feel in the same position, facing blindness, dementia, gradual starvation, with the possible key to succour well-wrapped in miles of red tape?

I know the drug may not work, but come on, let's try it, at least. Hurry, hurry, hurry, I beg silently and constantly. Time is running out, and we are bogged down in the endless, cruel and insensitive rules of the drug company. Peter is willing, eager, to be an experimental subject. Let him try. My heavy feeling of apprehension and frustration swells with each unending delay.

We spent three hours in the clinic, most of the time waiting. Peter has been very depressed the last few days. His fever is gone and his temperature is subnormal at 96.8 degrees. His blood pressure was 84/46, so low. His weight is down to 117 pounds. He complained that his jaw is tender and his teeth feel sensitive. God knows what that means, but assuredly it is significant. Sooner or later, all his complaints have meaning.

He has small, swollen nodes in the groin area, and Dr. McCutchan has given him more medication for the new herpes lesions. He also will set up the appointment for Peter's neuropsychological testing. Peter was dejected when we returned from the clinic, and sat on the couch, his tense body sinking slowly into the cushions. Be wanted to talk, and I sat down.

"I just feel like they don't give a damn," he started. "I feel like I'm always being ignored, they don't care. I don't think they heard a word I said."

"I don't think that's so, Peter, though I know you feel that way.

"Well, it seems to me that they don't really listen," he insists. "I know when something's wrong with my body. It's my body.

"And—I'm not ready to give up yet. But I'm worried about my weight, my ear still being congested after all these months, the diarrhea—everything."

He's angry. I'm angry. But it's his weakness that is reflected in his wispy voice. Vehemence is a luxury. Maybe the doctors do think he's whining, nitpicking at imagined symptoms for attention, because his voice is so soft and flatly unemotional. No, doctors. He simply doesn't have the energy to express any emotion.

I know Peter's doctors do care about his well-being, I'm

continually impressed by the concern and attention the AIDS patients here receive from doctors, nurses, technicians; the time and patience that they dedicate to the patients' physical, mental, and emotional problems. But perhaps they still haven't learned to listen.

This disease, in all its strange and myriad manifestations, demands an extra level of listening. I'm convinced that every little complaint is significant sooner or later, even though today it may not fit any known pattern. Every patient follows his own course of diseases; every patient reacts differently to medications, and new symptoms and forms of infection are always surfacing.

There is no cut-and-dry pattern here with familiar guideposts and little variation from them. AIDS is a completely frustrating and perplexing illness unlike anything ever seen before. It is understandable that at times the doctors do not respond. They are simply, completely baffled, and don't know what to say or do.

Saturday, July 28

Eating is becoming even more of a problem for Peter. He has so little appetite, and has commented with irritation recently that it hardly seems worthwhile. It just comes out unabsorbed in no time at all. He is down to 117 pounds and is still losing weight. When I encourage him to eat, he just says he'll try. But I don't see him doing it.

I've begun speculating on the possibility of his having a Hickman catheter inserted. A tube is inserted through the chest into a major vein. Then there is a procedure, called hyper-alimentation, for feeding predigested solutions directly into the bloodstream, bypassing the digestive tract and bowel. I've heard of other patients who have done quite well with this, and it is not a 24-hour process at all. He could live quite freely. I wanted to discuss it with him when he was hospitalized, but thought that surely the doctors would suggest it if they thought it was necessary.

Would Peter accept it? It's an artificial life-support system and, like dying, we have not discussed his feelings about mechanical devices for prolonging life. I think the subject is too negative, too threatening to his coping structure.

Again, verbalizing might make it too real.

Sunday, July 29

It's a perfect Sunday, the sky a clear, cloudless blue. Peter and I are meeting my friends, Tracy and Ray, in Balboa Park to see the Ansel Adams exhibit in the photography museum. Peter's walking very slow and, as always, I try to slow my pace down to his. His walk is steady, though, and he hasn't used his cane recently.

We meet Tracy and Ray and enter the gallery. I feel a flicker of anger as I see the crowd milling around inside— and not a chair or bench in sight.

"Just a minute, I'll be right back," I tell the other three, and run out to the ticket counter.

"Do you have any wheelchairs available?" I ask.

"No, you might try over at the park office," the woman suggests.

I run down the esplanade to the office.

"Do you have any wheelchairs?" I ask the elderly lady seated there.

"No, we don't, and we should. The only place in the park where you can get them is next door at the zoo, but they don't let you bring them over here," she informs me.

I race back to the photography museum, angry at the lack of consideration for elderly and handicapped people. Obviously, I have to get Peter a wheelchair, and think of a way that he can gracefully accept it. I hand my ticket stub to the attendant and look through the crowd for Peter. I can't see him. There is a second gallery, and I see a grand piano, a bench—and yes, Peter is sitting on it.

"There's nothing else to sit on." He looks up as I approach.

"I know. I went to look for a wheelchair, and there isn't one in the whole park. I'm sorry." I know the hard bench is painful for him.

"It's okay. I'll just look awhile, and sit, and get up and look again," he says cheerfully. "The trouble is that they should have seats right in the middle where you can see a lot while you're sitting. I'm getting very tired of that picture,'' he says, indicating the large photograph a few feet in front of him.

I laugh. Finally, he stands again and walks over to inspect other pictures, but it's difficult for him to push in and get a good view. People don't seem to notice that he can't move as they do.

"We'll have to come another day, Peter, when there aren't as many people," I tell him as we leave.

"Let me get a picture of all three of you." I unbuckle my camera as we emerge into the bright sunlight. The three line up, despite Peter's objections. He's so self-conscious about his appearance. I sight them in the view-finder and, Christ, he's so damned thin, looks so old next to Tracy and Ray. He looks thirty years older than them instead of the five years younger he is.

We meander slowly back to the parking lot, pretending to be looking about instead of measuring our pace to Peter's.

Driving home, Peter and I discuss the show. He liked it—there were many scenes of his beloved New Mexico—but feels that Adams used too much contrast. I disagree, and we discuss it.

But as we talk, I can think only of the wheelchair, planning how to make it a matter-of-fact acquisition and not another signpost downward.

Which, indeed, it is.

10

Wednesday, August 1

I have almost three hours free now. Peter is finally
having his neuropsychological testing at the Communicative Disorders Center. It will be a long, grueling ordeal for
him and he will sleep the rest of the day, but at least we
are finally making progress. The results will be evaluated
there, then sent to Drs. Spector and McCutchan. At last,
we will be one step closer to the DHPG therapy.

This frustrating delay has been driving us both crazy. I
wonder about the morality of the situation, that scientific
method has priority over possible alleviation of suffering. I
constantly hear talk about maintaining the "quality of
life" for the patient. And meanwhile, Peter is losing his
vision, facing recurrent seizures and dementia, and his
very life goes down the waste pipe in torrents of diarrhea.

Waste, waste, waste. I live with the wasting of a young
life. I walk behind Peter on the way to the car and see his
long, thin neck, his narrow shoulders hunched from constant tension, his legs and buttocks lost inside trousers too
big. He wears thick socks with his sandals or they would
fall off his narrow feet as he shuffles along. He can't find
shoes to fit. He is so thin that it's excruciatingly painful
for him to sit on an unpadded chair. He has no fleshy
cushioning and so we carry his "doughnut" in its old
pillowcase.

And always his eyes, those deep-sunk eyes, penetrating me with their mute plea: "Help me to live, rid me of this unending horror, don't leave me!"

I saw a patient once lie down on the grass outside the hospital, telling his friend, "Wake me up when it's over." These are mostly young men, used to being independent and self-reliant. They want desperately to live, but it's hard for them to ask for help, even harder to accept. And the asking is humiliating. Nor do they want sympathy. Sympathy means they're not normal, but pitiable, something less than they were and still want to be.

So I'm always guessing. Does Peter want a touch, a hug right now? Or will it be rejected as insulting sympathy, rather than an offer of love. Often, I want to hug him and cry with him, but I don't. If he saw me give in to the inevitable, then I fear he would, too, and he insists that he's not ready to give up.

So I feign a strength I don't have, create my own crying times and refuges. He is not ready for mourning. His will power is stronger than his body and carries it along in its powerful embrace.

That frail body, already besieged by tuberculosis, thrush, herpes, pneumocystis, CMV—and God knows what else— also has to withstand the onslaught of potent drugs prescribed to control those organisms. And who knows how much harm these drugs have caused? I have to admire him, this son of mine. I don't think I could do it.

So I cry alone. In the car without him, in the shower, on the patio in early morning or late night, in my bed. My fear wakes me in the early morning and during the night. I have known five patients who have died now, and I know he will die, too. But for his sake, I can't stop hoping.

Greater than my fear of losing him is the fear of the day when he realizes there will be no miracle and he will have to surrender hope. I am so afraid I might not have the strength to help him through the ending. But one day, this nightmare *will* draw to its inevitable conclusion, and I am bound by blood, heart, and brain to stay with it.

I hope I will be adequate. I have so many doubts about myself.

Saturday, August 4

I just returned from getting a wheelchair at the Disabled American Veterans Thrift Store downtown. I told Peter I was getting it to keep in the car, just in case, so that he could hoard his energy when we go out for the enjoyable part of the excursion, instead of wasting it on walking or standing.

He accepted this signpost without objection.

Tuesday, August 7

Peter and I sit side by side on the orange plastic chairs in the Owen Clinic waiting room. How many times have we sat here now, waiting?

James, an AIDS patient from a small inland farming town one and a half hours away, enters and sits on a chair opposite us. I look at him, startled at how well he looks. He walked in with a brisk step and his face is round, his color good. He sits up straight and his eyes have a bright sparkle they've lacked since I've known him. Until now, he has always come accompanied by his sister and brother-in-law, sometimes with their small children, and he has slumped into the nearest chair, too weak to sit upright. His hair has always been matted and lank, his body emaciated, his face pallid and his eyes dull. He, too, has been besieged by relentless diarrhea. He has attended Peter's support group meetings in the clinic from time to time.

"James, you look so well!" I exclaim.

"Yes," his soft, brown eyes light up. "I'm feeling very well. They gave me a Hickman catheter three months ago, and I've gained over 30 pounds. Actually, I'm getting too fat now." He smiles with pleasure.

"Oh, I'm so glad. Is the catheter a bother, or what's it like?" I ask him, curious.

"No, not really. I'm only hooked up to it for twelve hours, about ten P.M. to ten A.M., and it's no trouble at all. I can eat all I want, too, and my appetite is back."

''That's wonderful,'' I say. ''And how about the diarrhea?'' I hope Peter is listening.

''A little now and then, but not nearly as much as before. I also drink a special tea, made from herbs we got in Mexicali. Here, I'll write the name down. Maybe you can look for it in Tijuana for Peter.'' He searches for a pen and scrap of paper in his pocket and writes it down. ''Try this, Peter, it'll help. And, Peter, I drink a big milkshake made with papaya every morning. Everything helps,'' he says cheerily.

Peter's name is called by the nurse and we rise.

''It's good to see you again, James, and I'm so glad to see you looking so well,'' I say as we turn to leave.

''Thanks. Try the tea, Peter, see if it helps,'' he calls after us.

''All right, see you,'' answers Peter.

My mind is filled with newborn hope. If the Hickman catheter did so much for James, couldn't it be good for Peter, too? Why hasn't anyone suggested it?

Peter lies down on the examining table, and Phyllis rushes in, full of breathless energy. Peter sits up, reviving. Her energy is infectious. His vital signs are taken. His weight is still 117 pounds. Phyllis asks him about his appetite and food intake. He answers that his appetite is all right, that he's been eating fairly well. It's not true.

''How's your vision, Peter? Do you see any change, better or worse?'' Phyllis lifts his black eyepatch to examine his right eye.

''No, it seems about the same,'' he answers. ''At times I can see better than others, though.''

''Any pains in your abdomen, cramping with the diarrhea?''

''No,'' he answers.

But he's complained to me of abdominal pains all summer and nothing seems to alleviate them.

''Dr. McCutchan will be in in a moment to finish checking you. Probably you don't have to come back for another two weeks,'' she tells him. He looks pleased.

Dr. McCutchan enters, reads Phyllis' notes, then checks Peter over.

"Looks pretty good, Peter. Now, the latest on the DHPG is that we're still waiting to receive your psychological testing results. I don't know what's happened to them. I've called the Communicative Disorders Center and they say they sent them a few days ago, but I haven't gotten them yet"—how could they get lost in just a few blocks, I wonder exasperatedly—"so we're still waiting. We do have your eye photographs, though, so as soon as we have all the information together, I think we can go ahead."

I breathe a sigh of relief. Peter dresses slowly. We make his next appointment and walk slowly down the corridor outside the clinic. Elaine, the nutritionist who works with the clinic, comes toward us.

"Hi, Peter, how're you doing?" she stops and greets him.

"Oh, pretty good, thanks." He smiles at her. "Haven't seen you around for a long time."

"No, I've been on vacation in Tahiti," she beams.

"That's great," exclaims Peter. "I think we're going to Hawaii pretty soon. Not quite Tahiti, but almost as good."

"That sounds great!" She smiles widely. "Who are you going with?"

"With Mom. She's never been there and I'd like her to see it."

I am completely taken aback. I had no idea he was planning a trip to Hawaii, and I hope I'm showing pleasure and not the shock I feel.

"When do you think you'll go?" Elaine asks both of us. I look to Peter for the answer.

"Well, I just have to get a little stronger. Pretty soon, probably in September or October."

"Have a wonderful time, whenever it is, then! Bye." She waves and goes on.

"Tell me, when did you get this idea?" I ask with amused curiosity.

"Oh, I've been thinking about it for awhile," Peter tells me casually. "And I really want you to get over there.

You won't if I don't make you. And I want to show you around the islands. You'll just love it.''

''Well, okay! Sounds like fun and I'd like to have you show me the place,'' I agree.

I'll go to a travel agency tomorrow and pick up some pamphlets and information on Hawaii. I don't know how we'll afford it, but I'll give fuel to his dreams.

Maybe his dreams can give him the nourishment that food cannot.

Thursday, August 9

This morning, we went to the Communicative Disorders Center to learn the results of Peter's testing. There is evidence of brain damage. His verbal I.Q. is 134, his performance score is 91. The difference should be within a few points, and his full score—the average—is only 115. But his superior score on vocabulary testing indicates that he has had a much higher I.Q. Apparently, an extensive vocabulary demonstrates high intelligence and is an indestructible skill.

In addition, the abnormal discrepancy between his verbal I.Q. and his performance score reflects motor-visual problems. This explains his clumsiness and lack of coordination, and his lack of interest in piano playing and painting. Also, both left and right hands are equal in dexterity. Peter is left-handed, and the lack of dominance is another indicator of motor dysfunction. They also found his attention span to be short, though this could be partially explained by his fatigue.

The doctor summarized that Peter has problems learning visual material, forming strategies and logical thought, and absorbing and integrating new information into his functioning thought processes. This explains his inability to remember what the doctors have told him in the clinic, which is the reason I've accompanied him to the examining room for some time now.

The psychologist gave us several helpful suggestions for dealing with his inadequacies, most of which we've already developed. He should let others help him with numbers, have me write down phone numbers that are given to him. We already do this. I carry a small notebook with me at all times. She also suggested that, because of his short attention time and difficulty concentrating, he should try to isolate himself and the person he's talking to when there are many people around. This will help reduce distraction and allow him to concentrate on communication.

The report is saddening but not surprising. I already knew his mental functioning was impaired. At least, we now have definite proof of brain damage, and another prerequisite for the DHPG treatment is fulfilled.

Saturday, August 11

Saturday morning. It is early and my neighbors are still asleep. Nobody will be passing by on their way to work today. Later, they will be on the way to the beach, to picnics, or shopping. My Mexican neighbors will be on the way to their Saturday ritual, the swap meet.

Peter's still asleep.

I think the new plans for Hawaii have lifted his depression somewhat. He's been studying the travel literature I picked up, comparing hotel prices and airline schedules, telling me what we'll do and where we'll go. I told him he's the boss and should make the decisions.

He likes to feel he's in charge.

Wednesday, August 15

Walter is here this week. He and Peter are staying at a resort hotel near our apartment for two days. We hoped Peter might like the change. He must get bored in our apartment.

I've taken advantage of this to escape to Mexico for two days with friends. We are in Rosarito, a small, coastal town just below Tijuana. I was uneasy leaving Peter. I called him at the hotel last night to tell them where I was staying and he chatted lengthily. I think he misses me. Now I wish I had stayed home with him.

This morning, I walked alone to the beach, a block

away. It was deserted—a wide, long expanse of gray sand with curls of white waves slapping in, receding, slapping in again. I walked almost to the water and sat on the sand. The sky was overcast, murky clouds gliding across it, and the water was sullen. I looked ahead, as far as the fuzzy horizon. I looked to the right, no one; to the left, no one. I was finally completely alone.

My God, really alone! I've been longing to be alone for months, alone to cry, scream, to open up and let the daily horror, fear, frustration swarm over me. I sat and cried. I screamed once or twice, and I sobbed and cried and screamed and cried again. I stopped a minute, and saw Peter in front of me, and I cried again. I thought of this boy I gave life to, losing it, losing it faster and faster, and I am helpless to stop it. I felt like the Dutch boy with my finger in the dyke, and the waves, the death rolling in faster and faster, and I am too small, too weak. I can't stop it. I huddled, holding my knees.

I hope Rosarito is still here when it's all over.

Monday, August 20

It is one A.M. and I'm very tired. I gave Peter a massage tonight, trying to relax him enough to sleep. He's been tired and cranky all day.

"So far, I've been really lucky to have so little pain," Peter said as I gently kneaded his back muscles. All I could feel, really, was his ribs.

"But this time, those damned lesions are really hurting," he continued, "and I'm not used to so much pain. I've felt just rotten all day."

"I know, Peter."

"I felt like crying all day, I feel so bottled up," he confessed.

"It's okay to cry, Peter. It gets discouraging." *Cry, Peter, cry,* I implore him silently.

"I don't want to give in, though. I'm not ready."

"It doesn't mean you're giving in, Peter, not at all. You don't have to be strong all the time. You might feel better if you cry, and stronger, abler to go on. I wish you would cry."

His chin quavered and his eyes filled with tears, but they merely welled up without spilling over. I rubbed slowly, lightly, watching his face. His glistening eyes, the right one now almost sightless, gazed into the darkness beyond the lamplight. I saw him struggling to hold back the tears. Maybe next time he will cry.

I don't understand how he can hold them back. How can his will power not soften and let the tears, the anguish, the pain, the sadness out?

I am not so strong.

Tuesday, August 21

We're in Owen Clinic. It's been two weeks since Peter's last appointment—a small victory to have lasted two weeks. For once, we don't have to wait long.

"I have to apologize," Dr. McCutchan starts. "I'm afraid the DHPG treatment will be delayed even more. I didn't realize that you would have to be on the ninth floor in the Clinical Research Center at the hospital and couldn't be on 10 East where you usually stay. Dr. Spector has to be able to monitor you very carefully and the nurses on ninth are more accustomed to this. But there are less beds on nine and there won't be one available for another ten to fourteen days. I have you signed up now. I'm really sorry to have to postpone this again. I know you're anxious to get started."

I don't know whether to scream or cry. I glance at Peter. If he had the energy, I think murder would be his choice of action. I'm beginning to wonder if he will ever receive this drug, or will it simply be too late by the time they have all the rules and regulations fulfilled? I feel a desperate resignation. Maybe it doesn't even matter anymore. Maybe he's too far gone for help. He weighs 111 pounds tonight, six less than two weeks ago.

"Another doctor will be here in a minute to take a look at your eyes," Dr. McCutchan continues. "How's your appetite, are you eating well?"

"Oh, pretty good. Yes, I'm trying to eat a balanced diet," answers Peter as I cringe at his lie.

Phyllis hands the opthalmoscope to Dr. McCutchan as a young, blond doctor enters.

"Would you please put the light out?" requests Dr. McCutchan as he adjusts the instrument. The room is black but for the small, yellow light in his hand and the pinpoint reflection on Peter's eyeball. All three take turns looking into his eye as they explain what they are seeing.

"The CMV infection is causing blockage of Peter's peripheral vision," comments Dr. McCutchan. "The retina is almost completely covered."

Invisible in the dark, I can feel the familiar sting in my eyes as tears start welling. The small light shifts to the left as they examine the other retina. I don't ask what they see. Peter doesn't ask, either. I swab my face with the back of my hand. The light will be on in a minute.

"I'll let you know as soon as a bed is available on nine," Dr. McCutchan assures us as we leave.

"How soon do you want to see him again?" I ask.

"Oh, I think two weeks will be fine," the doctor answers, and I make the appointment at the desk.

We arrive home and Peter turns the classical music station on, a Beethoven symphony. He turns, sits on the couch instead of going directly to his room as usual, and stares sadly ahead. I sit on the other end of the couch, not speaking. I think he wants my company but doesn't want to talk. I'm not sure.

We sit quietly, surrounded by Beethoven's majestic chords. After half an hour, he stands, decides to go to bed.

I let him go.

Wednesday, August 22

This week has been such a nightmare. We both have been depressed and angry, feeling that time is running away from us and we can't catch up with it anymore.

Peter is sad. He lies on his bed all day, his hands folded across his chest, his eyes open and staring, or closed but not sleeping. I pass by his room and see him lying there as if already dead. He rouses to eat a small amount of yogurt, nothing more.

My impatience and frustration are unbearable. Why don't they give him a Hickman catheter? Why don't they give him the new drug? Why don't they do *something*? He's lost six more pounds, too quickly, and I don't know what to do.

I hear Peter up in the kitchen. It's only nine, too early for him to be up.

"What are you doing up so early?" I ask, concerned.

"Oh, that damn diarrhea. I had to get up and couldn't get back to sleep. Think I'll sit in the living room awhile," he answers, sitting on the couch. I follow, sit in the rocking chair. We must do something about his eating, we must talk about it.

"Peter, we have to do something about your eating," I start.

"No, we don't," he says, his voice surly and defensive. "I'm eating enough, stop worrying about it."

"No, you're *not* eating enough. I've been watching what you eat, and on the best days it's not even 1000 calories, and you know you're supposed to be taking in 2800 calories a day. You're not doing that," I say bluntly.

"Sure I am," he says angrily.

"Wrong. And this has to change. You still want to go on living, don't you?" I throw Bob Cecchi's question back at him, hating myself for the cruelty.

"Of course I do," he answers furiously, his chin quavering slightly.

"Well then, we—you and me—have to do something about it. You are going to eat everything I put in front of you. I won't fix big portions, but you've got to eat it all, and you're going to have to let me fix your food. This piddling around with a spoonful of yogurt here and there is simply not enough."

I look at him. He's angry and upset and I want so much to put my arms around him. He wants so much to be in control, and I am taking his control away from him.

"All right," he finally concedes.

"Okay, now what do you want for breakfast?" I ask. "How about some canteloupe, French toast, juice?"

I prepare his breakfast and he eats it all, slowly and without pleasure. I watch, raging inside at what we have come to.

He goes back to bed and sleeps and I rinse the dishes and stack them in the dishwasher. I am a bundle of nervous, angry energy. There isn't enough to do in the apartment and I want to cry.

It is one-thirty, time to leave for my art lesson at John and Tom's house. I hope Peter will come along. I feel safe to leave him alone, but I don't want to be away from him.

"Peter?" I say his name softly.

"Yes?" he answers.

"I have to leave for the art class, do you want to come, too? You could just lie down inside, where it's cool," I suggest.

"No, I think I'll stay home and sleep."

"Are you sure? I'd like you to come."

"No, I'll be all right here."

"Well, if you want. Look, I'm leaving their number right next to the phone. If you need me or want me to pick anything up, call me, okay?"

"Okay," he murmurs sleepily.

I park outside John's house, go around to the back gate. Tom comes out to greet me. John has gone to the store and will be right back.

"Well, how are you today?" Tom asks, putting an arm around me.

"Fine," I start to answer automatically, but the touch of his arm triggers the pent-up tears. "No, no, I'm not fine, I'm a mess. I don't know what to do. Peter's so down, he's lost six pounds these last two weeks. He won't eat, nobody in clinic last night seemed concerned about his weight loss, and I don't know what to do, I just don't know." The words spill, tumble out.

"It's just so damned frustrating. The diarrhea is worse, this new drug won't be started now for up to two weeks or more, and he's lost all this weight. And he lied to Dr. McCutchan last night, told him he was eating pretty well and balanced meals. Tom, he isn't eating anything! And McCutchan seemed to believe him."

"Listen, I think you ought to call McCutchan and tell him the truth," Tom suggests. "You can call him from here, right now, and get it all settled."

I go inside the house and dial the telephone. Dr. McCutchan answers.

"I'm very worried," I tell him. "Peter lied to you last night about his eating. He isn't eating anything, and as of last night he'd lost six pounds in two weeks. I don't know if you realized it."

"Two weeks? No, I'm sorry. I thought it was six weeks. By all means, I think it's time for intervention," he answers. Thank God, I sigh.

"I think we should bring him in tomorrow and schedule him for a Hickman catheter. Do you think you could talk to him about it and then call me back tonight to let me know?"

"Oh, yes, I will. Thank you so much." Thank God I called.

I go back to the patio. John has returned. A suffocating load has been lifted temporarily, and I can now work freely with John on his painting.

Six P.M. I sit in the darkened living room. Dinner is cooking in the oven. Peter comes around the corner and sits on the couch. He was asleep when I came back.

"How are you doing?" I ask.

"All right, I guess. I think I slept most of the afternoon. What time is it?"

"It's about six," I answer. "Peter, I talked to Dr. McCutchan this afternoon. I was worried about your weight loss and wanted to ask him about it. He thinks you should have a Hickman catheter put in." I stop, wait for a vehement rejection, but he's quiet.

"I really don't want one," he says finally. "I don't feel that I'm that far gone."

"It doesn't mean you're far gone," I tell him. "But you do need some assistance. Malnutrition is dangerous and can leave you more prone to infection. You don't have any appetite and I hate nagging you to eat, but you need the nourishment. You need to get built up again so you can fight better. Things simply can't go on like this.''

He is quiet, thinking it over.

''And your intestines need a rest from the diarrhea, not to mention your poor rear end. Look how well James is doing. It doesn't seem to bother him at all. I told Dr. McCutchan we'd talk about it, and let him know tonight how you feel about it. It's your decision, it's completely up to you.''

''I feel like it's another signpost,'' he finally says after a long silence. I look up, startled at his reference to the symbols of his decline as ''signposts''—my own term.

''I don't think you need to,'' I assure him. But I know it's another signpost. I wish they'd prescribe Hickman catheters earlier in the disease so it doesn't have the stigma of being a last recourse.

''I think I'll lie down awhile before dinner,'' he says, standing.

''Okay. I can turn the oven off till you're ready,'' I tell him.

I turn the television on, but I can't concentrate. I sit, staring at the box, my mind wandering as images flash on and off the screen. Violence in Latin America, killing heat waves in the midwest, they mean nothing to me. My only concern is the life and death of my son, here in my house.

Eight-thirty P.M. Peter rejoins me silently, gazing without interest at the television.

''Goddamnit!'' he shrieks suddenly, leaping up and moving as fast as he can down the hall.

I wait a minute, cringing. I hear the shower through the wall and his soft, plaintive moans. I race down the hall and into his bathroom. It's all over everything. Peter is in the shower, still moaning softly. I slip rubber gloves on quickly, grab a rag and the bottle of bleach, and start cleaning everything, saying nothing, but cursing, boiling, hating the obscenity this damned disease has made of his life.

''Do you think Dr. McCutchan could find me a room in

the hospital for tomorrow?'' Peter asks from inside the shower stall.

"I'm sure he will,'' I answer.

Thank God! I stop scrubbing a second and fight back the tears of mixed exhaustion and relief that rise to my eyes. I grab a towel from the rack and hold it for Peter as he steps out, and I guide him to his bed. He sits on the side, I next to him. I put my arm around him and rub his back gently, trying to smoothe away his dejection and despair as if it were a sore muscle. If only I could kiss it all away for him, like when he was small.

"Would it be all right if I called Dad?'' he asks finally.

"If you want to, but it's after midnight there, you know he'll be asleep. Do you want to tell him about the Hickman?'' I ask.

"What I really want to ask him is if he thinks it would be all right if I lance that herpes blister, it's gotten bigger.''

"I'm sure he would advise you not to, and you could ask Dr. McCutchan here about that,'' I tell him. "Why don't you call him? We don't have the sterile equipment at home to do it and probably it shouldn't be lanced, anyway. Probably that would make it spread.''

Peter leaves the room, still wrapped in his towel, and dials Dr. McCutchan on the kitchen phone. After a few minutes, he returns.

"What did he say?'' I ask.

"He said not to lance it, to put gauze on it and leave it alone.'' He sits down again. "And he said I should go to the clinic at five tomorrow evening and be admitted from there for the Hickman catheter. He's not sure he can get me on the surgery schedule for Friday, but he said they'd at least start me on IV feeding.''

Thursday, August 23

We're in Owen Clinic, Peter in his support group and I in mine. Peter wanted to go to his support group meeting before being admitted to the hospital.

Tim comes late to our meeting, his handsome, amiable face is lined and tired. Tim is Ron's roommate, the young man with the terrible cough who was in the hospital when Peter was. He's been taking care of Ron in their apartment. Others stand quickly and embrace him with compassion. I watch, sensing immediately what has happened. Someone turns, speaks to me.

"Barbara, Ron died last night," they tell me.

"Oh, no, Tim," I turn, touch him. I can say no more. It is too close to Peter and me. Ron had been in the hospital seven weeks, but we heard that he was given a Hickman catheter, gained about nine pounds, and was sent home finally.

Peter felt close to Ron in their support group. Will he be discouraged by the failure of the Hickman catheter to revitalize Ron? He died only nine days after it was put in.

Tim talks about his deep affection for Ron through seventeen years, and how glad he was that he was able to die at home. It was very quick. One day he was playing handball, the next he was complaining of abdominal pain, was given morphine, and died two days later, surrounded by his family and Tim, as he wished. Tim talks on, and I listen carefully. He's grateful he could be with Ron at the end. His pain was so unbearable that Tim had prayed for Ron's release. After his death, Tim felt strangely detached, clinical. He watched the mortuary people come for Ron's body and was impersonally fascinated by their precautions in handling an AIDS patient.

"It's awful, but it's also funny in a macabre sort of way," he says. "They dress up in these plastic suits and helmets and zip them closed. They look like space men. Then they have to put the body in a special plastic bag and zip that up. It's horrible, but I just found myself watching everything with scientific interest, I don't know why. Actually, it's pretty gruesome."

"Is Ron around?" asks Peter when I meet him in the hallway. "He wasn't at our meeting."

"No," I answer, wanting to wait until we're alone to give him the news. But Richard comes toward us from the clinic waiting room.

"Come back in here, I want to talk to you both," he says, holding the door open. We sit around the table.

"I wanted to tell you that Ron died last night," he says gently.

"Yes, I know. I just heard it in my group," I tell him. Peter is silent, unreacting.

"Well, he never had the right attitude," he says after a moment. "He always said he would die when his leave of absence from work was over and his medical benefits ran out. That was just a couple of days ago, you know. He just decided he had nothing else to live for."

No tears, an impassive face, yet I know Ron's death must affect him. The impassivity is a wall, not insensitivity. Once again, it is his defense against the terror and fear of his own death. The "right attitude" is his weapon.

Peter and I return to the waiting room. His bed is ready upstairs, and a nurse accompanies us to 10 East. Peter goes to the nurses' desk to greet them.

"Hi, Peter, what is it this time?"

"Oh, they're going to give me a Hickman catheter," he says nonchalantly. "And some more acyclovir. I've got that herpes back again."

"We'll fix you up," one nurse says cheerfully. "Come on, let me show you your room." We follow her down the hall to Room 4, on the corner.

Peter changes out of his clothes and into the white hospital gown. An intern enters with charts in hand to take Peter's history. This detailed repetition of the medical history has become the most tedious part of every admission.

As usual, there is confusion over his medications. Somehow, someone new to his case can never find the previous list of drugs and dosages on his chart. I get the list of drugs out of my notebook and hand it to the intern to copy. He finishes the history and examines Peter. But, Peter refuses to let him do a rectal examination. It is too painful.

Nurses and technicians come and go. His IV line is started for the acyclovir infusions, blood samples are taken for the lab, and I hang up his clothes and arrange what he'll need on his bedside table.

At last, I pull a chair close to the bed and sit down, tired but relieved that he is going to get some help. He speaks positively of the hyper-alimentation formula that will be provided through the Hickman catheter. He anticipates an increase of strength and energy and a decrease of diarrhea. He does not fear the surgery needed to implant the catheter. It is simple and relatively safe. Two two-inch incisions will be made in his upper chest, below the collarbone. A slender plastic tube will tunnel under the skin from one incision and feed into the vein beneath the second incision. About twelve inches of tube will be outside the body, and the incision above the vein insertion will be allowed to heal. The tube will have a removable cap, replaced after each feeding. Several feet of thin tubing will feed the hyper-alimentation solutions into the catheter mouth and then directly into the bloodstream.

Peter seems calm. We ask the nurse if she knows what time the surgery is scheduled, but no one seems to know.

"I think I'll go home now, Peter." An hour has passed quietly and he seems all right. "Give me a call if you find out when you're going to surgery, okay?"

"Okay. Get a good sleep," he admonishes me.

"I will. You, too," I tell him. "Call if you want to talk or need anything. Here, I'll put the number next to the phone." I write it on a slip of paper and tape it to the table. I hesitate, turn at the door.

It's so hard to leave him.

Monday, August 27

Peter wanted to reach me at home last Thursday night, after checking in, but he said he couldn't read the number I had so carefully taped to his bedside table. I found out Friday that he felt dizzy throughout the night, and that no one would come to him.

Friday was a horror, too. Nothing was being done for Peter—the IV feeding wasn't started until late afternoon, no one knew when his surgery was scheduled—he felt ignored, angry at the doctors. "They're wasting my time," he kept saying.

Worse yet, he feared a seizure all day. I, too, saw his

dizziness and anxiety as possible signs of a seizure. I called Dr. Rothrock early, but he couldn't get there until 9:00 P.M. He decided to take Peter off of the Dilantin for awhile, fearing that his weight loss has changed his metabolism, and that he needs less.

Peter seemed settled down by Saturday morning, resigned that nothing would be done until today. The rest of the weekend was calm, but this morning, Peter is anxious and irritable. He will finally have his surgery today, but no one seems to know at what hour.

Maria is arriving from Aspen at noon. I can't believe the summer is over already. Time is passing much too fast. Because of the uncertainty about Peter's operation, she's coming straight to the hospital when she arrives. She'll be here a week before returning to Baltimore for her sophomore year at Peabody Conservatory.

A nurse enters and tells us that Peter is scheduled for surgery at one o'clock. At noon, I go outside to wait for Maria, and sit on a concrete bench in the sun. A cab pulls to the curb and out steps Maria, tan and energetic. What a contrast between her vitality and the heartbreaking torpor of her older brother upstairs. If only he could have her health for one day. We greet, hug, and hurry upstairs.

"Hi Peter, how're you doing?" she asks as we enter his room.

"Hi, how was your summer?" he asks her, his face wrinkling into a smile. He weighed 108 pounds this morning and when he smiles, his teeth appear unnaturally large under his moustache. We visit quietly. I can see that he's glad his sister is here.

"Okay, Peter, here we go," a nurse wheels a Guerney bed into the room. Slowly, painfully, he transfers himself to the other bed, refusing help. We walk alongside his bed down the hall, to the elevator, and into an anteroom in the surgical suite. Now he seems anxious, apprehensive. I hate to leave him.

Tuesday, August 28

Peter's hospital room is hot and stuffy. Unlike previous visits, when he wanted the door open to stay "connected to the world," he insists on keeping it closed, saying there is an obnoxious cigarette stench that even seeps in under the closed door.

"You're Peter Vom Lehn?" asks a young woman with glasses and a sheaf of papers in hand.

"Yes," Peter answers.

"I'm Jane Donahue, your nutritionist," she introduces herself. The Hickman catheter was inserted successfully, and she begins to explain what will be done now. "We are starting your hyper-alimentation, or hyper-al, at 800 calories a day and will gradually increase it to 2500 a day. You'll be connected 24 hours at the start, then we'll gradually taper it down to 12 hours a day, and you'll be free the other 12 hours. Then, as soon as we're sure you're tolerating it well, and you and your mom can take care of it, you can go home."

"How long will that take?" Peter asks.

"Usually, about a week; but we won't let you go until we're absolutely sure you can manage it yourself.

"Now, Peter, it is extremely important that you gain some weight and strength back. You know you're down to 108 pounds, and have almost no fat or muscle tissue. An infection could strike, and you'll be in serious trouble with no tissue to absorb it. Even with the hyper-al, I want you to eat all you can and drink as many fluids as possible. I'll be in to check you every day, make sure everything's going okay. See you tomorrow."

Peter looks distressed. I think she could have delivered her information less dramatically. Surely she must know that AIDS patients are all too aware of their vulnerability to infection. Peter himself is almost phobic about exposure to infections.

A white-coated doctor enters the room. I have never seen him before. He looks like an Old Testament prophet, with thick, black hair, thick, black beard, and piercing, intelligent, dark eyes.

"I'm Doctor Spector. I'm here to talk to you about the DHPG treatment, Peter," he introduces himself.

"Oh . . . how do you do, I'm Peter's mother," I tell

him, trying not to laugh at my amazement. By his telephone voice, I visualized him as an older, heavy man with short, white hair.

"I think we have everything arranged now for you to start the treatment next Tuesday," he tells us as he sits in a chair by the bed. "I want you both to understand that this drug is so new it's not even in the experimental stage. You'll be just the seventh person in the country to receive it, Peter. This means that we cannot guarantee any results, nor do we know much about possible adverse effects, though so far they've been nil. There have been excellent results at killing off CMV in the lab, but varying results so far with humans. You will be a guinea pig, Peter. But if it helps to know, you can be sure that even if the drug doesn't help you, your experience with it may help someone else down the road." He smiles kindly at Peter.

"Yes, I know that," Peter responds. "That's part of why I feel it's worth trying."

"Good. Now, let me explain what will happen. Tuesday, we'll move you down to the CRC unit on nine. We'll start the treatment on Wednesday, and we'll be taking blood every half hour the first nine hours, checking it immediately on the floor for any possible adverse effects. Then we'll take it every hour for four hours, then just once a day till the last day, when we'll repeat the procedure. We'll probably administer it right through your Hickman catheter, for an hour every eight hours. The treatment will last ten days. How does that sound?"

"Will I be able to get out on pass during that time?" Peter asks.

"I don't see why not. By then, you'll only be on the Hickman twelve hours, the DHPG every eight hours, so I think that can be arranged."

"Okay, sounds fine to me." Peter smiles.

"Good." Dr. Spector rises. "Then we'll plan on that. If you have any questions, give me a call. You'll have to sign a permission to be an experimental subject, you know, before it starts."

"Yes, that's all right," says Peter.

The doctor leaves. I look at Peter. We are both relieved.

"He looks like one of the Smith Brothers on the cough drop box," Peter comments, laughing.

"Frankly," I tell him, "I thought it was Moses himself in a white coat."

We both laugh. I know that Peter, with his penchant for naming everyone, will now refer to him as "Dr. Smith," just as Drs. McCutchan and Matthews are "the Drs. M & M"; the regally beautiful and reserved Philippine secretary in Owen Clinic is "Mrs. Marcos"; and Tom and John are "The Bobbsey Twins." Sam, who drops in to visit from time to time, is referred to as "Mr. Jack-in-the-Box."

"Why that? You mean because of the deep-frying smell?" I asked, assuming that Sam's clothing might carry the odor, as he often stops at the Jack-in-the-Box restaurant near the hospital to pick up snacks for patients. I've never smelled anything, but Peter is always picking up odors that no one else does. I think it has to do with his brain infection.

"No, no," he said. "It's the pickle relish—don't you notice it? I can smell him coming when he gets off the elevator."

Despite the tremendous discouragements of his daily life, Peter still maintains his sense of humor.

I leave Peter to rest and dash over to the outpatient building, run inside the elevator before it closes. Sam is inside, going upstairs.

"Did you hear about James?" he asks.

"No . . . ," I answer hesitantly. Oh, God. Please don't tell me what I don't want to hear . . .

"He died over the weekend."

"Oh, no!" I clap my hand to my mouth in shock. "He was doing so well. We just saw him in clinic. How could that happen?"

"It seems he was down in Mexicali and he suddenly went into seizures. They brought him up here by helicopter, worked on him in ICU a couple of days, but couldn't pull him out of it."

"Look—*please* don't tell Peter if you see him. I don't want him to know," my voice is urgent. "He's just started on hyper-al, and if he hears this, he'll be terrified. He mustn't know.''

''All right, I won't say anything.''

I rush out the elevator door. I'm almost hysterical. Peter already knows about Ron's death, only nine days after starting hyper-al, and now James. Our world is so crazy, there's just no sense to it. James was doing so well—and now he's gone. He's dead.

How long can it go on, senseless death after senseless death?

Wednesday, August 29

''There's something important I want to talk to you about,'' Peter starts as I drag a chair close to the bed. He looks a little better today.

''What is it?'' I ask, sitting down.

''Well . . . now don't get any funny ideas. This is just in case,'' he prefaces.

''Yes?''

''Well, just *in case* something should happen, I want you to know that I've decided that I don't really care what you do with my things afterward. I don't have much of value. You can give them away, or sell them—whatever.''

''Okay, that's fine,'' I promise, feeling a sudden sadness. This is the first time he's actually admitted the possibility of death. Are his doubts about surviving growing?

''I'm planning a trip to Hawaii. Will it be possible to take the hyper-al and use it there?''

''Oh, yes,'' answers Joanne, the nurse in charge of the hyper-al program. She has just arrived to start our instruction today. ''We have patients who travel all over the world with this set-up. Just tell us in advance, and the company that makes the formula arranges for everything to be waiting for you when you arrive. I have one patient who goes to Seattle once a week on business, and they have it all ready at her hotel when she arrives.''

"Is there any way it can run on battery, so I don't have to be tied down to the machine?" Peter asks.

"Yes, they make a vest that has pockets for two batteries, and you can walk around with that on. It's rather heavy, but I have one patient who just hangs it on the back of a chair and then can be anywhere in the house he wishes. Of course, you can also use an extension cord for the pumps. I've got another patient who uses a 50-foot cord and just pulls the pumps around with him all over the house while he's hooked up. You really can be very free."

"Would it be possible to let me have one of the vests, so I can learn to use it before we go?"

"Oh, sure. I'll order one and show you how to use it," she tells him.

"I'd like one when I go home, so I can start getting used to it. I'm hoping we'll be able to go in early October," Peter tells her.

I gulp inaudibly. Only an hour earlier, he was talking about the disposal of his property. Here he is at 108 pounds, sicker and weaker than ever, and now he still talks of traveling to Hawaii.

"All right, I'll order one to be sent to your house after you get home," Joanne promises.

"One other thing," Peter says. "Mom already takes care of so many things for me, so I want to learn this procedure and do my part."

"That's a good idea," Joanne agrees. "You should know all about it. Now, let's start with this model."

She pulls a flesh-colored, plastic torso from a box and ties it around her neck. We laugh. It is the torso of a nude woman and hanging in front of Joanne, like an apron, it looks incongruous. It has the facsimile of a Hickman catheter inserted in its plastic incision.

Step by step, we go over the procedure, starting with changing the incision dressing. The tapes must be pulled off carefully, the skin swabbed with peroxide, Betadine Solution, then Betadine Ointment—all antiseptics. Then a sterile gauze pad is laid over the incision and taped back down. The same procedure is followed with the incision where the catheter enters the body, though the tubing must also be carefully swabbed.

Joanne then shows us how to cap and uncap the catheter mouth, swabbing it with alcohol, then Betadine Solution, air-drying it a minute, and recapping it. She shows us all the tubing that must be connected from the catheter to the two hyper-al bags, and how to inject the dextrose solution with vitamins immediately before connecting the tubing and hanging it on the stand. The whole procedure looks so complicated—so many joinings to be Betadine-swabbed and taped—my mind reels.

But I will learn it. I must.

Thursday, August 30

The phone rings, startling me awake. I look at the clock, eleven-thirty.

"Mom, were you asleep?"

"No. What would you like?" I ask.

"Well . . . there's something serious to talk about."

"What's that, Peter?" I ask apprehensively.

"I don't think I can go right to the ninth floor next Tuesday without getting out of here for a few days first. I think I'll go crazy if I have to be in here another six to eight weeks, at least without a short break first."

"Dr. Spector said it would only be a ten-day course of treatment, Peter, not six weeks. Remember?"

"No, he said six weeks, at least."

"Maybe you heard him wrong, Peter. I'm sure he said ten days," I correct him gently.

"I don't think so," he insists. "I don't know that I can really trust him anymore."

"Yes, you can, Peter," I assure him. So many delays with both the DHPG treatment and the Hickman catheter placement, added to his growing phobias and suspicions, have made him distrustful and fearful of the medical people.

"I tell you what, Peter, why don't you call Dr. McCutchan tomorrow and get it straightened out? And if you still feel you need a few days out, tell him so they can reschedule you. You know how hard it is to get a bed on the ninth floor.''

"All right, I'll do that in the morning. Sorry if I woke you up, good night.''

"That's okay, I told you to call if you needed to. Good night. Try to have a good sleep.''

How confused he gets. I wonder, for the thousandth time, how the patients who live alone ever manage to keep their lives straight.

Friday, August 31

Peter's birthday is Monday, and all the kids will be here to celebrate. Maria is already here. David arrived at noon today from Austin. And Jonathan is flying in from Las Vegas at 10:30 P.M. tomorrow.

Even Nani is coming at noon tomorrow from Tucson. She is my "Dominican daughter." She came to live with our family when she was 13, after Walter served ten months in Santo Domingo as a Peace Corps staff physician. She has shown so much concern for Peter, and for me, calling often since this ordeal began. But circumstances in her life have prevented her from coming to visit before now. I'm so glad she will be here for Peter's birthday.

Sadly, because of their jobs and other obligations, there will be only 24 hours when they are all five together. Nani and Maria are leaving Sunday noon, Jonathan Monday night, and David Tuesday morning.

The last reunion, I fear.

11

Saturday, September 1

Nani arrived, amidst a tumult of hugs and giggles. Maria, David, and I spent a short time with Peter this morning, then went to the airport to pick her up. We will let Peter rest all afternoon and return about seven-thirty, when all but Jonathan will be together. We will start his birthday celebration tonight. Peter ordered sushi for his birthday dinner, so we'll pick it up on the way to the hospital.

At seven, the four of us pile into the car, collect the sushi from the Japanese restaurant, and troop up to Peter's room. He is completely free of any IV tubes for a few hours and has dressed neatly in a red plaid shirt and khaki trousers. David takes him for a slow walk around the hall while Nani, Maria, and I decorate his room with paper ribbon, balloons, and a big ''Happy Birthday!'' banner across the upper window.

Peter lies semireclining on his bed while we open the boxes of sushi and pass them around. I watch Peter carefully. The energy and enthusiasm of the others must exhaust him, but he appears happy. I hope he is. Oh, God, I hope he is, on his last birthday. I turn away a moment. I wonder if he thinks of it as his last.

I feel nothing but pain as I listen to my children laugh and joke.

Sunday, September 2

Jonathan's plane arrived late last night. We all went to meet him and then returned to the hospital, as Peter had wanted us to. As I expected, though, Peter was asleep when we arrived, still dressed and one light shining on him. We left him a note and went home.

Midday. Peter is dressed but I see he's exhausted. He had several bouts of diarrhea during the night. That, the loss of sleep, and so much unaccustomed company, have depleted his energy. I expected this and only left half an hour to visit before we take Maria and Nani to the airport. I brought my camera and I group everyone quickly around Peter, take two or three shots. David, Jonathan, and I leave Peter alone with Maria and Nani. All of us would be too much.

"Come on, ladies, we have to go." I open Peter's door. The three have been laughing and I'm glad, but I can see Peter needs to rest. "Peter, we'll leave you alone and come back later, okay?"

"Okay, I think I'll sleep for awhile, anyway."

I take more pictures of David, Jonathan, Maria, and Nani at the airport before Nani's plane leaves. She runs to board the plane as we wave goodbye, then we walk to Maria's gate.

"Mom, I want you to be sure to call me if you need me," she says as we wait.

"You know I will. Let's just hope I won't need you," I say, my eyes filling, feeling that the next time I see her, all will be different. "Just go ahead and get a good start on the semester, and we'll see what happens."

"I'm going to come home for Thanksgiving, anyway. I've decided not to go to Maine to Nanna's. I want to come home."

"I'm glad," I tell her. And, of course, the tears spill, tears not just of fear for Peter, but of gratitude to my children. David, Jonathan, and Nani have already decided to come, too. We have another goal for Peter to aim for. I love these kids. Thank God I have them.

Monday, September 3

Today is Peter's birthday. By coincidence, he was born on a Monday twenty-nine years ago in New York City.

He wanted us to take him out for more sushi tonight, but we have called and all Japanese restaurants seem to be closed for the holiday. We can't rouse him enough to see if he wants to go elsewhere. He's been sleeping all day.

I think he's more depressed than tired. The company has been exhausting, and surely their energy, compared to his, is depressing. I wonder if it was a good idea to celebrate his birthday this way.

Jonathan's plane leaves at eight tonight, David's at seven tomorrow morning. Tonight will be Peter's last chance to see them. We have spent the afternoon on the lawn outside the hospital, hoping Peter might revive. But by five, we go home for a quick dinner, planning to return for half an hour at seven before going to the airport.

Peter is up and dressed when we return. His hair is wetly slicked down; he must have washed it in the sink.

"Do you want to go to the airport with us, Peter?" I ask.

"No," he answers after thinking a minute. "I want to go for a walk . . . *alone*," he says firmly.

"Can't you wait a few minutes?" I ask. "Jonathan has to leave." I am piqued by his strange rudeness.

Without answering, he walks straight to David, shakes his hand, and says, "Thanks for coming, I hope you have a good trip back." Then, passing by Jonathan as if he weren't there, he rushes out the door, saying, "I have to hurry. I have to get out while there's still light." We sit, stunned, looking at one another.

"Well," I say at last, "I guess that's that. Come on, let's go." I am infuriated. Was he confused, didn't know who was leaving, or what? And why so rude?

"I don't understand that at all," I tell David and Jonathan as we descend in the elevator. "That was really rude. I'm sorry, Jonathan."

"Oh, that's okay, Mom. Don't worry about it. He's sick. He doesn't always know what he's doing."

"Well, sick or not," I say indignantly, "he could at least have walked to the car with us, as long as he was going out anyway. He could have said goodbye. Listen, you all came especially for his birthday, and gave up your own plans for him. I'm really mad." I slam the car door shut. I feel hurt for them.

"It's all *right*, Mom," Jonathan repeats.

We leave Jonathan at his gate. There is barely time to say goodbye.

"Let's go get some dinner, David. Tracy and Ray are going to visit Peter tonight. He won't need extra people around."

I'm afraid I'll explode at him if I go back.

Tuesday, September 4

I awoke angry and tired today, still upset by Peter's rude behavior last night. I took David to the airport at six A.M., had coffee and read the newspaper in the airport cafeteria. I knew if I went home, I would fall back in bed for twelve hours, and I must be at the hospital to disconnect Peter's hyper-al today.

"Good morning, Peter," I greet him when I get there.

"Where's my breakfast?" he asks in a surly tone. He's walking back to his bed from the sink. His hyper-al tube only allows him to walk that far.

"Your breakfast?" I ask, puzzled.

"Yes, my breakfast," he repeats sarcastically.

"I don't know," I answer, bewildered.

"Well then, fuck you!"

"Wait a minute!" I explode. "You don't need to talk to me that way, and I don't need to hear it. Besides, I'm tired of you talking to me as if I were stupid. I'm not stupid and I don't like being talked to as if I were."

The anger, the pain, the hurt—everything is boiling up and out of me—rage with everything, the whole world, AIDS, Peter, myself. I don't even know what it is.

"I've been taking it quietly, making excuses for you—'he's sick'—but I'm not going to take it anymore, it's just not fair . . ." My voice starts to rise. I start to speak of his rudeness to his brothers, but a nurse enters and I choke back the words.

"Think about what I said, I'll be back in a while," I tell him as calmly as possible, storming out of the room.

I don't want to be angry with him, God knows. I know why he's acting this way, but I can't help it. What is this awful, pressure-cooker world we're locked in, that makes us scream at each other when we should be loving? There's so little time left, so little.

I push into the bathroom, dry my eyes, shove the anger back inside, and go to the cafeteria. I cannot go back upstairs until I am in control of myself.

Finally, I return upstairs. Peter is quiet, docile. We chat about insignificant matters. Any minute, a nurse will bring a wheelchair, and we will take Peter to his new room on the ninth floor. He will now be a human guinea pig for ten days.

Oh, God, Peter. What the hell are we doing here?

Wednesday, September 5

At last, the DHPG treatment has begun. Almost eight weeks of anxious and frustrated waiting have ended. Now we will see if the waiting was justified. If this drug doesn't work, Peter will eventually be blind, the diarrhea will worsen, and his brain will be eaten by this wretched virus. Peter knows that the CMV may remain unaffected by the drug, but it is also important to him to feel that his experience may help others later.

With Joanne's supervision, I've been changing Peter's incision dressings and learning to connect him to his hyper-alimentation apparatus, gaining confidence each time. We have to be extremely careful that new infections do not enter at any juncture in the tubing and get into his blood-stream directly. There are two plastic bags, one with a high dextrose solution and the other with fats and lipids, that are connected to the tube in his chest. The two infusions are controlled by separate pumps fastened to an IV stand, and the rate of infusion is tapered up three times in the first hour to avoid insulin shock from too much sugar at once. The same procedure is reversed when he's disconnected after twelve hours. Tedious but worth it. He has gained four pounds already.

Today, he can barely sleep. A heparin lock has been inserted in his arm—an IV needle that can be capped after each use, rather than having to reinsert it over and over. How wonderful—this is much more comfortable for Peter. Blood is being drawn every half hour for the first eight hours to monitor for adverse effects. Now that the treatment finally has started, Peter is in a better mood. We are both optimistic, glad to be hoping again.

I think we both deserve a break, for a change.

Friday, September 7

"You'll never guess what happened here last night," Peter greets me as I sit by his bed.

"What happened?"

"I woke up about three-thirty, heard a funny noise, and there on the top window frame was a big, fat pigeon!" he exclaims, his face animated.

"Oh, my Lord. What did you do?"

"I let out a bloodcurdling yell—they must have heard me all over the hospital—and a nurse came running in. She must have thought I was flipping out. I yelled, 'There's a bird in here!' and she grabbed a roll of tape and threw it at it." He pauses for breath. "You know how I've always been scared one of those dirty things was going to get in the window."

"Yes, I know. So what happened next?"

"Well, it fluttered and flew back out. God, I was so scared I couldn't stop talking about it afterward." He grins ruefully.

"That must have been really scary," I sympathize.

More than frightening, it is bizarre. He has brought this fear of the pigeons through each hospitalization. It's almost as if the pigeon were a malevolent harbinger of Peter's fate. I feel a sudden chill.

Dr. Spector knocks on the door and enters, accompanied by a tall, blond woman in a white coat.

"Peter, this is Wendy Young, the nurse practitioner who assists me. She'll be coming around to see you, too."

"Hi." Peter greets her, smiling. "How are you?"

"Fine, thanks, Peter. We'd like to check your eyes today, see if there's any change yet."

"Okay, though I don't see any change yet." Peter props himself up.

"Now, close your left eye and tell me what you can read." Dr. Spector holds up a miniature eye chart and masks off the smaller lines with an index card.

"Wait till I put my glasses on, I can't even see the card," Peter says, fumbling around the objects on his bedside table. He puts the glasses on, moves his head slightly up and down, right to left, then reads a few letters.

"All right, fine. And how has the diarrhea been this week?" the doctor asks.

"About the same," answers Peter. "I think the rectal pain is coming back, though I don't think there are any lesions yet."

"Hmm, all right. We'll continue checking you. See you tomorrow, Peter." They leave.

"How the hell do they expect me to see the letters when I can't even see the card itself?" asks Peter, a frustrated edge in his voice.

"You mean, you can't see the card at all?"

"Well, I can move my head around, there's sort of one little spot I can see through if I focus on the object, but I have to search for it first. Like tunnel vision, I guess."

No. Please, no.

Saturday, September 8

I took Peter to get his hair cut today. He still insists on maintaining a good appearance, but I also think he needed to get out of the hospital for awhile. I waited for him outside the shop, and he was quite excited when he joined me.

"He was very nice," Peter said as we left. "And, you know—I feel I did some good in there."

"Why, what happened?"

"He saw my heparin lock and asked what it was. I told

him and said I was out on pass from the hospital and had AIDS. He didn't flinch at all, didn't shrink away or anything, just kept on cutting my hair. I told him the whole story. He was very interested, and I told him to be very careful, to take good care of himself. He was really nice, very sympathetic. He wished me good luck when I left.''

I saw that the encounter gave Peter an unaccustomed feeling of value, a renewed self-esteem. He's been concerned that others not find themselves in his situation, and has wished he had the strength to be of more help to others. The barber did not shy from him in fear or revulsion, but listened and asked intelligent questions. I'm glad Peter got this opportunity; glad the barber was tactful and compassionate.

Wednesday, September 12

''What are your plans for Thanksgiving?'' I look up, surprised at the question.

''Why, you know . . . I'll be right here, of course,'' I answer. ''Why do you ask?''

''Oh, I thought you were going somewhere, up to Charlotte's in San Francisco or something.''

''No, no. I wouldn't leave you alone like that. I'll be here, of course. And all the kids are planning to come, remember?''

''Oh, I didn't know that,'' Peter says, looking bemused.

''I told you so, after they were here for your birthday.''

''Well, that's good,'' he says, lying back more comfortably. ''What kind of plans should we make?''

''Oh, I don't know, a big dinner at home, I suppose. The rest we'll have to think about, we have more than two months,'' I tell him, glad that he is setting himself another goal for living.

Thursday, September 13

''Well, what do you think is a good word for AIDS?'' Peter asks me. Two days ago, Wendy, then later Phyllis, referred to AIDS as a terminal disease. Peter gave Wendy a stern lecture when she said it, and now he has asked me to invite Phyllis back to speak to her about this. She should be in momentarily.

"Let's see . . ." I answer, thinking. The word "terminal" is very offensive to Peter, as is the word "victim," instead of "patient," to many others.

"It *is* a chronic disease, but it's more serious than that. I've seen it referred to as life-threatening. That implies the inherent danger but not the absolute finality of terminal."

"Yes . . . yes, I think life-threatening is good," Peter agrees.

"Good morning, Peter. I got the message that you wanted to talk to me," she says cheerfully, her heels clicking briskly across the linoleum floor.

"Yes, I did. I just wanted to talk to you about calling AIDS a terminal disease," he starts.

"I expected that might be it, and I was thinking about my choice of words yesterday. What word do you think might be better?"

"I think life-threatening is more suitable. After all, you can't call a disease terminal when only 45 percent of the cases have died, not 100 percent. Some have lived three to five years, and records have only been kept since 1981. How do you know that they're all going to die? I think that terminal is insulting, offensive to the patient, because it takes away all his hope and can discourage him immediately. And hope is a very important part of the patient's mental and physical health, and essential if he's going to get any better and not give in. It's not fair to take away someone's chances for survival by taking away his hope, and if he's told he has a terminal disease, that's just what you do, right at the start," he pauses a minute, tired from such a long speech.

"You have a good point, Peter," Phyllis agrees pensively.

"It just makes me angry to hear people call AIDS terminal, that's all," he tells her.

"I really appreciate your talking to me about it," Phyllis says. "The medical community often gets so wrapped up in its professional and technical approach to disease that it forgets about the patient's feelings, and that those feelings are very important to his well-being. I'm glad you told me this, because we need to know what the patient feels. We can empathize only so far. The patient ultimately is the only one who knows how he feels.''

They chat a few minutes more, then Phyllis has to return to her work.

I do think Peter has a valid point, and he has become an expert on survival, after all. His physical resources have been hopelessly inadequate without the emotional impetus his hope has given him.

His indomitable will to survive continues to amaze me. Despite all his talents and intelligence, Peter has never been able to set goals for himself and fulfill them. He's always been too easily discouraged and let plans fall apart at the slightest setback or disappointment. And now, here he is, barely surviving—but indeed surviving. It's as if he's made survival the purpose of his life, to prove to himself and others that this strange and vicious disease can indeed be battled, and that Peter Vom Lehn is going to win. It is his greatest challenge and he has met it head-on and unflinching. I don't think he has any long-term goals such as what he would do with his life if he should be cured. Maybe he'd find himself with nothing to do. But at this point, it hardly matters.

Friday, September 14

Today is the ninth day of the DHPG treatment. Peter is increasingly impatient to go home, sleep in his own bed, not be awakened for his vital signs, IV's started or stopped, and no more poking and prodding by many hands. Especially annoying is being awakened before seven A.M. to be weighed. It does seem rather contradictory that a patient hospitalized for a wasting disease should be wakened from his much-needed sleep.

His mental status appears excellent. He still has some memory lapses, but he's far better than even two months ago. Dr. McCutchan tested him the other day and was astonished. Peter could repeat eight digits back to him speedily and correctly. ''He's really quite bright. I couldn't do that," the doctor remarked. But names are difficult. I risk his anger and correct him, hoping repetition will help his memory. I wonder if his bursts of anger are caused by his brain infection—a personality change like his phobias and reclusivity, or are they his way of angering at his disease?

Dr. Spector and Wendy enter, interrupting my thoughts, and greet us.

"Well, Peter, we've been discussing the possibility of further treatment," Dr. Spector starts. "You probably think that the DHPG hasn't done much because you still can't use your left eye, but actually the vision in it has improved, even if only through that small tunnel. The peripheral vision is still no better, but your vision through that opening has improved from 20/200 to 20/50."

"The eye is still virtually useless to me, though," Peter comments.

"I know, for all practical purposes, it doesn't function," agrees the doctor. "But I'm hoping the peripheral vision might still improve. Also, your diarrhea seems to be better, and the CMV is not culturing as fast as before, which could indicate that the drug is having some effect." He sounds hopeful, encouraging.

"What we would like to do is to give you a back-to-back treatment; that is, initiate a new course of ten days."

"I don't know about that. I have to get out of here for awhile first. I just couldn't stand another ten days right away."

"Well, maybe that could be arranged, or perhaps we could arrange somehow for you to get the treatments on an outpatient basis."

"Good, thank you." Peter smiles.

"All right. We'll be discussing the idea of more treatment between ourselves, and then with you later." He smiles kindly at Peter and they leave.

Sunday, September 16

Peter and I walk slowly along the sidewalk outside the hospital. It won't be a long walk today, but a little fresh air and exercise is better than none. The sun is low, but the

vivid sunset colors he loves haven't appeared yet. Peter's
gait is slightly irregular and he's leaning slightly to the
left. He doesn't seem to be placing his feet down properly
with each step. Maybe it's just the new sneakers he's not
used to, they are too big.

We approach the outpatient entrance on the east side of
the building.

"Let's go back, I'm tired," Peter says.

"Okay," I answer, and we start up the sidewalk to the
door. The glass doors open automatically and he suddenly
rushes in, heads to the right, his feet tripping, and almost
falls to the floor. An Oriental man sitting on the floor with
his two children jumps up quickly to grab him. Peter tries
to struggle to his feet and the man helps him to a chair.

"I'm sorry," Peter mumbles. The two small children
stare at him, eyes wide. Peter is upset, shaken.

"Let's just sit here a few minutes," he says.

"Of course, as long as you want," I reply.

"Okay, let's go upstairs now." Peter rises and I stand,
ready to help him, but he wants to walk alone.

Back upstairs, Peter eyes his bed gratefully and changes
back into his hospital gown. The brief foray outside has
tired him more than expected, and I feel apprehensive.
Why the imbalance?

Monday, September 17

I was up at five-thirty this morning so as to be here in
time to take Peter off the hyper-al. Tonight will be my first
time to hook up the IV feeding alone. There will be no
buzzers, no nurse to answer it, if I have problems. Even
though the nurses assure me I'm doing well, I feel uneasy.
I hope everything will be ready for Peter to leave by noon,
though I have my doubts.

A nurse comes in, Peter gets in a wheelchair, and we
are off to the eye clinic, for the required series of photographs after the DHPG treatment. We wheel him to the
photography room. A technician enters, asks Peter to sit
behind the camera lens, and adjusts the lens. Fortunately,
everything seems to be moving quickly today, for a change.

I sit beside a small table that has all of Peter's past slides of his retina laid out on a light table. I glance at them and can see the fuzzy, white masses obscuring the retina. Not a happy sight.

We return upstairs. The intern enters and removes the sutures from the catheter incision site. The incision has healed well and the scar will be barely noticeable.

Miraculously, the familiar brown bag of medications arrives before eleven. There are fourteen different drugs, and the pharmacist explains them carefully. I am relieved to see that the medications have been vastly reduced. The Dilantin is down to 200 milligrams, and there are now just two drugs to treat the tuberculosis—ansamycin and clofazimine.

By eleven-thirty, we are on our way home. The day is hot and sunny as we park in front of the apartment. Peter breathes deeply in the cool shade of the living room, then goes directly to his own room. The window is open and a pleasing breeze wafts through the room. He surveys the new arrangements made to accommodate life with a hyper-alimentation apparatus. The IV stand to hold the two pumps and the two plastic bags will be in the bathroom corner nearest the door and his bed so that he can get to the bathroom at night. Extension of the IV tubing and the pumps' electric cord will give him enough slack. I found an inexpensive, small TV stand on wheels, the top shelf at bed height, to keep his glasses, water, and books easily available, and all the hyper-al supplies I will need when connecting and disconnecting his tubes.

Apparently satisfied with the new arrangement, Peter strips down to his underpants and goes into the bathroom, glancing in the large mirror over the sink—and glances again, in pleased surprise at his improved appearance. At last, with a heartfelt "Aah," he lies back on his own bed.

I hear a knock on the door. Joanne, the hyper-al nurse, is here to help us unpack the supplies and set everything up. She helps me unpack and assemble the stand and the pumps, and we store the supplies: boxes of rubber gloves; Betadine and alcohol swabs; gauze pads of different sizes; rolls of paper and silk tape; cotton-tipped swabs; bottles of

Betadine Solution; two sizes of syringes and needles; plastic tubing, extension tubing, and tube filters; catheter caps; plastic clamps. In the hospital, the nurses brought me only enough supplies for each session. Two weeks' supplies take up a lot of space, and I shall have to clear another shelf.

The company that manufactures the hyper-al supplies delivered a small refrigerator to store 1000-cc. bags of central formula, heparin for flushing out the catheter, and small bottles of multivitamins. Two more boxes contain 500-cc. bottles of the white fats and lipids solution. These need not be refrigerated.

"Okay, you're all set," Joanne tells me. "Think you'll be able to manage it alone tonight?"

"I hope so." I laugh nervously.

"You'll do just fine," she says. "Just in case of problems, this is our number." She hands me a card. "There's always someone on call, and if I'm not there, they'll know where to find me and I'll call you back. In an emergency, be sure to tell whoever answers that it's an emergency, though."

"Thanks so much," I tell her gratefully as she leaves.

Peter sleeps all afternoon, his first sleep in three weeks without interruption. Walter arrived in town last night for a medical conference, and is staying at the Intercontinental Hotel downtown. He calls from the hotel after his meetings to see how we are and visits later for an hour. Afterward, I connect Peter to his many tubes, working slowly and nervously. I prime the tubing, connect it, and am pleased it all went well. We watch television in his room, go to sleep early. We are both happy and relieved not to be in the hospital anymore.

Saturday, September 22

Peter's spirits have been good this week, but a new complication worries me. Whenever he gets up, he complains of dizziness, lack of balance, nausea, and a bothersome pain in his right ear. Two nights ago, he vomited when he got up for the bathroom.

And this afternoon, Walter took him to see his hotel.

"Guess what," Peter said wryly when they returned. "I managed to upchuck all over the Intercontinental Hotel."

"You what?" I asked.

"Yup. We went up in the elevator to Dad's room, and I barely made it into his bathroom. God, imagine if I'd done it all over the elevator."

"Do you think the elevator made you sick?" I asked. Peter has always had motion sickness, but a short ride in an elevator is hardly upsetting.

"Yeah, probably," he answered nonchalantly.

"What did you do the rest of the afternoon?" I asked.

"After we got through with that act, we talked in Dad's room for awhile. Then we decided to go over to that shopping area by the bay, Seaport Village. It's connected to the hotel by a wooden walkway. We used the wheelchair, but what a bumpy ride. It's all very quaint but really rough on a wheelchair. Funny, though, when Dad stopped the chair, I felt sick again, like everything was spinning. At least I didn't throw up again. Wouldn't that have been cute, in front of all the little old ladies from Des Moines?"

Tuesday, September 25

"Okay, Peter, come on in," the nurse calls us in at Owen Clinic. "Let's weigh you first . . . 121 pounds, good," she comments. We help him off the scales. He lists unsteadily.

"Well, that's funny," I say. "This morning I took him to the hyper-al clinic and he weighed six pounds more. I think the scales aren't adjusted the same."

"It's all that running around I did today," jokes Peter. We follow the nurse to an examining room and Peter lies down on the table.

"Hi, babe!" Phyllis bubbles into the room, chart in hand. "What can we do for you tonight? How've you been since you left the hospital?"

"Pretty good, really. Though I managed to upchuck all over the Intercontinental Hotel last Saturday when I went there with my father," he tells her, smiling tiredly.

"Well, nothing like going in class, I always say. Go on," she urges him.

"I've been nauseated off and on, throwing up some, especially when I get up, but sometimes if I just change position lying down," he continues.

"How's your walking?" she asks.

"I get really dizzy when I'm up and I'm afraid of falling, though I haven't yet."

"How long has this been going on?"

"The dizziness started when I first went into the hospital at the end of August, and has been getting worse slowly," he answers. "Dr. Rothrock took me off Dilantin for a couple of days to see if I was getting too much, but it didn't really help."

"I thought you said it did," I interrupt.

"No. The first day or two, I thought maybe it did. But I think I was trying to convince myself that was the cause. It kept on." He hadn't told me—or anyone. I hadn't noticed it until he fell that night in the hospital lobby.

"I've had a painful earache for about two weeks, too, in my right ear," he adds.

"Okay, we'll take a look in there," Phyllis assures him.

"When you walk, do you lean to one side or the other?" she asks, helping him to sit up slowly and carefully.

"To the right," he answers.

"All I can see in there is a lot of wax, I don't think there's any damage. The eardrums look intact." Phyllis squints through the small, lighted eye instrument. "Do you have a sore throat, any trouble swallowing?"

"Yes, my throat feels sort of irritated. I thought maybe it was the drugs. That's just the last two or three days, though," he replies.

"Okay, Dr. McCutchan will check your ears, too. Now, how about the herpes?"

"I'm not sure, but I think something's coming back— it's not very painful, though."

"Let's take a look at your eyes. Do you feel there's any change in your vision?" she asks.

"No, I think it's the same. I just can't use the right eye at all," he says resignedly.

Dr. McCutchan pushes the door open, greets us, and checks Phyllis' notes. "I think I'll give Dr. Rothrock a call in the morning about your vertigo and ear pain, Peter. You could have an ear infection." He turns to me. "Why don't you call me tomorrow and I'll let you know what we've discussed. See you here in a week, Peter."

I don't believe it's just an ear infection.

Wednesday, September 26

"And if it is this ear infection—labyrinthitis—causing his vertigo, is it possible it could spread to the brain? I mean, because the ear is so close to the brain?" I ask Dr. McCutchan.

"Oh, yes, most definitely," he responds. "If it hasn't already."

There it is. My worst fear.

Thursday, September 27

"It looks like we're not going to make it to Hawaii in October, Peter," I say, sitting on the chair in his room. "We've got to get you over this vertigo thing before you can go anywhere. Do you think we should plan for November, except that's Thanksgiving, or wait till after Christmas?"

"No, no, we should plan for November. We could be back in time for Thanksgiving, we're only going for two weeks. Maybe the first two weeks in November."

"Okay, let's plan on that. We'll have to decide pretty soon and start making reservations," I tell him.

Why not?

12

Monday, October 1

I am so discouraged. I wanted with all my heart for
Peter to regain a little strength—just a little—to enjoy
living for a while. But it is being denied. His life for the
last nine months has been nothing but fight, fight, fight. I
don't know how he continues motivating himself.

AIDS is constant warfare, an unending siege. The patient is like a small, weakly defended country surrounded
by mighty powers. It fights fiercely to defend itself from
invasion, but its weapons are few and primitively inadequate. And, little by little, the big powers overtake the
small one, gobbling its territory bit by bit. One day,
nothing will remain. No one will remember it ever existed.

Peter has been sleeping almost around the clock this
week. He's been told to stay in bed and, strangely, the
enforced bedrest has not made him impatient and restless,
as I expected. Indeed, he seems patiently resigned to it.
We still talk about the trip to Hawaii, making detailed
plans, but it's a fantasy game. Every day, I feel more
frightening apprehension. I can't sleep more than four
hours a night. And yet, I don't feel tired. Tension has its
own energy.

And Peter's strangely peaceful resignation frightens me
most.

Tuesday, October 2

Joanne took more blood this morning at the hyper-al clinic, and told us that the results since two weeks ago are very encouraging. Peter's general nutritional state has improved and they are unexpectedly pleased. I don't understand why he has less stamina and energy than before if he is better nourished. Here he is, relatively well-nourished, weighing more than since he left New York, even looking healthier—and yet something still eats away his life strength. He is wasting, wasting, wasting.

I hate pushing him around to all these clinics. He barely had the strength to get himself out of bed today, and I feel it's cruel. The end of his life is near and it seems unfair to waste his time with more futile poking, prodding, testing. I know they can do nothing, and I think he is losing hope, too.

Another appointment in the Neurology Clinic. Dr. Rothrock finishes the usual litany of neurological tests with good results. Peter's acuity and memory are intact and he's alert, conversing intelligently. The doctor examines his eyes carefully, asks him to stand. Peter lurches suddenly and the doctor grabs his arm and assists him upright.

"Now, Peter, close your eyes."

Peter closes his eyes and immediately falls to the right. Dr. Rothrock grabs him again.

"What do you feel like when you're standing?" he asks.

"I feel as if the world is moving to the left," Peter answers. "And I have this weird feeling, like sloshing in my right ear."

"Mmm. I don't like the way this labyrinthitis is lasting so long. Usually, it's self-limiting, about a week's duration," he muses.

"I'm going to send you to the ENT Clinic. I want them to check out your ear more carefully than I can, then I'll consult with them. I'm also going to put you on Antivert®

That's aimed at vertigo specifically, and take you off Tegretol and Dilantin for now. I'll give you 120 milligrams daily of phenobarbital instead, for anti-seizure medication. It's possible we may have to do another spinal tap, too, if this thing keeps up.''

"Oh, no," groans Peter.

"I'm sorry." Dr. Rothrock smiles apologetically.

We go home and Peter drops into bed. His walking has been terrible today, lurching wildly, but he refused to use his cane or to lean on me. He takes an extreme lurch to the right, a big step, then a smaller lurch to the left, two short steps, as if to right himself. And he continues to plant his entire sole on the ground instead of heel-toe. I walk as closely behind him as possible to catch him as he zigzags.

I'm considering sleeping in his room again. I hear him up, bumping and banging during the night, and I am terrified that he might lurch and tear the catheter out of his chest. And the diarrhea is back in full strength, though without incontinence. I am again leaping out of bed at the least noise.

Wednesday, October 3

"How do you plan to pay for the test?" the bored secretary asks.

"He's on MediCal, don't they pay for it?" I ask, surprised.

"No, not unless you petition for payment," she answers.

"And that surely takes three weeks, right?" I smile ironically.

"That's right."

"Well, I guess you better start the petition," I tell her. "Would you please let me know right away when it's accepted? And how long does it take to get an appointment for the test?"

"At least a week."

My God! Four weeks at least! We don't have that much time to wait around. Controlling my voice, I tell her, "Please let me know right away, we're in a hurry to get it scheduled."

"Yes, of course," she replies.

I feel tears of desperation in my eyes. Peter has just been examined by the doctor here in the ENT Clinic, who cleaned out the wax in his ear and found nothing abnormal, but recommended an ENG, or electronystagmographic test, to determine whether the current infection causing vertigo and nausea is based in the ear or the brain.

Doesn't anyone understand we don't have time to waste? If it's another brain infection, we must treat it right away, at least do our best. Even another week could be too late. If it's an ear infection, it must be treated promptly, so that it doesn't spread to the brain.

Insensitive bureaucracy raises its head again, and the bucket empties faster and faster. Is Peter right, that nobody listens and nobody cares?

Thursday, October 4

"Hello, Dr. Robertson?" I have finally located the doctor who saw Peter yesterday in the ENT Clinic. "I'm Barbara Peabody, mother of the AIDS patient you saw yesterday in ENT, Peter Vom Lehn."

"Oh, yes, what can I do for you?"

"The clinic secretary told me that the ENG test will take three weeks to be approved by MediCal," I start. "I was wondering, how much does the test cost?"

"I think it's $130," he answers.

"And how long to get the results?"

"About one week," he replies. The addition is easy: three weeks for approval, another for scheduling, another for the results. Five weeks till we'd even know where the infection is, and if in the brain, *more* testing to determine the area, if possible. By then, he could be dead.

"All right," I say resolutely. "I'm going to pay for the test. I'll call the clinic to schedule it. Thank you."

I call the clinic, introduce myself to the secretary, tell her to cancel the petition and make Peter's appointment as soon as possible. "The earliest would be October 12," she tells me. My God, that's nine days!

"Do you ever have cancelations?" I ask anxiously.

"No, not for that test," she tells me.

"All right," I say hurriedly. "Please make it for then and let me know if there are any cancelations. It's very important." I hang up, angry and frustrated.

If that test is so important for so many people, why don't they have more people doing it, schedule them faster?

Monday, October 8

I'm back to my midnight vigil on the patio. Everything is a mess. I feel it's all running away from me faster and faster, and I can't control it. But then, for ten months now, control has been only an illusion.

Yesterday, Peter didn't wake up till eight P.M., when I started preparing his hyper-al. I was almost frantic with worry. Every time I spoke to him, tried to rouse him, he opened his eyes halfway. His eyes were unseeing and he didn't respond, as if he were drugged. Maybe the phenobarbital and the Antivert are drugging him. I don't know.

And today, Peter slept till six P.M. All he ate was a few teaspoonfuls of white rice or yogurt. Two teaspoonfuls of white rice or yogurt are all he ever wants now. He went into the bathroom an hour later and I heard him vomiting. I thought the Antivert would stop the vomiting. I cleaned him up and he accepted my help passively. A bad sign.

Later, he roused a little and we tried to watch a movie on television, but the reception on his set was so bad we decided to watch it in the living room. I helped him stagger to the couch to lie down, and I sat in the rocking chair. Because of the movie, I didn't even start the hyper-al till eleven o'clock. He's asleep now while I taper up the formula. I hope the damned thing doesn't start beeping tonight, as it often does, signaling a malfunction.

The diarrhea is back in full force. It's not as frequent as before, but he can't get to the bathroom in time. "When will it ever stop?" he moaned downheartedly last night. The truth is that it never will.

I can't persuade him to go outside for a short walk, and I'm afraid his muscle tone and circulation will deteriorate even more lying in bed all the time. I know that he's afraid people will laugh at him because of his staggering gait, thinking he's either drunk or crazy. But he won't even go out when it's dark and no one would see him, not even for a few steps.

He staggers and lurches so erratically that I have taken all the pictures and paintings off the hallway wall so that he won't be hurt if one breaks. He literally ricochets down the hall. I am wondering, too, if the sight in his left eye is starting to go, though neither he nor any of the doctors has mentioned it.

He's afraid now to take a shower, afraid he'll fall and hit himself on the tiled walls. Nor will he take a bath. It's too painful to sit on the porcelain, he says, but I think he's afraid he might slide under the water. When he has to shower after an attack of diarrhea, we hang the IV tubing over the shower door. I try to hold it up there with one hand while scrubbing him rapidly with the other. I tell him to stand facing the corner of the stall so he can hold the walls with his hands, then I quickly squeeze soapy water over him. He has only had sponge baths now for five days.

Strangely, Peter has been discouraged but not depressed. His few spells of bad humor have been brief. However, he did admit last night that this newest infection causing the vertigo has him discouraged. Discouraged! It has me frantic with pain, terror, anxiety. I'm sure it's in the brain, not the ear, and I'm sure it's the damned CMV. And above and beyond my frenzied fears hovers not only anger but a desperate helplessness that I cannot quell anymore.

He still talks of going to Hawaii, though now that even November is out of the question, he thinks it best to wait until April. I suggested January again, but he says there are too many tourists there then and the prices are too high. "It'd be better to wait till April, no tourists and the flowers will be blooming," he told me.

Oh, Peter, you know we're not going to go, you know your time is too short. Are you carrying on the Hawaii dream because you don't want to hurt me with the realization of how little time is left? I know you are starting to let go and I can't hold you back.

Tuesday, October 9

"I'm going over to Bertha's for half an hour," I tell Peter. It's about eight P.M. and he's lying in bed watching television. He looks relaxed and as if he won't need any help. "How about a sponge bath when I come back?"

"All right," he agrees.

I am always fearful now of leaving, since he can't get to the kitchen to use the phone without help. But surely half an hour will be safe.

I return. Peter is sitting in the rocking chair, wrapped in a large towel, his hair sticking up in damp spikes.

"What are you doing up?" I ask him, alarmed.

"I did 'caca' in the bed," he explains with an apologetic smile.

My heart sinks. Why do things *always* happen when I'm not here?

"I took a shower," he adds.

"Oh, Peter, don't do that without my being here," I say anxiously.

"But I got too dizzy, couldn't even get all the soap off in time, and I'm afraid the bed's a mess," he apologizes.

It is, indeed. I hurriedly strip the sheets, pillowcases and mattress pad off the bed. I throw them quickly in the bathtub and fill it with hot water and bleach. I go back to his bathroom. I am so angry at this disease, at myself for not being here.

I scrub everything with ammonia and bleach, put clean sheets on the bed, and help him back in. He lies down, relieved.

"How about a backrub?"

"Oh, that would be good." He turns on his left side, facing the wall. I rub his back and legs. As before, they are aching from being bedridden. Suddenly, without warning, he vomits.

"Just a minute!" I run for more towels and gently pull the pillows from under him to change their cases again. Luckily, the sheets are untouched. Everything clean again,

I resume the backrub, sitting on the edge of the bed and talking quietly to reassure him.

"You know, I had some ideas the other day. Maybe, as soon as we can get rid of this vertigo, we could make a small, local trip, over to the mountains or up the coast."

"Maybe we could go to Arrowhead," he suggests.

"That would be nice, neither of us has ever been there. Or maybe up the coast, there are some nice places just in Del Mar or Oceanside." I see his eyes brighten. "Just go for a couple of days and stay somewhere really deluxe. You know, really blow our wad. What do you think?"

"We could go visit Miriam and Seymour," he suggests. I am taken aback. They live north of San Francisco, somewhat further than what I had in mind.

"Well . . . we could," I agree. "They've invited us. Aunt Charlotte has, too, and they're only an hour apart so we could combine them in one trip. But if it takes you awhile to recover from this thing, maybe we should try a small, closer jaunt first," I venture. I don't want him to set impossible goals anymore.

He nods in agreement.

"I wish we had one of those mini-vans," I tell him wistfully, rubbing his calves and feet. "Then you could lie down in back and be comfortable while we travel. All the hyper-al stuff would fit in, too. Maybe when you're up and around again we could go out looking at vans."

"Yeah, that'd be good," he agrees.

But I cry inside. I know we'll never get the van. We'll never go anywhere. I know, and he knows, that the fight is almost over but we cannot admit it to each other. Neither wants to accept defeat.

Wednesday, October 10

Peter has had an ugly blemish on his left temple for over a week now. It started as an angry pimple, then became brown and cratered in the center and very tender to the touch. It is now the size of a quarter. The doctor in the ENT Clinic asked Peter about it last week, and he said he thought it was a pimple.

Yesterday, I noticed another smaller spot on his left shoulder. And this morning another on his back. And as I disconnected the hyper-al, I saw one more on his right forearm.

They could be Kaposi's sarcoma lesions.

Late this morning, I contacted Dr. Matthews. Dr. McCutchan is out of town. I described the spots to him and he was immediately concerned and made an appointment for us at two-thirty in the Urgent Medicine Clinic. I waited till one to try to awaken Peter. He didn't want to go, but I finally rousted him from bed and into clothing.

"Hello, Peter, I haven't seen you for a long time," Dr. Andia, his intern during the July hospitalization, is now on duty in Urgent Medicine.

"Hi, how are you?" he asks listlessly.

"Oh, I'm fine. Let's see those spots I heard you have," she says, helping him to take his shirt off. She inspects the purplish spots carefully, then examines his chest and abdomen and listens with her stethoscope.

"Any cough recently?"

"No."

"And the diarrhea?"

"Yes, I still have it," he replies dejectedly.

"Peter, I'm going to take some scrapings of these lesions to send to the lab. It won't hurt. Then the dermatologist will be in to look at them, too." She carefully takes minute scrapings from two of the lesions and smears them onto a slide. An older woman in a white coat enters, and Dr. Andia introduces her as the dermatologist. With a magnifying glass, she inspects the lesions, then straightens up.

"No, they're definitely not Kaposi's sarcoma," she states firmly. "Most likely, they're herpes lesions. The lab results should tell us by tomorrow. Meanwhile, put acyclovir ointment on them and come back tomorrow to see Dr. Matthews."

I exhale. I feel as if I've held my breath for days.

Thursday, October 11

"Your weight is holding steady at 122 pounds, Peter," the nurse tells him. "Blood pressure 200/70, temperature

94.7 degrees. Come on in here and lie down to wait for the doctor.''

We follow the nurse. She helps Peter onto the table and puts a pillow under his head. Dr. Matthews enters.

''I'm going to take another scraping, Peter. The ones they took yesterday came back negative for herpes, but I want to run them through again.'' He bends over Peter's forearm. ''Give me a call tomorrow to see what the results are.''

''How's the vertigo today?'' he asks Peter.

''It's pretty bad,'' Peter answers. ''I just stay in bed all the time, then it doesn't bother me as much. My right ear—well, actually, the right side of my face and my eye—sort of burn when I touch them.''

''Hmm.'' The doctor peers closely at his face. ''No lesions on that side,'' he comments. ''Well, I want you to discontinue the acyclovir on the lesions. Just use hot, wet compresses for a while.''

''Okay.''

''Make an appointment for next Thursday night, or call me if you have any problems.''

Peter dresses and we leave, after making the appointment for next Thursday. He refused to let me bring the wheelchair with us and had lurched and staggered into the clinic when we arrived, refusing my help irately. Instead, he had stumbled to the wall and walked slowly alongside it, his hands stepping their way across it and barely holding him up. He had come to a recessed doorway and I ran to keep him from falling, but he said angrily, ''I can do it!'' and I moved back.

Now, as we leave the clinic, he staggers across the waiting room from one chair to another. Outside in the hall, he again refuses my help and we make our way erratically to the elevator. Everything must be turning around him as if he were inside a kaleidoscope. It must be so terrifying, and I feel my heart beating wildly in fear of his falling. Yet I admire his steadfast insistence on walking alone, his attempt to keep control of his environment.

Peter leans tiredly against the elevator wall, his face lined and his eyes half-closed.

"Would you mind bringing me that wheelchair over there?" he asks me weakly as we leave the elevator on the first floor. His strength is gone.

"Sure, just a minute." I run to bring it. He has trouble seating himself, doesn't know where to put his feet. I wheel him quickly to the car. I must get him home and in bed as soon as possible.

I park him in front of his door, unlock it, and help him into the car. He is so weak I have to help place his legs and body inside, but at least he is not mentally confused.

At the apartment, I help him out of the car and he takes off up the sidewalk. I run after him. "Wait a minute!" I cry. But he mumbles something about doing it himself and rushes headlong, zigzagging and stumbling along the walkway. He reaches the wooden fence enclosing our small patio, grabs for its support. He careens as he crosses the gap between the fence and the building wall and I leap, thinking he'll fall, but he rights himself. I unlock the door quickly. He blunders down the hall to his room. I don't know how he did it without falling or bruising himself, but he did. And I collapse into the rocking chair with relief, amused, now, at his stubborn pride and independence.

He lies quietly on his back, staring thoughtfully ahead. Does he want to talk? I'm not sure. I sit on the edge of his bed a moment.

"What are you thinking about?"

"I don't want to talk about it," he answers, turning his head away. I wait a minute. Nothing more. Every day, he is loosening more threads, knotting them and clipping them off, and I can't splice them back together.

It's getting late.

Friday, October 12

Peter had his ENG test done in the ENT Clinic this morning. The results won't be available for a week.

When I took him there, they told me the test would take three hours and I told them I would be in the cafeteria. There's no place else to wait. I returned to the clinic 15 minutes early and found him asleep, stretched across several benches. All the personnel had gone to lunch, apparently. Someone had just helped him out to the waiting room and left him. I was angry that they abandoned him there, after telling me that the test would be three hours.

Tuesday, October 16

I've been sleeping in Peter's room for several nights now. Though he told Dr. Matthews that the diarrhea wasn't bad, actually it's been relentless for almost two weeks. I have become very adept at sliding rubber gloves on in two seconds flat. I keep four or five towels hanging on the towel racks, and a pile of eight or ten clean washcloths on the toilet tank next to another pile of clean underpants.

I also keep an opened box of adult diapers next to the toilet, so he can get them out easily. Now that it's not as hot, he can bear to use them again, though they aren't very efficient. I also keep a plastic wastebasket half-filled with a strong bleach solution so that he can throw used underpants there, and a plastic-lined wastebasket next to that for the diapers.

We are quite organized.

A week ago, he decided to stop eating anything solid in hopes that the diarrhea might halt if his intestines were empty, but to no avail. The diarrhea is a relentless destroyer.

Last Thursday, I asked Dr. Matthews if the diarrhea could be due to the hyper-al, could it be too rich and need readjustment. He was writing on Peter's chart. He paused a moment, a strange, sad look on his face, and mumbled softly, "No, it's from the CMV."

He gave Peter a kind, apologetic smile, turned back and said quietly, "There's nothing more we can do."

I don't think Peter heard him. Oh, God, I thought, please don't say that, the words I have feared for so many months.

I feel desperately discouraged, but also confused. I see Peter starting to let go, loosening. And yet, when he does speak, his voice soft and slurry, it is of a trip. We still discuss where we might go and the postponed trip to

Hawaii. I can't tell if he really wants to give up now or not. Maybe he's not aware that he's loosening. Maybe there is a force inside, unclenching his tensely clutched fists, slowly opening his fingers out and relaxing his grasp. Or maybe he's so tired that he's unaware of its touch on his thin fingers.

All I know is that if he does still want to fight, something must be done to help him. I am not ready to let him go. I see death coming, and I resent it angrily. I'm willing to bargain, I'm willing even to let him go, if he could only have one or two good weeks—no, even four or five days. I just want so passionately for him to feel normal for a little while. Then I'll let him go in peace. I know he has to.

I've been rubbing acyclovir ointment into the four original lesions for three days now, even though the doctor said not to. They seem to be scabbing and healing, but yesterday I found two new lesions: one on the left shoulder, the other on his stomach. Another may be starting on his right leg. I think the ointment helps and I apply it to the new spots, too. What can it hurt?

The lack of coordination and the vertigo are so upsetting. His signature on his last Social Security check was completely illegible. When he takes his pills, I have to place the glass of water carefully in his hand or it will spill. It did, once, and he shrieked in angry surprise at the cold water. He cannot fish the pills out of the small, plastic cup I use for each dosage. His fingers fumble, drop the tablets, and I hand them to him, making sure he feels them in the palm of his hand. I wonder if he sees them.

Last night, I convinced him to take a bath in the tub, and I lined the bottom with thick towels. He wanted me to stay with him but didn't want my help. He has not bothered to shave (and I am reminded of Ron) for days, even though he complains of how uncomfortable his beard is. I have offered to shave him but he refuses.

But last night while bathing, he decided to shave and asked me to bring his razor. For 40 minutes, he shaved his cheeks as if in slow motion. He could not coordinate his hands, and his face was left with uneven patches of black beard. He looked so pitiable. He has always liked to be clean-shaven. But he didn't care.

There is only one more thing I can do, one small hope—another course of DHPG. This was discussed both in the hospital and when Wendy drew Peter's blood for the follow-up tests. I feel sure the CMV has invaded his brain and want to know what the decision is regarding more treatment, but Dr. Spector has been away. Yesterday, I left several messages, hating myself for being a nuisance but driven by anxiety. He finally answered my calls last night, apologizing graciously for not being able to call earlier.

"We would like to repeat the treatment, maybe at a double dosage, as you mentioned," I told him, trying to talk sanely. "Peter's diarrhea is back, very severely, but it almost disappeared while he was on the drug and for a short time afterward. He's also developed lesions on his body that look like herpes even though twice they've tested negative. Topical acyclovir seems to help them. And the last few weeks, he's had vertigo, getting steadily worse. He's completely bedridden now."

"I'm still very interested in giving him another course, especially to see if it arrests the diarrhea again, as I think that's due to CMV colitis," he told me. "But first, I'll have to do some preliminary investigation. I think that a prolonged course at the same dosage would be more advisable than a shorter course on a higher dosage. It's been used on 16 patients now, and I need to know if any have taken it for a longer period and, if so, what the results or side-effects might have been. I'll let you know when I find out."

I felt better after speaking with him. His voice was kind and concerned. I know it's not a cure for the primary disease, but maybe—if it works—maybe he'll have a little good time, just a little.

That's all I ask for now.

Thursday, October 18

Peter is lying across a row of benches in Owen Clinic. His father arrived today for a four-day visit and is with us.

I was relieved that Peter wanted to bring the wheelchair tonight. And sad. At least, his former insistence on trying to walk meant he was still fighting.

"Okay, Peter, come on in," the nurse says. We wheel Peter to an examining room, help him to lie down on the table.

"Peter, I don't like this weakness." Dr. Matthews is sitting at the desk, writing on his chart after examining Peter. "I'm going to put you in the hospital. I want a dermatologist and a neurologist to see you."

No, no, no. I don't want him to go in the hospital again. He doesn't want to be there. This time, finally, I am terrified he won't get out again and I know he is, too. We've never discussed it, but I know he does not want to die in the hospital.

"Peter, is that all right with you?" I turn to him. *Please say no.*

"I don't want to go back in the hospital," he protests softly.

Good. Don't go back in. There's nothing more they can do for you. Stay home.

"It would be easier on you to have consults if you're in the hospital. You wouldn't have to make so many trips," Dr. Matthews urges.

"I suppose that's true," I have to agree. I already feel so cruel rousing him from comatose sleep, forcing him out of the house for his many clinic visits. After all, he could leave the hospital if it were unbearable. He could sign himself out against orders.

"Okay," agrees Peter, finally. "But I don't want to go in from here, they always take so long to get a bed," he bargains, still unwilling to give up all control. "I'd like to go in the morning."

That would be wiser. After waiting, giving his history several times, reviewing his medications—all the interminable admission procedures—it would be midnight before he could sleep.

"That's fine, Peter," Dr. Matthews concurs. "You call admissions in the morning to see when his room is ready," he tells me. "I'll see you there tomorrow, then." He smiles sadly at Peter, collects the charts and leaves. I wonder how many times he has shepherded these young men to their inevitable deaths, has witnessed the end of hope.

Peter allows us to help him. Walter and I wheel him to the car, later to the apartment and down the hall, and he falls back into bed.

"Mom," Peter addresses me. I have started assembling his hyper-al, and his father sits in the rocking chair, watching, before returning to his hotel.

"Yes?" I answer.

"Would you please make me two signs to take to the hospital?"

"Sure, I'd be glad to. What do you want them to say?"

"I want one to ask that nobody disturb me before . . . mmm . . . I guess before eight A.M. I don't want any more of that being hauled out of bed to be weighed at dawn," he requests. "And the other is to say, 'No Visitors.' "

"Okay." Walter and I laugh. He still fights for his rights and his privacy.

Friday, October 19

I start calling the admissions office at eight-thirty. No room, call later. Apparently, part of the hospital is being remodeled and rooms are scarce, especially private rooms.

Three-thirty. Peter's room is finally available. I wake him, help him dress. I already packed his suitcase and laid out his clothes. Walter waits with the wheelchair in the hall. I know Peter won't insist on walking.

"Why are you taking all that money to the hospital with you, Peter?" He's stuffing a wad of bills into his back pocket.

"Because I want to," he answers gruffly.

"Peter, I don't think you should take so much money. Things get stolen in hospitals, you know. How much have you got there?"

"Ninety dollars," he answers.

"That's an awful lot. What are you going to need it for there? There's nothing you can buy."

"I don't care, I want to take it with me," he insists.

I say no more.

We stop in the admissions office to get Peter's room number. But there is confusion over his room assignment and the girls are chattering, gossiping among themselves while I stand waiting impatiently.

An hour passes before a woman finally comes to take us upstairs. Peter signs the admission form illegibly—a few slashed lines—and we follow the woman up to 10 East. She takes us to the nurses' station and leaves a sheaf of papers there. The nurses come to greet us. We are old friends now. "Well . . . here I am . . . again," Peter smiles weakly. I see the concern in their faces. They have seen him admitted six times, each time sicker, and they know he is nearing the end. How do they bear it?

Ironically, Peter's room is the first he had on 10 East, on the north side. I have always liked this room best. It is large and light, and the built-in cabinets are painted a bright, cobalt blue, cool and restful. I slide his clothes off gently, tie the hospital gown at his neck. He lies back, pale and depressed, but resigned. The admitting nurse takes his history and his vital signs. I can recite his history by memory, a common enough tale of AIDS.

Walter appears at the doorway, carrying a container of fresh, autumnal flowers, and hands it to me. I look at it in surprise, then at him.

"No . . . it's from Peter, not from me," he says, smiling. I look at Peter and open the small envelope. "Thanks. Love, Peter," reads the message in the script of a flower store employee.

"Oh, Peter . . . thank you so much."

"I thought they might brighten up the house for you," he says.

"Oh, they will, they certainly will," I exclaim. "I'll enjoy them. I'll put them on the dining table so I can see them all the time."

Tears beg release. How can he be so miserably ill and be thinking of doing something for me?

Saturday, October 20

I get to the hospital at noon. I wanted to come earlier but resisted, fearing I might disturb Peter if he were asleep.

He's awake, settling himself down again. A nurse is finishing mopping the floor by the bed.

"Hi," Peter greets me weakly. "Something awful just happened."

"What was it?" I ask, sitting down.

"I could feel the diarrhea coming, and I buzzed and buzzed and no one came, so I got up by myself and my IV wouldn't reach to the commode. Then I got terribly dizzy and fell down and threw up and the diarrhea came. I screamed, I was so scared the Hickman had come out, but no one came for about ten minutes, and I was lying in all that mess."

"Oh, damnit, Peter. I'm sorry I wasn't here. I could easily have been here earlier but I didn't want to disturb you." I curse vehemently. How could this happen? I boil with anger and frustration, indignant that he had to lie, helpless, in his own excrement and vomit. Where is the dignity in this wretched disease?

"Is the catheter all right?" I ask anxiously.

"Yes, I guess I just panicked," he says more calmly.

With reason, I think. He could hemorrhage if the tubing were pulled out.

I know one thing now. I can't leave him alone, even here in the hospital. I'll simply have to be here, and Walter can help till he leaves next Wednesday.

Sunday, October 21

Evening. Walter is here. Peter turns the TV on with his remote-control switch, but we are talking.

"Do you mind if I turn it off, Peter?" Walter asks. "We're not watching."

"Sure. I can't see it anyway," he says, slight irritation in his voice.

I glance at him quickly. His face is impassive. Oh, no, has he gone completely blind? He has said nothing about more loss of sight. Could he not want me to know?

I start the hyper-al procedure. The light is too dim for me.

"Peter, do you mind if I turn this overhead light on? I can't see what I'm doing."

"Sure, it doesn't matter," he answers quietly.

No, of course it doesn't.

Monday, October 22

"And how long have you had this pain on the right side of your face?" Dr. Rothrock asks Peter.

"About two months, I think, but it's only been bad the last two weeks." How odd. He only started mentioning it recently.

"Just what does it feel like, can you describe the pain?"

"It burns, feels hot, but also feels like pressure." He thinks a moment. "You know how you feel when you eat ice cream too fast?" He nods. "Well, that's how it feels, starting here, in the forehead,"—he raises his hand to his right temple—"And going to the top of my nose"—his hand traces the route—"all around my right eye, and almost to the hairline. It feels like it's just on top, my skin, it's not deep." He lowers his hand.

"Is it persistent, and does your position or coughing or straining affect it?" he asks as he writes notes.

"No, doesn't seem to make any difference what I'm doing. It's persistent, though Tylenol helps."

"I'm tentatively calling this an 'atypical trigeminal neuralgia.' Probably it and the headache are due to some ongoing infection, maybe CMV," Dr. Rothrock tells us. "It could be associated with the lesions, which could be herpes zoster, but I don't see the usual pattern of its erupting over nerve pathways, and we can't confirm it in the lab."

With AIDS, there are too many inconsistencies and contradictions that defy convenient labels. I wonder if all this poking, pushing, pricking, and prodding is worth-while.

Tuesday, October 23

I try to imagine how Peter feels. I cannot conceive of a world I can neither see nor hold. A world where every-thing swirls in a vortex around me, where if I try to place my foot, the ground flies away, and if I reach out, an object swoops away. I can't imagine it.

I can only guess at the terror of a familiar world lost forever.

Wednesday, October 24

I hear Peter speak, his eyes closed.

"What did you say?" I ask. But he isn't talking to me. He's talking to someone else, waiting for an answer, resuming his conversation. He's hallucinating. I catch an occasional word, but most are meaningless, though his tone of voice is conversational in cadence.

Peter, please come back to me.

Suddenly, he sits up, tries to slip his legs between the two side-rails.

"Just a minute, Peter, I'll help you." I jump up.

"No, I can do it alone, I don't need any help," I lower the side-rail and grab his arm. He veers sharply to the right.

"Let go, I can do it myself!" he insists angrily. We struggle as he lurches. I grab him, finally seat him on the commode.

"Damnit," he sputters. "I'm all right. It's just that you get in the way."

I chuckle at his indignant stubbornness.

"It's not funny," he snarls.

"I'm not laughing at you, Peter," I assure him. "It's just that I'm glad you have so much spirit."

"Hmmph," he mutters, as I help him back to bed.

*   *   *

Walter left for Virginia this morning. In a way, I'm glad I'm alone. I can simply turn off the world for awhile.

Thursday, October 25

"The CT scan shows a mass in the cerebellum that wasn't in his last CT scan in May," Dr. Matthews tells me in the evening. "We can't tell if it is blood or calcium; that is, a lesion, hemorrhage, or calcification. Calcification seems unlikely, though, because that takes longer than five months to build up."

"If it's a lesion, what's causing it?" I ask, knowing the futility of the question.

"It could be one of several things," he answers. "It could be the MAI, but he's already being treated for that. Could be toxoplasmosis, cryptococcidiosis—probably not herpes because of the location. And, of course, it could well be CMV. Other than that, toxoplasmosis is most likely."

"What can we do?" Another futile question, but hope dies fighting.

"There are three things we can do. Follow it along, doing nothing, and take a repeat CT scan in a few weeks to see what else develops. Or assume it's toxoplasmosis and treat him with pyrimethamine. The problem with that is that it lowers the white blood cell count, and that he doesn't need."

"No," I agree. "But if it did, is it reversible if you take him off the drug?"

"Yes, it is, and we'd be checking his white cells often for that reason.

"The third choice is to do a craniectomy and biopsy,"—I cringe—"and see what organisms grow out of that. Neurology has asked Neurosurgery to discuss that with us. The lesion is deep inside the head and we need to know how dangerous it would be, if the benefits outweigh the risks."

"I don't especially like that one," I say. "Besides, along with the danger of the surgery, it could all come out negative, right?"

"Yes, it could," he answers.

"Could this mass in the cerebellum be causing his facial pain?"

"No, it's not likely. We still don't know what that is. Probably herpes zoster, even though it doesn't fit the typical pattern. The neurologists and neurosurgeons will see Peter tomorrow, and probably by the next day we'll have something to tell you," he tells me, his face compassionate.

"All right. Thank you," I reenter Peter's room and look at Peter. He lies on his back, hands folded, face peaceful.

Oh, Peter. You don't know it, but I'm still fighting for you. I know it's near the end but I don't want you to go.

I don't want to lose you.

Friday, October 26

"How is he today?" the fourth-year medical student asks, starting his morning rounds.

"The same," I answer, smiling tiredly. Peter has been talking almost ceaselessly with his invisible people for three days now. The relentless activity in his brain gives him no rest, nor does the diarrhea, which is now uncontrollable. I lie on the other bed in his room, listening for every sound, jumping up at his slightest move. He tries to get out of bed, catching his legs in the side-rails, angry at the restraint. I am so tired.

"How do you feel today, Peter?" the student asks at the bedside.

"Fine," Peter answers laconically. He lies on his side with eyes closed.

"What day is it, Peter?"

"Mmm . . . October."

"And the year?"

"1984," Peter answers groggily.

"He seems fine to me. What did you mean by 'the same?' " the student asks skeptically.

"I meant that he's the same as he's been the last three days—hallucinating, talking to people, trying to get out of bed. Didn't you hear him say October for the day? Now ask him something more complex or detailed," I tell him, trying to keep my voice placid but screaming inside. He's gone crazy—can't you see it?

The student returns to the bedside. "Peter where is the hospital, what city are we in?"

"In Santa Fe . . . I mean, Santo Domingo," Peter answers, perplexed.

"We used to live in both those cities," I tell the student.

"Are you sure, Peter?" Probing.

Silence.

"Yes," Peter finally mumbles.

"Who am I, Peter?"

"Dunno."

"Who's the president?"

"Reagan."

"And before Reagan?" the student persists.

No answer. Peter has gone back into his own world. The student probes, tries to pull words out. Silence. Peter turns slightly onto his back, looks blankly in my direction.

"Give me that milk carton, please," he requests.

"There's no milk here, Peter," I tell him.

"Yes, there is, right on the table," he mumbles semicoherently.

"No, Peter, and you haven't been drinking milk since July, you know," I tell him firmly and look at the student. He nods, understanding.

"Okay, Peter. See you later." The student leaves.

"Mom?" Peter calls softly.

"Here I am, Peter," I move to the bedside. "What do you want?"

"I still want some milk, please."

"Peter, there isn't any milk. Remember? It's not on your diet."

"What do you mean, there isn't any milk? What do you think is in that carton on the table," he asks, irritated. "Please, just hand it to me, and a straw, too."

"Okay, Peter." I don't want to agitate him and turn, pretending to reach for a milk carton, and place it in his outstretched hand. "There it is," I say. Will he believe me?

"Thank you," he mutters, bringing the imagined carton closer, holding an invisible straw and starting to sip.

It is so real to him. He's so far away. But if this keeps him calm and secure, fine. Maybe this is better than reality.

I know now that I cannot go on without help. David has told me repeatedly that he can arrange to come if I need him. I've decided to call him.

"Hi," I turn, see my friend Lee in the doorway and join her.

"How's our boy doing?" she asks, concerned. She's just left her own son, recently hospitalized again at the VA Hospital in La Jolla with AIDS. We've become very close through the support groups and keep in touch with each other daily.

"Oh, Lee, he doesn't know where he is or what's happening. He's been hallucinating, he's just not here. Could you stay with him a few minutes while I make some calls downstairs?"

"Oh, sure, of course," she says, nearing the bed.

"Lee, is that you?" Peter asks, eyes closed. Lee and I look at each other, startled, and smile.

"Sure is, Peter. How did you know?"

"Oh, I could hear the New York accent," he answers, smiling faintly.

"Well, you're right," she smiles lovingly. "I'm going to stay with you a few minutes while your mother goes downstairs."

"I figured as much," says David as I tell him of the new developments and my need for help. "I was afraid of that, I've been trying to call you."

Plans are made. David can take time off work easily and will be with me tomorrow. I call my mother. I haven't been able to speak to her for a few days.

"How's Peter? I've been trying to get you, I've been so worried," her first words, taut and anxious.

"I haven't been able to call, I've hardly been home. He's much worse . . . Oh, Mother, it's awful, he's not here anymore!'' I'm crying, voice tripping over anguished sobs.

''Oh, Barbie, do you want me to come? I can come right away,'' she offers.

''No, not yet.'' I bite my lips as if that could sever the pain of the words. ''They may try another drug, a shot in the dark, try the CMV drug again. David's coming tomorrow. I'll let you know what happens. It'll be easier once he's here. I can't leave him alone at all.'' More words. I hang up and go back upstairs.

Lee leaves and I resume my watch in the yellow vinyl chair.

''Peter?'' Dr. Spector bends over Peter, trying to elicit a response. ''Peter?''

Nothing.

''Peter, do you know who I am?''

Peter's eyes remain closed, his face impassive. The doctor remains bent a minute, straightens up. I watch his face.

''We've been talking about putting him back on DHPG next week, but I'm afraid that if his mental status doesn't improve, it isn't worth doing the treatment,'' he tells me, his dark eyes kind.

''Peter? . . . Peter?'' Dr. Matthews bends over Peter. ''Peter, do you know who I am?''

No response.

''We're going to start him on pyrimethamine,'' Dr. Matthews tells me, walking toward the door. ''His tests are negative for toxoplasmosis, but that's not always significant. It will be a week's treatment, then we'll test him again.''

''We might as well give it a try,'' I answer. But I feel sure the infection is CMV, and now it's too late to even try another DHPG treatment for that.

All I can do now is be with him and make him comfortable.

Saturday, October 27

I greet David gratefully. ''It's okay, Mom, I'm here now.''

''Tell Peter who you are,'' I instruct him before we

enter the room. "It helps to orient him, sort of brings him
back for a few minutes."

I hate having to share the hurt and pain with David, but
I simply cannot do it alone anymore. I show David what to
do to clean up the "accidents," warning him of the importance of always putting rubber gloves on to avoid contagion. I warn him that Peter tries to get out of bed, and how
to handle him when he does. I tell him that I suspect he
may be totally blind now. I see the look of hurt, but he has
to know everything. David looks around, assesses the
situation.

"I can handle it Mom. I'm glad I'm here."

"I am, too," I tell him.

I'm at home, finally, on my patio. Peter is safe with
David. The sun is reflecting on the eastern hills. I see gray
night approaching and the bronze glow of sunset to the
west. Lavender puffs of cloud merge into salmon streaks.
Soon the sun becomes a burning globe of red as the dark
hand of night pushes it below the horizon. Peter would like
this sunset.

But Peter will see no more sunsets.

Sunday, October 28

I'm wearing out or wearing down, I don't know which.
But I know time is short, and I think I can carry Peter
through if I ration my own strength. David can help,
physically and morally, and the hospital has arranged for a
night-sitter so we can both go home to sleep. And Walter
arrived tonight. He called me last night, said he couldn't
bear being 3,000 miles away and was returning.

Despite moments of lucidity, Peter is leaving. He's
going away on his own private journey. His spirit, inside
the emaciated pod of his body, is losing its hold and leaves
to wander among old friends, old places, freeing itself
gradually from its shell. It is too tired to fight now, and the
enemies within have multiplied and are winning, pushing
the spirit out. All that is left is the shadow of a shadow.

I weep silently, already mourning.

Monday, October 29

Peter sleeps all day long, only waking slightly when a nurse takes his vital signs—he half-opens his eyes and speaks, but his words are confused and inappropriate. He frequently pantomimes taking his pills, as though this routine is a subconscious habit he cannot control. I go along with it, handing him the imaginary cup of water.

Touching his face appears painful to him. I see him grimace and shrink from me if I try. I comb his hair and moustache as gently as possible, but I can't shave him, and his beard is growing in thick and black. He has never liked beards, but at least it hides his gauntness. He seems unaware of it, and I'm glad. A careless appearance was another signpost to him.

I give him sponge baths, and he seems to enjoy the warm touch of the washcloth. But I dare not massage him now for fear of disturbing the lesions, and I know his muscles must ache terrible. He has not complained of the pain, but maybe he is incapable of complaining.

His only lucid statement today was, "It hurts too much to talk or smile . . . or even think."

Tuesday, October 30

The doctors have been giving us more information. Everything appears to be at a standstill pending results of the treatment for toxoplasmosis—if that's even what Peter has. Though Peter continues coughing up thick sputum, his chest X-ray yesterday was good and he's breathing without difficulty. The sputum sample taken Saturday was negative, too, though CMV grew out of a throat wash and urine sample taken a week ago. It is not as elusive as it once was. The EEG taken yesterday was normal, no seizure activity. They finally determined that the skin lesions *were* herpes zoster, and they are improving now, after completing acyclovir treatment. They still appear to be very painful to Peter, though.

Although a layman, it seems to me that Peter is already

so infested with CMV that it must be the cause of the vertigo, nausea, and almost complete lack of voluntary movement. However, as long as his white blood cell count stays within safe limits, there's nothing to be lost in treating possible toxoplasmosis.

Last night's CT scan also indicated that he's not having seizures. The neurologists and neurosurgeons have decided against a craniectomy—nor would I give permission for it. He does not need the pain it would cause, even if he survived the operation. The only justification for surgery would be evidence that fluid is accumulating in the tissue. Then a shunt would be required to decrease pressure on the brain. The prospect is so horrible I can't even think about it.

The diarrhea seems to be decreasing, happening only three or four times a day, though always with incontinence. I'm glad that he's unaware of it. In a perverse way, the hallucinations and disorientation are a blessing in disguise, rendering him unaware of the abominable degradation of his body. He eats no solid food, only sips apple juice or water now and then.

This afternoon, he thought a nurse was Maria as she stood talking to me from the foot of his bed. "What's Maria doing here?" he asked.

"She's not here, she's in Baltimore," I told him.

"No. I heard her voice in the hall," he insisted. He couldn't understand that it wasn't her.

He always knows me, though. I say, "Peter, it's Mom, I'm right here," whenever I go to his bedside or he calls me, and he seems to feel safe. I wish I had the stamina to stay here at night still. I'm not sure if he knows David, though when David said good night to him last night, Peter answered, "Good night, David." He knows his father, too, but doesn't seem to realize he was gone for four days.

I don't know how we've survived for so many months now. Hope. Foolish, silly, human hopes, were what kept us going. His, that he could exist, in whatever way, until a cure could be found. Peter has always been such a dreamer. And mine—not quite as grandiose—that he'd have a year or two more and the energy and strength to fulfill some of his dreams.

I remember when we talked about death and reincarnation last summer, and Peter said to gather everyone close when the time came and then we'd talk about it. The time approaches fast. But unless this black cloud in his brain lifts, he will be unable to tell us what he wants. I'm through bargaining and hoping for the impossible, but I do have one little plea left, just a small one.

Please, God. Give him a few hours to do this. It's not too much to ask, after all we've been through, is it?

Wednesday, October, 31

I have read that, toward the end, you finally wish for the patient's death and release.

I don't.

I don't want Peter to suffer more, but neither do I want to let him go. I still cannot hope for his death.

13

Thursday, November 1

Cindy, one of the nurses, comes in with Peter's small cup of pills and greets me brightly. Together, we rouse Peter and I put the pills in his mouth and give him water while Cindy holds his head up to drink.

"Now, just suck on this, don't swallow it," she tells him, putting a clotrimazole lozenge in his mouth. The lozenges are for thrush and are foul-tasting, and Peter grimaces with displeasure.

"Oh, come on now, Peter, is it really that bad?" she asks.

"Smile, Peter. It'll taste better," I tease.

"How do you expect me to smile with anything this awful in my mouth?" he says in mock disgust.

Cindy and I glance at each other, surprised at his alertness, and laugh. His infrequent returns to reality are surprising interludes in the midst of so much delirium.

And I wonder how he feels in his own world. Is he comfortable floating around, drifting casually from one imaginary person or situation to another? I no longer try to reorient him to our world. He got angry at my cutting off his delusions and trying to pull him back to this reality. All that angers him now is our holding and supporting him when he's up. He must think we are trying to restrain him and fights us as he used to fight the seizure restraints.

I also wonder how long he can live like this. His physical strength is minimal. I have to hold his head up to drink. I don't understand whether the limpness of his limbs, his inability to move them at all, and their insensitivity to stimuli are due to his overwhelming weakness or something neurological.

Does it really matter anymore?

Friday, November 2

I met with the hospital's social worker and an administrative nurse from Hospice this afternoon. Recommended by the social worker, Hospice is a private, non-profit organization that lends support to terminal patients and their families. They will be arranging Peter's home care. He'll be released soon.

The Hospice nurse will find side-rails for Peter's bed at home. I've already picked up a portable commode from the Disabled American Veterans. She offered to deliver a hospital bed, but I told her that I don't want one until absolutely necessary. Peter wants to be in his own bed. She will also arrange for two shifts of L.V.N.'s. We don't need R.N.'s unless narcotics are administered.

Neither David nor Walter were with Peter while we met in the social worker's office. Peter seemed to be sleeping soundly, and the nurse and I thought that we could leave him, returning to check from time to time. The nurse went back twice. Sound asleep.

Walter met me at Peter's door when I returned, grinning. "You'll never believe what just happened," he said. "When I came in, Peter said, 'Dad, would you please empty what's in the commode?' I thought he must be hallucinating, but I peeked, and sure enough, he'd gotten up, used the commode, and gotten back in bed again— alone! And with the side-rails up."

"Oh, my God—" I gasp. "That little stinker. Stubborn to the end!" I chuckle, but I respect his stubborn independence.

I knew then that I was right not to get him a hospital bed. We'll not give in all the way yet.

*   *   *

Evening. I'm alone now with Peter, and Dr. Matthews comes in to examine him. I stand, anxious to ask the question whose answer I don't want to hear . . .

"Dr. Matthews, no one has said anything and I don't know if they've noticed it, but I think Peter's vision is gone in the left eye, too. Would you mind checking it?"

"Hi, Peter, how are you feeling tonight?" He stands next to the bed. No answer. "Peter, do you know who I am?" Nothing. Dr. Matthews looks into Peter's left eye with the ophthalmoscope, straightens up, and looks across the bed at me, nodding silently.

It's true. He is blind. I didn't want to believe it—that unfocused gaze, his eyes looking slightly beyond me when he speaks to me.

I follow Dr. Matthews out of the room. I don't want Peter to hear what I want to ask, though he probably knows the answer himself.

"How much longer can he go on like this?"

"He could go on for several months. I just don't know," he answers frankly.

How could he endure so long? My instincts had estimated a few weeks, maybe just a few days.

"His white cells are staying at the same level, which is good. I really expected them to go lower. The pyrimethamine will finish tomorrow and we'll do another blood culture, and another CT scan on Monday to see if the lesion has changed. I want to be sure you have his home care arranged before discharging him, and then you can take him home on Monday."

Take him home to die. This is it. Nothing more can be done. What I've feared, dreaded, fought for so many months—now it's here. It's all over.

I feel the doorless walls of my screaming room crumbling around me.

Sunday, November 4

"I can't wait to get home," Peter says longingly as I lightly rub his back, avoiding the scabbed lesions.

"I can't wait to have you home. I've missed you."

"I want to get back in my own bed," he says. "I'm so sick of this damned hospital."

"I know you are. David and I have your room all fixed up and clean, ready for you."

"Good. Does it smell all right?" he asks.

"Yes, just fine." I lie. I can never get rid of that smell.

"Good," he murmurs. "What about my voting? Am I going to be able to vote absentee?"

"A volunteer came by on Friday to sign up patients who need absentee ballots. I gave him your name and he'll be back tomorrow with the ballots."

Peter has been so concerned about voting in this election, anxious to cast his vote against Reagan, to have his say against his plans to cut federal medical spending, research funds, and support of AIDS research. With so much disorientation, it's peculiar that he can focus on the election. It must be terribly important to him.

Monday, November 5

"I have the chair ambulance ordered for four this afternoon," the social worker informs me. "And I understand that Hospice has arranged with a nursing service for a practical nurse to come tonight at eleven."

"Oh, good. Thank you," I tell him.

"I hope everything goes well for you," he says. "Be sure to call if you need anything."

"Yes, I will. Thank you for all your help." We shake hands.

Peter is wheeled back from his X-ray and CT scan on a Guerney bed. He cannot move at all, and it takes the attendant and myself to transfer him back to his bed. I must call the social worker and tell him that we'll need a bed ambulance. Peter cannot sit up.

Medication bags arrive at noon—another brown grocery bag full of modern medicine.

The intern appears to discharge Peter, telling us the morning's CT scan indicated that the brain mass remained unaffected by the treatment, just as I feared, and the chest X-ray appeared normal.

At four, two ambulance attendants arrive and suggest that we wait an hour. President Reagan is making a speech at a rally in Fashion Valley, and traffic is stalled all around the area that we have to pass through. Ironic that Reagan, whose political demise is Peter's last goal, is keeping him from going home. We agree to wait until five-thirty.

Peter sleeps. David and I watch the traffic below, waiting for it to thin out.

The volunteer enters with Peter's absentee ballot, but when I inform him that we're checking out shortly, he refuses to give it to me, saying that we'll have to go to our local polling place. I'm glad Peter is asleep and doesn't hear our conversation. I can't believe this.

"All right, let's go now," the ambulance attendants, a husky young man and woman, return. David picks up the suitcase and leaves to drive my car home.

"Peter, can you help by moving your legs over for us?" the girl asks.

"No, he can't," I tell her. It takes the two attendants, a nurse, and myself to transfer Peter to the Guerney bed. Straps are buckled over him and he doesn't object. The bed moves quietly on rubber wheels to the elevator, out the first floor exit, and down the hall to the emergency room exit. Dr. Rothrock comes toward us and stops.

"Where are you going?" he asks, surprised.

"We're going home," I tell him. "There's nothing more."

"Oh . . . well, good luck," he tells me, evidently at a loss for appropriate words.

The ambulance engine starts. I sit in front with the driver to give directions, the girl in back with Peter.

"Mom?" Peter calls.

"Yes, Peter. I'm right here in front."

"Who are all these people in here?" he asks, puzzled.

"There are just four people, Peter."

"No, no, there are lots of people in here. Who are

they, why are there so many people in here?" he asks insistently.

"There are just four, Peter," I repeat. "You, me, and two attendants. We're going home."

He starts mumbling, his voice curious and inquisitive. The girl talks to him, trying to reassure him.

We park, the attendants roll him into the hall, transfer him to the wheelchair, then lay him in bed. Peter gives a deep sigh.

"Mom?"

"Yes, Peter?"

"Why were all those Japanese people in the ambulance with us?"

"There weren't any Japanese people there, Peter," I correct him.

"Yes, there were," he insists. "There must have been about 18 Japanese people coming home with us."

I stifle a giggle. The picture is amusing. "Well, I didn't see them, then," I tell him.

"They were there," he insists confidently. "I wonder why."

Thank God we have him home. No more hospitals. No matter what, I will not take him back. His comfort is all that matters now.

Tuesday, November 6

I hardly slept last night. It's difficult to relinquish care, learn to trust a stranger's capabilities. Al, the male nurse, a stocky, middle-aged man, arrived at eleven, and seemed quite competent. Peter greeted him lucidly.

I heard every little sound from next door—Peter mumbling, Al's hearty voice answering. Nothing unusual. I went back to sleep. Louder voices. I jump up. Al is helping Peter to the commode, encircling Peter with strong arrns. Peter seems to trust him.

Up at five-thirty to take David to the airport. He's going home to Austin. I will vote on the way home. Al will leave at seven.

*　　　*　　　*

"Be sure to call me if you want me back. I hope everything will be all right for a while," David gives me a hug, picks up his suitcase, and enters the airport.

Next stop, the voting booth. I ask the registrar about an absentee ballot for Peter. She tells me I must call the voters' registration office. The registrar is indignant that the hospital volunteer refused to give us an absentee ballot yesterday.

Home before Al leaves. I will be alone with Peter for an hour until Michael, who has pre-AIDS symptoms and is an L.V.N., arrives to help me for six hours. I hope I won't have to battle Peter to stay in bed during this hour.

Eight A.M. Michael arrives. I explain our problems, show him where the supplies are. Peter has to use the commode and we struggle with his limp body. I hold Peter upright, embracing him lightly from behind. Peter is anxious about voting. I relate what I've been told, and he asks me to keep trying to get his ballot. I will keep calling the voters' registration office, but I'm sure the lines will be busy all day.

I must also call the AIDS Project. They've called periodically, offering help, and I've always refused. But I won't be able to take care of Peter alone, even for a few hours. Walter probably will be going home soon, and to continue long-term, I see now that I must have more help. That's okay, though. I'm just glad Peter is home, at last. I call the project and request someone with a strong back, arms and stomach.

Michael calls me urgently and I run to Peter's room. Peter has had diarrhea, and the sheets, Chux liner—everything—are soaked. Peter seems unaware. Again, we struggle to move Peter's inert body and change all the bed linens, wash him, and settle him back again.

I keep calling the voters' registration office. Peter is insistent, but the line is always busy. I call the AIDS Project. They're still working on getting volunteers. Michael will be leaving at two-thirty and I can't locate Walter. I feel a small wave of panic. I can't take care of Peter alone.

*　　*　　*

Michael has to leave. I finally located Walter, though, and he arrives. The voters' registration line is still busy. The AIDS Project will send a volunteer at six, is still trying to line up more volunteers for me. Dr. Matthews calls. He will come at six.

Six P.M. The volunteer from the AIDS Project, Leonard, arrives, bringing me a bouquet of flowers and I'm touched by his thoughtfulness. Dr. Matthews arrives late. He examines Peter and beckons Walter and me to the living room. Peter has lost contact again, didn't respond at all to Dr. Matthews.

"I'm afraid someone read Peter's last X-ray wrong," he starts as we sit down. I stiffen with fear. "The radiologist's report came back today. There is a new density in his lungs, and we think it's pneumocystis again."

I sit rigidly as the doctor continues. Peter can't possibly survive another attack of pneumocystis.

"We have two choices," he says. "We can go ahead and treat him for the pneumocystis again, or we can not treat it." He pauses while we ponder his words.

"I know that's a terrible decision to have to make. But Peter already has so many other complications that even if we treat the pneumocystis successfully, his quality of life will be nil."

He's asking me to give up. Tears sting but I feel as if I'm outside myself, watching myself swirl blindly in a black nightmare. I know he's right.

"How long will it be if we don't treat it?" I ask finally.

"He might have a week," the doctor answers.

"He's so stubborn, it might even be two weeks," I smile sadly through the tears filming my eyes. Walter is silent.

"How will it be?" I ask quietly.

I have accepted.

"We'll do everything to make him comfortable. I'll order oxygen to help his breathing, and nurses around the clock. They'll have to be R.N.'s in case we have to use narcotics. I'll give you a prescription for Dilaudid® in case he has pain.''

I look at Walter. He remains quiet, looking at me. I have to make the decision, speak the words.

"All right," I hesitate. "We won't treat it."

Oh, God. How can I say that? How can I condemn Peter to death? But I knew this anguishing moment would come. I've known for months. I just can't believe it's here. But there's really no choice. It's either now with pneumocystis, or later with CMV, and possibly a more horrifying and painful death. No choice, none at all.

"I think you've made the right decision," Dr. Matthews says with compassion. "I know how hard it is. I had to do it last year for my mother. She had cancer."

I look at him with sympathy. He had to do that for his own mother, and he's had to help others like us with AIDS-stricken children. I know each time has wounded him, too.

"I'll make the nursing arrangements. Do you have the agency's number?" Dr. Matthews asks. Walter brings the nursing service's card and the telephone, glad to be able to do something.

I go back to Peter's room. He's sleeping peacefully. Leonard is reading. I look at Peter a moment, go back to the living room.

Arrangements are completed. The nursing director will be here tomorrow to talk with me. The bills will be paid by Walter's father. MediCal does not finance terminal home care. They only pay if the patient is hospitalized.

"I'll be in Los Angeles for two days," Dr. Matthews tells us as he leaves. "Here's the number where I'll be staying if you need me, and you can call Dr. McCutchan while I'm gone." He writes on a small card. "You've done the right thing," he tells us. He smiles but his eyes are sad.

Leonard leaves. I thank him profusely for his help. I go back to Peter's room, watch him sleep. His breathing is so easy, so regular. How could he have pneumocystis again?

Now is the time to gather everyone around. This is what

Peter wanted. My mind wanders erratically between planning what needs to be done and my anguish, overwhelming fear, numbing sadness.

Walter stays with Peter and I carry the telephone to the patio. It will be easier to make the calls enveloped in the soothing blackness of night. My body suddenly starts to tremble. I'm freezing-cold. It's the same shiver I felt last December, the day I heard the fatal news from Walter. I dial the first number.

The calls are completed. My mother will be here tomorrow at noon. She said I was doing the right thing. I was angry for a second. I'm not doing the right thing. I have no choice. The right thing would be that Peter lived. My sister, Charlotte, will be here from San Francisco in the morning. Maria will make plans and call, probably will arrive Thursday. Jonathan has to arrange time off; probably Thursday. David will come Thursday. I hope they'll be in time. Though Louise, Sandy, and Nani wanted to come, I told them to wait. I'll need them later.

Wednesday, November 7

Are his kidneys closing down? I wonder fearfully. Michael and I have tried to get Peter to urinate but he can't, neither with the plastic urinal nor on the commode. He's even weaker and limper than yesterday and can't speak. His lips move but we can't distinguish words. Michael touches his abdomen lightly and Peter groans. There is a slight swelling, and we decide his bladder is distended and we need to catheterize him. We call Phyllis. Michael will go to the hospital and pick up a catheterization set.

Michael leaves and I am alone with Peter, trying to console him. The distension must be causing him great discomfort. He moans now and then and tries to speak, finally manages to ask when Michael will be back. At least he's oriented. I wash him, change his dressings, disconnect the hyper-al.

Charlotte arrives, greets Peter. His eyelids flicker but remain closed. Alice, the nursing supervisor knocks on the door. I forgot she was coming. Michael returns, starts opening the catheter set. I try to talk with Alice, the nurse. Everything is confusing. Michael isn't familiar with this kind of catheter. Fortunately, Alice is, and she and Michael finally insert it properly. The plastic bag fills promptly, Peter's belly flattens out, and he sleeps restfully. Alice and I resume our talk.

"I've gotten you some excellent nurses," Alice tells me. "I didn't want anyone here who would be afraid of AIDS or have the least negative feelings. I asked each one how he or she felt, and if I detected any hesitancy, I turned them down. All those coming had no hesitation at all."

She asks questions, fills in the answers, then files her papers in her briefcase.

"Now, I want you to remember that you're the boss. The nurses are just here to do the menial work so you have the energy to be with Peter, give him your love. You can't do that if you're exhausted. Anything *you* want, goes. Get your rest."

She leaves.

I sit on the couch a minute, looking at the bright sunlight outside. Its brightness seems to mock me. Or is it just saying that the world keeps on turning, life keeps going, no matter what? I don't know. I'm too tired, too confused, to even think.

Michael leaves at two. Charlotte brings in my mother from the airport. The new nurse arrives. The Hospice representative arrives. Grand Central Station. I show the new nurse around, discuss details with the Hospice lady, take my mother to see Peter.

"Hi, Peter, it's Nanna." She leans over, strokes his arm. "I love you." His eyelids flicker slightly. He knows she's here. I wonder if he realizes that this is the gathering, his farewell. I hope so.

Peter's lips move. I can't hear anything. He hasn't enough strength to blow breath through the words, to make them audible.

"What is it, Peter?"

He tries again. Nothing.

"Peter, I can't tell what you're saying. It's all right, Peter." I wish I could read lips. I smooth his hair back on the painless side, raging at my helplessness.

I go to the kitchen. The nurse is with Peter. I don't know what to do, where to start. I'm floating in a confused, bewildering dream of sorrow. My mother and Charlotte bring groceries. Walter arrives, bringing flowers. I can't find a vase, don't know what to do with them.

Walter and I go to Peter's room, stand looking at this grown child we created. He is so thin, his face gaunt under the black beard. His unseeing eyes are slightly open. The right eyeball shows whitely, only the left pupil can be seen. His lips move. We try to understand his voiceless words. Damn. Now when he needs to speak, he can't. Not even my last dim hope is answered.

I hear metallic clanking in the hallway. The oxygen tank is being delivered. I watch as they install it at the foot of the bed. It stands like an unexploded World War II bomb dropped into our house, ugly and ominous. I hate it.

Another delivery—the aspirator, to suck out mucus that might impede his breathing. Oh, God. It's all so horrible, horrifying. I hate these machines, hate what they mean, hate the pneumocystis.

Dusk falls. The family is going out to eat, urges me to go, but I don't want to leave.

Everything is happening so fast. I feel helpless, confused, dazed. I can't keep up. I wanted more time. Peter wanted more time. I thought it would be slower, a few weeks. Now it's down to days. The bucket is empty, the last drop falling out and I can't catch it in my hand, scoop it back like I could before.

Oh, Peter. I hope I'm doing what you want, I hope this is what you meant when you said we'd gather everyone around when the time came and talk about dying then. I'm gathering them for you, Peter, but you've been cheated, you can't talk about it. It's a cruel, tragic trick.

"Peter, it's me, it's Mom." I kneel next to the bed, laying my hand on his. His lips move, form words. I lean closer, looking directly at his lips. "Say it again, Peter," I implore. His lips move voicelessly again. Damn! I scream silently. I can't understand him! I stroke his arms, his head, say little but that I'm here, everyone's here, it's all right, Peter.

Thursday, November 8

All I really want to do is sit next to Peter, hold him in my arms till he leaves, but it's physically impossible. I don't even know where I can touch him. I don't know how much pain he feels anymore, now that he can't communicate. We have him propped up on a pyramid of pillows to facilitate his breathing and he seems to be comfortable, but how can we tell?

I stopped giving him his pills this morning. I put a pill on his lips and it stuck there. I nudged it inside, gave him water, but he couldn't swallow. The water dripped down his chin. I guess it doesn't matter now. Another giving up. The little surrenders of control are accelerating faster and faster, almost smothering me with their inevitability.

The sun shines again today, mocking me. My mother and Charlotte are busy in the kitchen. They stayed at a nearby motel last night. They will pick up Jonathan. Walter will bring David. I will meet Maria at five. We dispatch Walter for liquid Tylenol and an eyedropper. Peter may still feel the head pain and this is the only way we can give him the medicine.

I still feel outside myself, in my own screaming room. The bond is shredding, fiber by fiber. I am trying not to let go of my end, but Peter's gentle strength is stronger than mine and I can feel him pulling from the other room.

At least everyone will be here now, assembled and expectant. I have my supports around me. They will catch me when I fall. And Peter will have his wish. His tortured, valiant spirit can rest now, surrounded in the warmth and love that only shared blood can give.

David and Jonathan arrive and I take them to their brother. The nurses all tell me that the hearing goes last and to keep talking to him, I tell them. I see the pain on their faces as they tell Peter they love him. David, who has been here more, is accepting. Jonathan's face is confused, marked by bewildered anguish.

At five, I go to meet Maria at the airport. She has arrived with boxes and cases, suitcases. I ask why she has brought so much luggage.

"If I'm going to be here six weeks, I'm going to need to study and practice," she tells me.

"You mean you're not going back to finish the semester?" I ask.

"No, I've got it all arranged. I can make up the work and take the finals, and the semester is almost over, anyway," she tells me. "Besides, I want to be with you."

I must have done something right in raising this child.

"Hi, Peter," Maria calls softly. "It's Maria, I'm here." She touches him.

Peter's head turns slightly in our direction and his lips move. A single tear rolls from his left eye, tracing a delicate line down his cheek. Yes, he does know what is happening. He knows Maria would only be back for the dying, the farewell.

The living must be fed. The decision is dinner in a nearby restaurant. My mother urges me to come. I don't want to leave. I can't. More urging. I tell her when I'm upset, my stomach turns off, don't worry, I'll be all right. Finally, I accede, tell her I will join them after connecting Peter's hyper-al. They leave.

I gaze at Peter before I start working. I think I have aged a thousand years this week. His right eye has stayed closed all day. The left one is half-open but the pupil has turned upward. Only the white is revealed. He looks so bizarre, so pitiable. I suppose the ocular muscles are gone now, too.

Poor Peter. My poor, poor Peter. This shouldn't have happened to you. You never hurt anyone. It's not fair. All you wanted was to live, and you finally found the strength

*to fight—your first real fight—and you lost. I'd give
everything if you could have won.*

I start preparing the hyper-al apparatus. It seems so
futile, but at least I'm doing something. A small flame
flares in me. Of course, I must do it. What if he survives
the pneumocystis?

Stop!

Friday, November 9

A strange gurgling awakens me. I jump and run into
Peter's room. The nurse stands over Peter, feeding the
plastic tube of the aspirator into his throat. Oh, God. He's
having trouble breathing! I stand tensely watching as white
globs slide up the tube and into the glass jar. The nurse
slides the tube out, back in. "One more time, Peter," she
says kindly, then deftly runs the tube around his mouth
and back out.

"He was having trouble breathing," she tells me. "I
think he'll be all right now for awhile."

I kneel next to Peter, tell him I'm with him, stroke his
arm. If only I could help more.

"I don't know what to say to him," Jonathan confesses.

"Just tell him you love him. That's all he needs to
know," I explain simply.

I know he's still thinking and feeling, albeit in a different level. His lips still move almost imperceptibly. I wish I
could blow air in and he could blow it out, making words
of the silent syllables.

More incontinence, more sheet-changing, bathing, running to the laundry. The aspirator gurgles frequently and I
try to be with him every time, let him know I'm with him.
In between, I wander back and forth from the living room
to the bedroom.

I mock myself. How could I have thought yesterday that
maybe he could survive this? My foolish hope dissolves,
melts away like wax on a burning candle. He can't move,
can't see, can't talk. I pray now that he can't feel pain,

either. My hopes are gradually twisting, turning, changing into hopes that he can go soon and end his anguish. If I can't hope for life anymore, then I must hope for death.

The afternoon light dims. The sun falls and the sky is illuminated by streaks of brilliant crimson and flaming, defiant orange. I go out on the patio, alone.

Oh, Peter. You should see this one, you'd love it. You should go now, tonight, Peter. Go in a beautiful sunset, your time of day. Hurry, go. Wrap yourself in the brilliant colors and fly!

Dr. Matthews arrives at seven. He examines Peter quickly, asks where he, Walter, and I can talk alone. I lead them to my room and close the door.

"How long do you think he has?" I ask immediately.

"It's hard to say, maybe 24 hours," he guesses. Walter's eyes glaze with tears.

"I think you can stop giving him the hyper-al now," the doctor suggests.

No! I scream inside. Don't ask me to stop feeding him. That's all I can do!

"But . . . won't he get dehydrated?" I ask, desperate for an excuse.

"Well, just give him the hyper-al formula, leave off the lipids," he says. He knows—he understands—that I will fall apart if I can do nothing.

"You can stop his medications now, too," he tells me.

"I already did this morning. He can't swallow them," I say. "He won't—he can't—drown, suffocate, in his own fluids, can he?"

"No, I don't think so. The nurse seems to be keeping him well-aspirated," he assures me. "You're doing all that can be done."

He leaves, telling us to call him over the weekend if we need him, even though he will be off-duty.

I turn to the family waiting in the living room and the tears break through. My mother holds me. I pat my sister's shoulder. "Here's your good, fat, old Aunt Charlotte," I say to everyone jokingly and laugh through my tears. Why did I say that? But she laughs good-naturedly.

"David," I say, standing. "I guess you'll be the oldest now. You'll have to take care of these two." I hug him. I reach out to Jonathan and Maria and pull them into my arms. "We're all together," I tell them, and we cry, laugh, sob, hug. "Do you all want to go see Peter, say goodbye?"

One by one, they file in, talk to Peter. David and Jonathan stand together. "I'm going to miss you," Jonathan blurts out, his voice breaking. They tell him they love him, pat and stroke him, reluctantly leave. Everyone is crying.

"Barbie," my mother starts. "Have you thought of what you want to do afterward?"

"Yes," I answer firmly. "I will have him cremated, then I want to take him back to Santa Fe, to the mountains. He never wanted to talk about it, but that's what I think he wanted."

More tears. It sounds so final to talk of this before he even dies.

"Good, I'm glad you want to do that," says Walter.

"Would you like to leave his ashes on Uncle Park's property?" my mother asks.

"Oh, yes, that's what I really hoped to do. He loved that place so much."

"All right. I'll call tomorrow and ask. I'm sure it will be all right with them."

Night. My mother and Charlotte have gone to their motel. David, Jonathan, and Walter will stay here tonight, sprawled all over the living room. Maria will share my bed. I go outside on the patio, alone, and look up at the vast blackness above.

Is it tonight? I ask the stars. Will you take him tonight? Please do. Please end his suffering.

Saturday, November 10

Three-forty A.M. Again, the gurgling. I run to Peter's room, lower the side-rails, put my hands gently on the sides of his head.

"It's all right, Mom's here. It'll be over in a minute, it's all right."

The nurse takes a final swish around Peter's mouth, replaces the tube, and leaves me alone with Peter. I want to talk to him.

"Peter," I know he hears me. I kneel beside him, my hands on his arms across his chest.

"Peter, you can go now, whenever you want to. You don't have to fight anymore.

"Peter, we're going back to Santa Fe. We're all going to take you back, together." Tears run freely down my cheeks, off my nose. I stroke his arms. "We're going to Uncle Park's house. You're going to be free in the mountains . . . in the piñons . . . with your beautiful sunsets . . . your favorite place." Tears strangle my words.

Peter's lips part. He wants to speak. His body turns slightly toward me, his left arm rises and reaches for me. I lean forward as much as I can and put his arm on my left shoulder, holding it there with my hand. I put my left arm around his head as far as I can, and we stay in this embrace several minutes, my tears flowing unrestrained onto his arm and sheets. For the first time, I can cry freely with him. His left eye, open, glistens, and a tear slides out.

"Oh, Peter," I sob quietly. "You've fought so hard, so hard. We all love you so much." I feel a light pressure from his left arm on my shoulder. Thank God, you can respond. You *can* hear! Joyfully, I squeeze his hand in answer, hold it tightly. Words are not needed now.

The nurse slips quietly back into the room. I remain motionless, kneeling, until Peter's arm starts sagging. Gently, I lay his arm back on his chest. His face is relaxed, content.

"You can go whenever you want. We're all here with you, and we love you. It's all right," I wait, watching.

I have said goodbye. I have let go.

The dawning sun casts rosy light and lavender shadows across the sky, heralding another day. I wonder if it's

Peter's last, tiredly pulling on my clothes. I hope not.
I want him to go at night. He's always been a night
person.

Everyone is asleep. I take scalding coffee to the patio
and watch the sun rise, its rays nudging into the shadowed
crannies between my potted plants. I inspect my flowers.
They have kept me company through so many anguished
hours here on this little patio. They will be with me after
Peter leaves. I hear birds singing and chirping in the trees
above, traffic noises as the city wakes up. A door bangs. I
hear breakfast sounds as neighbors start the day. I must
suck in all the sounds of living around me. This might be
Peter's last day.

We take turns visiting Peter throughout the day. "Hi,
Peter, it's David." "Peter, I'm here, it's Mom." "Peter,
Nanna loves you." Jonathan stands quietly next to him.
"You're a good boy, Peter," Walter. Maria gives him
another backrub, talking softly.

Shadows lengthen, I go outside to see the sunset. No,
it's nothing great today, Peter. Wait till tomorrow. Make it
perfect!

Sunday, November 11

Peter will die today. I know.

I look at the lavender-gray hollows in his temples, his
cheeks, his eyes, the skin stretched taut over the contours
of his bones, and I know. My only remaining hope now is
for a beautiful day, a brilliant sunset, and a soft, dark
night. He deserves that.

"I think it will be today," I tell everyone gathered in
the kitchen. "Remember to talk to him when you go in so
he knows we're still here with him."

I sit in a kitchen chair, feeling as if I haven't slept for
almost twelve months. My mother stands next to me and
puts her hand on my shoulder.

*   *   *

Eleven A.M. The nurse calls me. Peter's temperature is rising. We try to give him liquid Tylenol but it seeps back out. The nurse gives him his first injection of Dilaudid. I hold my dying son, praying his temperature will descend. I want him to be comfortable. His left eye is open, the white eyeball showing.

"I love you, Peter," I whisper. I wonder if he hears me. "Go whenever you want, Peter. We're all here with you." But I think he will wait until night. I straighten his body. He has fallen to one side. I rearrange the pyramid of pillows. There, that's the best I can do. Walter comes in and I leave him alone with Peter.

Two P.M. The nurse calls me. Peter's temperature is up to 105.4 degrees. The nurse administers another injection of Dilaudid. I touch Peter's forehead, his arm. He feels cool.

"Are you sure it's that high? He should be burning up."

"Feel underneath him," he answers.

I slide my hand under his back and am shocked by the intense heat of the sheet. "My God! Might he have a seizure with that fever?"

"I hope not," answers the nurse.

"Would it help to bathe him with alcohol?" I ask. We've come full circle from St. Vincent's.

"I think it would be a good idea," he agrees.

I bring alcohol, a basin, washcloths. We pull down the sheet and swab Peter's burning body. No reaction.

"It's coming down a bit, let's keep on," says the nurse, taking Peter's temperature again.

"Good, it's down to 102 degrees," the nurse announces with satisfaction. "I think we can stop. It'll probably keep going down as the Dilaudid takes effect."

Three P.M. The night nurse arrives, a motherly woman who was here last night. Together, we straighten Peter's body, rearrange the pillows. I kneel by the bed and hold his left hand lightly. His long, slender fingers are gray next to my white hand. I lift the sheet, look at his feet.

They are puffier than yesterday and are bluish. The circulation is failing. Walter comes near and I make room for him.

"Peter, Dad's here, Dad and I are here," I say.

"You've made a good fight, Peter," Walter tells him, his voice full of grief. "You're tough." He touches Peter's leg.

David, Jonathan, Maria and my mother stand together by the bed.

"I love you," says David.

"I love you, too, Peter," says Jonathan, his voice trailing upward. Maria is crying.

"We all love you," my mother says firmly.

They stand quietly, then leave, one by one. Walter and I wait, then leave the room. Everyone sits in the living room, waiting.

"Barbara," the nurse calls urgently. I run to the bedroom.

"I think he's going to have a seizure. His temperature is up to 105 again. Just hold him. I'm going to give him some Valium."

I lower the side-rail quickly, sit on the edge of the bed, facing Peter, and put a hand firmly on each arm.

"It's all right, Peter," I say as I have many times before. Yes, there it is. I feel tremors shake his body and my heart tightens. No, don't let him have a seizure, he hates them so. The tremors flow up my arms, into my body, into my heart—and then cease. There is not even enough strength for a full seizure. Thank God, that's all. I relax my grip carefully. The nurse injects his upper arm and the seizure loosens its hold, fades away and I let go, sigh with relief.

"There, Peter, it's all right now, it's all right now," calming myself.

"Good. His pulse is down to 140. It was up to 160," she says. "His fever should go down now, too."

"Peter, it's all right, Mom's here, it's all right, everything's all right," I repeat over and over. Keep talking to him. He'll hear you. Keep talking. "Oh, Peter, my baby. Go, go now. It's all right."

"Would you like to start his hyper-al now?" the nurse asks.

What? Why start his hyper-al? Doesn't she know he's going to die—or does she think he has more time? I hesitate, confused. I don't want to leave Peter, take the last minutes away from him. I stand reluctantly, slowly, arrange the paraphernalia, glancing constantly at Peter's face.

"I think we'll give him some oxygen. Do you see how he's breathing, sucking in deeply below the ribs?"

"Yes." I pause, watch as she slips the oxygen mask over his face. Peter's breathing steadies and the nurse removes the mask. She lifts the sheet, checks his toes. I know she's checking the color.

"Peter, you can go now, we love you," I tell Peter, bending over him and touching his hands. I hope he still hears me.

His breathing is irregular again. One deep, deep gasp, three short breaths, one long, three short, forming its own rhythm. The deep gasps suck in the hollow at the base of his neck as he strains for breath and the nurse gives him more oxygen. I turn to hang the hyper-al bag, connect two tubes.

I feel bewildered, anguished. Maybe he'll wait a little longer, maybe he won't, yes, no, maybe, the struggle for breath starts again, deep gasp, three short ones the nurse brings the oxygen mask I turn to do something Damn! I'm not going to bother with this what am I doing I want to hold him when he goes . . .

"Barbara . . . he's stopped breathing," the nurse says quietly and I drop everything turn run hold him in my arms his mouth is wide open frozen in its last gasp he looks like he's singing and I clutch him feel the salt-sting of tears that don't fall paralyzed in place and my mouth opens in a silent scream my last scream of protest of horror I hear a cry of No-o-o echoing through the chambers of my head echoing and echoing reverberating as I clutch my baby my heart tears completely its flesh rips off and splatters on the walls of the room.

"Oh, Peter . . ." I finally wail, and the tears come, falling on his hair, his tortured face, dripping on the pillow, his chest, his arms, as my whole body wilts, crumbles, caves in, I don't have to be strong anymore, the strengths built up during months and months of tension, of angry energy, dissolve, and I am just another mother who has lost her child, who holds his empty, wasted body in her arms and mourns, grieves, cries for loss of part of her own body and soul.

I lay his head gently back on the pillow, lean over, touch his hand by his side. Both arms lie by his sides, palms turned upward. I see his stilled chest, the white catheter tube taped to his shoulder. Yes, that was good. It kept him living two extra months. His thin shoulders, the clavicles leading to the base of the neck, his Adam's apple, the golden voice forever silenced now. I see his head, tilted to the left and downward. His black beard. The hollows on the temples, under the cheekbones. His mouth, forever open in song. The left eye open, the other closed. Peace. Quiet.

I look at my watch. Eight forty-five. He must have died at eight-thirty. What does it matter?

"Would you like me to pack everything up for you?"

"What?" I ask stupidly, numbly.

"Would you like me to pack up all the medical supplies?" The nurse is speaking to me, her face solicitous.

Oh. Yes. Things have to be done. I have to tell the family.

"Yes, I guess so," I answer vaguely. I don't know what she's talking about, but it seems to be important. I turn slowly, walk to the living room. Faces look up expectantly.

"He's gone," I tell them and tears crash through. They cry, hug, swirl around me, we cry, my mother embraces me, I cry, I hurt, I'm numb, I hurt.

I don't know what I feel.

Someone calls Dr. Matthews. He'll be over right away. We sit, waiting, I go look at Peter again, yes, he's still dead, he's dead—No!—the others go look, quickly, come back with faces reddened with tears.

Someone opens the door. Dr. Matthews. Walter and I take him to Peter's room. I stand by Peter's head. Dr. Matthews checks, yes, he's gone, he steps back, I hear a harsh, gasping sob, it's the doctor, poor man. I step close, give him a quick embrace, compassion.

"All these boys, they're so young," he blurts in pain, in a voice angry at the unfairness, hurt by so much useless pain. I know, I understand the hurt, the pain, the sadness I have always seen in his eyes. We stand for moments, the two parents, the physician, facing our defeat, our wasted anger and labor. We turn, go back to the living room.

Dr. Matthews calls the mortuary for me. Yes, I want cremation. Yes, also an autopsy. Anger flashes—yes, I want to know what killed my son. I see my son's body being dissected, his flesh cut—a twinge of horror, protest—stop that, he won't feel it and you won't see it. The anger smothers the horror and I repeat, "Yes, an autopsy, by all means."

Walter and I take the doctor to the door.

"And how do you cope with all this?" Walter asks sympathetically.

"Oh," he laughs ironically. "I used to go to a psychiatrist, now I play a lot of tennis." He laughs again apologetically.

"The mortuary people will be here in an hour, Walter. I know what they do, and I don't want the kids here," I tell him.

"All right, I'll take them out for dinner," he agrees.

"If you all want, you can say goodbye to Peter before going," I tell them. "If anyone doesn't want to, that's perfectly all right. You don't have to."

"We'd like to," they tell me and one by one each gives Peter his silent farewell.

Oh, my children. My heart cries for you three, a part of

you is gone, too. I watch their young faces as they stand by Peter.

Then Walter, the father. I wonder if a father feels the loss as physically as a mother. And my mother, the grandmother. I watch her face, see her sorrowing acceptance. Her second baby, her husband, her only brother—and now her first-born grandchild—she has known death well in 81 years.

"I'm so sorry, Barbara," the nurse is ready to leave. I'm glad she was on duty tonight. She has four sons, one Peter's age. "I hope everything goes well." She embraces me.

Maria stands next to me, looking down at Peter. "He looks like Christ, with that black beard," she comments sadly, wistfully. I put my arm around her.

"That's just what I was thinking," I tell her.

"You all better hurry. It's late," I tell them, anxious that they be gone before the mortuary people arrive. And I want time alone with Peter.

"Do you want me to stay with you?" my mother offers.

"No, thanks. Help Walter with the kids," I urge her.

I'm alone. It's my turn to say goodbye.

Peter's body is so white. Where did the blood go so fast? I pull the sheet down gently. I want to see all of him one last time.

No more pain now, Peter. No more fears, no more worries. The horror is gone. You're at peace. Twenty-nine years of you in front of me. I'll miss you so much.

I pull the sheet up to his waist, fold it neatly across his waistline, caress his hands, his arms.

It looks like you were caught in mid-song, Peter. Is it mid-song or mid-breath? My eyes go to yours, see the one closed and the other still open, the blind, white eyeball still staring—and I break, the tears tumble over each other and I hear myself wailing, keening softly, and I caress your face, trail my fingers around your cheeks, nose, forehead. Oh, why, why did you have to be blind? I stroke your hair, combimg it with my fingers away from your forehead. "Oh, my baby, my poor, blind baby," I croon

as I caress you, and the tears fall relentlessly on as both
as I make my farewell.

I walk heavily down the hall, out to the patio. I hear a
van parking outside, go to the door. Two uniformed young
men, a Guerney bed behind them.

"Do you want more time alone with him?" one asks
kindly.

"No, that's all right. I'm ready."

"Ma'am, it might be better if you wait out here," the
other suggests.

"Yes, I know. Thank you." I return to the patio. I feel
empty, a hollow, scooped-out shell. I hear zippers, the
dull crackle of plastic being unfolded. I don't want to hear,
don't want to see them. I just hope they hurry. I look up at
the moon, shining fully. Yes, it cared.

Thank you for taking him tonight.

Epilogue

We buried Peter's ashes on the windy Santa Fe hilltop where my Uncle's adobe home stands. A chilling wind swept down from the snow-whitened Sangre de Cristo peaks, whining through the foothills. Snow would fall soon. Far to the west, the vermilion sun fell slowly behind the purpling Jemez range. We waited until sunset for Peter's farewell.

Peter had finally come back to Santa Fe, and we were all with him. Huddling together against the wind, we said goodbye to Peter, one by one, each in his own way. We buried his ashes deep in the pit Sandy and David had dug earlier. Deep in the hard, red soil.

Now his spirit was free—free to watch the seasons change on the mountains above, free to see his sunsets, free to sing eternally through the groves of cedar and piñon and smell their pungent smoke rising from squat, adobe chimneys.

Free, at last.

The autopsy was completed three months later. As I read the results, I wondered for the thousandth time how Peter endured such overwhelming physical devastation for so long, wondered at the fortitude and unwavering hope that turned him from boy to man.

The immediate causes of Peter's death were the destruction of white cells throughout his entire system, CMV pneumonia, and congestive heart failure. CMV, cytomegalovirus, was the principal killer, causing not only the blindness, the terrifying vertigo, the final paralysis, the many cerebral and neurological changes, but also the last pneumonia which had been assumed to be pneumocystis. CMV had also infiltrated his adrenal glands extensively, wiping out his immune defenses, causing progressive wasting and emaciation, and totally depleting his white blood cells. The DHPG treatment had not been enough. There was also severe damage to the cells of his kidney, liver, spleen, pancreas, and pituitary gland.

Our cruelly relentless enemy, diarrhea, had been assumed to be caused by MAI, mycobacterium avium intracellulare. Ironically, no MAI appeared in the autopsy. The antibiotics must have been effective.

The physical autopsy is complete, but the survivors' healing is still in progress.

My mother, 82, helped establish an AIDS support organization in Portland, Maine, when the first patient was diagnosed there in the winter of 1984. The hospital calls her in to talk with patients' parents, to console and advise.

All my children, though busy with work and school, have found time to work with AIDS organizations where they live. It's not easy. They see their brother in the eyes of other patients.

Walter has lectured on AIDS to students at Virginia Polytechnical Institute, where he works in student health, and is helping establish an AIDS Task Force there.

I gradually found my way out of my screaming room by sorting out and writing down all that happened to us. I have closed the door, but scars and bruises will always remain inside. Tears still come when least expected.

Returning to more intensive artwork with other AIDS patients—the parade is unending—helps to soothe my own pain and sorrow. I feel Peter's spirit with me every time I walk down the exhibition gallery my students named for him. The anger? Only the end of this vicious disease will quell that.

I am currently on the board of directors of the AIDS Project in San Diego. As a volunteer, I also work under Dr. McCutchan in the AIDS office at UCSD, counseling AIDS patients and their desperate families, and as manager of the San Diego Research Foundation. In August of 1984, two other mothers and myself founded MAP, Mothers for AIDS Patients. AIDS is such a terribly lonely disease, for the mother as well as the patient. We know what they are struggling with and offer our support and ourselves as "substitute mothers" for rejected patients. We also lend support to increased government funding for AIDS research, home care for AIDS patients, and more inclusive support programs.

Peter lives on in each of us.

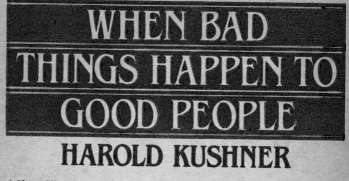